# TEACHERS OF THE ETERNAL DOCTRINE

## VOL. II: INDIAN AND TIBETAN TEACHERS

# Theosophy Trust Books

# TEACHERS OF THE ETERNAL DOCTRINE

## VOL. II: INDIAN AND TIBETAN TEACHERS

BY

ELTON A. HALL

W. Q. JUDGE

H. P. BLAVATSKY

RAGHAVAN IYER

—

THEOSOPHY TRUST BOOKS

NORFOLK, VA

# Teachers of the
# Eternal Doctrine ~ Vol. 2
# Indian and Tibetan Teachers

Theosophy Trust books may be ordered through Amazon.com, CreateSpace.com, and other retail outlets, or by visiting:

https://theosophytrust.org/theosophy-online-books.htm

ISBN-13: 978-0-9992382-5-7
ISBN-10: 0-9992382-5-6

Library of Congress Control Number: 2018961984

Printed in the United States of America

Dedicated to

Raghavan Narasimhan Iyer

Master Teacher

*Lux Theosophiae, Lux Terrarum*

For a truly fundamental understanding of good and evil, along with all the other pairs of objective opposites, one must turn to the quintessential distinction between the manifest and the unmanifest. This distinction is a modern formulation of that drawn by Shankaracharya between the Real and the unreal. Given the relationship between the Good and inward acknowledgement of the source of illumination, it is significant that Shankaracharya, when expounding the Teaching concerning the Real and the unreal, invokes the Upanishadic sages and their revelation of the Path leading from death to immortality. As Shankaracharya explicitly states, there can be no realization of the Atman and its unity with Brahman apart from a reverential and grateful recognition of predecessors and preceptors. It is only when one realizes the true meaning of the posture of authentic humility, assumed by even so great an Initiate as Shankaracharya in relation to the ancient Rishis, that one may begin to understand the unwisdom of the modern age. The ingratitude of latter-day Europeans towards Islamic scholars who transmitted the teachings of the classical world, the earlier ingratitude of Christian theologians towards the children of Israel, and the even earlier instances of ingratitude between Greece and Egypt, between Egypt and Chaldea, between Chaldea and India, and between Brahmins and the Buddha, have all left a heavy burden of unacknowledged debts which contribute to the moral bankruptcy of the modern age. The sad consequences of this spiritual ingratitude are to be discerned in the moral blindness of contemporary society, in the restrictiveness of its range of vision, so that the succession of events is seen as a random series of amoral happenings.

*Hermes*, November 1981
Raghavan Iyer

# CONTENTS

# PREFACE

In the last quarter of the nineteenth century, the Masters of wisdom through Helena Petrovna Blavatsky communicated to the world what we know as Theosophy. Theosophy is what in our times can be shared of the divine wisdom at the root of the world's religions and philosophies - or *theosophia*. Much of *theosophia* is "esoteric" in the sense that it cannot be fully comprehended without following exacting moral discipline and mental preparation on the part of the disciple, and some of which would only be a danger to one not so prepared to assimilate it for the good of all humanity. The world's religions, drawing on more or less partial inspirations from and insights into *thosophia*, invariably degrade over time through concretizing intuitive symbols, dogmatizing universal teachings, reifying abstractions, and taking literally great spiritual concepts. Add to that the mixed motives of adherents from selfishness and self-aggrandizement to power-seeking and exclusivity, and religious traditions tend to lose the golden thread that gave them their profound meanings.

Siddhartha Gautama, the Buddha who founded the Buddhist tradition, is said to have predicted that Buddhism would pass through just such stages of loss and degradation to the point of vanishing in about 2500 years, which would be our present time. It is also said that Buddhas before Gautama arose to restore the sacred teachings, and that such figures would appear again to restore the divine current of spiritual truth. The Great Master, known as the Maha Chohan, wrote a letter at the beginning of the modern Theosophical Movement declaring that "It is time that Theosophy should enter the arena." In the same letter he said "Buddhism, stripped of its superstition, is eternal truth...." Theosophy is as much of that eternal truth as can be shared with and assimilated by humanity today.

While not pretending to discern exactly what is encompassed by the Great Master's term "superstition," it is possible to examine the lives and contributions of those profound Buddhist teachers who sought to reform the practices and clarify the thinking of their days. The articles in this volume constitute a selection of just such teachers.

Between 1975 and 1989, articles on great thinkers and teachers were published monthly in *Hermes*, the organ of the United Lodge of Theosophists in Santa Barbara, California. The articles in this volume consist of a selection of remarkable Buddhist teachers and promulgators of the Bodhisattva Path, the path of service to all humanity. There are many illustrious teachers of this path who have labored for the world in the last two and a half millennia, and this selection is designed to give a sense of the immense range and richness of the Indo-Tibetan Buddhist tradition. This is the second volume in the collection of teachers from diverse spiritual schools of thought. The first volume presented those figures associated with the Seven-Century Plan initiated by Tsong Kha Pa for the Western world, culminating in the founding of the Theosophical Movement. There Tsong Kha Pa was discussed in terms of this Plan and its esoteric meaning. In this volume, Tsong Kha Pa is presented as the Buddhist teacher who rejuvenated Buddhism in Tibet, creating the Gelukpa Order, of which the Dalai Lamas are spiritual leaders. The third volume will focus on Chinese teachers—Confucian, Taoist and Buddhist—and Japanese Buddhist exemplars.

Since these articles were written, an enormous amount of scholarship has emerged, especially regarding the teachers and schools found in this volume. Many Tibetan texts have been carefully translated into English by highly trained individuals and teams of translators, thanks to the spread of Tibetan centers across the globe. Much of this ocean of material is profound but quite technical. The articles in this volume can serve as a general introduction to what is rapidly becoming a vast library of Buddhist history, teaching and knowledge. And they intimate the deeper meanings of the Bodhisattva Path which become clear only as a student or disciple assimilates the Teachings over a lifetime of study, self-examination, and self-sacrifice.

In addition to the articles on these remarkable individuals, there are articles by the great Theosophical teachers Helena Blavatsky and Raghavan Iyer which place fundamental Buddhist ideas in a broad context. These include essays on the Bodhisattva Ideal, esoteric Buddhism, reincarnation in Tibet, and the soul of Tibet, among others.

Taken together, the intuitive reader will not only gain a sense of the magnificent heritage of Buddhist thought over 2500 years but also glimpse the deep spiritual impulse working its way in and through the strivings of humanity. Contemplation of the core ideas in these articles will nurture the deepest aspirations of each individual who is actively seeking Buddha's Path to Enlightenment. One's perspective on the world and reality will be radically altered through a mature study and reflection on Buddhist thought in these essays.

Prof. Elton Hall
Ithaca, NY  November 2018

*****************************************

NOTE: All of the articles and readings in this work can be found in their original forms on the Theosophy Trust website at https://theosophytrust.org

Editor, Theosophy Trust

# TIMELINE OF INDIAN AND TIBETAN BUDDHIST TEACHERS

Ashoka .............................................. c.304-232 BCE

Nagasena ..................................................c.150 BCE

Ashvagosha .........................................c.80-150 CE

Nagarjuna .........................................c.150-230 CE

Aryadeva .......................................3rd Century CE

Asanga .........................................4th Century CE

Dignaga ...............................................c.480-540 CE

Vasubandhu .............................4th-5th Century CE

Buddhaghosa ...............................5th Century CE

Dharmakirti .............................6th-7th Century CE

Chandrakirti .....................................c.600-650 CE

Shantideva .........................................c.685-763 CE

Shantarakshita ...................................725-788 CE

Padmasambhava .........................8th Century CE

Atisha .................................................980-1054 CE

Marpa ...............................................1012-1097 CE

Milarepa ...........................................1052-1135 CE

Tsong Kha Pa ..................................1357-1419 CE

First Panchen Lama .........................1385-1438 CE

Taranatha ..........................................1575-1634 CE

Fifth Dalai Lama ..............................1617-1682 CE

Seventh Dalai Lama .......................1708-1757 CE

Seventh Panchen Lama ...................1782-1853 CE

Fourteenth Dalai Lama ...................1935-Present

# THE BODHISATTVA IDEAL

The attempt to understand and assimilate the central spiritual core of any religious tradition or collective religious heritage is most difficult. This is especially true of the Buddha's man-affirming doctrine that one must work out one's own salvation with diligence, that one must assimilate teachings so that they manifest in practice. The principle that there is no distinction between doctrine and practice constitutes the metaphysical underpinning of all Buddhist thought, no matter how much it may be lost in sectarian Buddhist theologies. This doctrine emanates from and is utterly dependent upon the centrality of the possibility of enlightenment, and it lays bare our difficulty in assimilating the teachings of the Buddha.

The difficulty takes the form of a paradox: on the one hand, one must pay careful attention to the scriptures, for one will never achieve salvation by blind belief nor will one achieve salvation by fuzzy thinking, being constantly victimized by *maya*. Discrimination must be developed; Buddhi must be activated. On the other hand, mere scriptural analysis, higher criticism, pedantic argumentation over the origin and meaning of particular words and over the historical development of formulations of doctrine, will not in any sense lead one to true understanding or realization. The need to develop discrimination is itself indicative of the necessity of handling the concepts taught by the Buddha, and applying them to our daily experience in such a way that we may articulate the teaching in our own words, from our own experience. Every doctrine, every scriptural point, is valid in a true Buddhist sense only to the extent that we 'engage' it and embody it in our own learning, experience and illumination. The Sixth Patriarch went so far as to say of enlightened men:

> Since they have their own access to highest wisdom through the constant practice of concen tration and contemplation (*dhyana* and *samadhi*), they realize that they no longer need to rely on scriptural authority.

While he could say this of enlightened men, the rest of us have to be a good deal more cautious. Nevertheless, the point he is making is germane to every individual who wishes to assimilate the basic teachings of the Buddha. Religious experience will reveal itself neither to the scholar nor to the tea-table conversationalist, but only to the man who makes the central conceptions of Buddhist thought the basis of his mental activity and the subject of his deepest meditation.

This is paradigmatically the case with the Bodhisattva ideal. Neither the nature nor the reality of the Brotherhood of Bodhisattvas, the grand fraternity which devotes its entire effort with one mind, one will and one overriding thought, to the welfare and liberation of all beings, can be grasped by other means. To assume that such a lofty conception as that of the Bodhisattva could be understood by the worldly mind would be to fall into the error of thinking that its subject could ever be understood in a realm where *samvrittisatya* ('relative truth') necessarily reigns. Nevertheless, if we put aside the rare case of the brilliant intellect which is refined by a fine attunement to its inner nature and warmed by a full devotion to the idea that there is no religion higher than truth, we may say that any man who continuously meditates on the ideal conception of the Bodhisattva can come to some understanding of the nature of such a being and its role in the world.

While the term 'Bodhisattva' means a number of different things and refers to various levels of spiritual attainment, we may take it that the Bodhisattva is reflected most archetypally in the Kwan-yin pledge. Kwan-yin is said to have been a Chinese princess who married a Tibetan king and led him to become a follower of the Buddha, but Kwan-yin is also assimilated to Avalokiteswara, a Buddha of inexpressible stature. Kwan-yin is said to have taken this pledge:

> Never will I seek nor receive private, individual salvation; never will I enter into final peace alone; but forever and everywhere, will I live and strive for the redemption of every

creature throughout the world from the bonds of conditioned existence.

This noble pledge immediately reveals two things about the Bodhisattva. The pledge can only be authentically taken by a very high being who cannot use speech in the degraded and careless fashion that we do in making cavalier claims and commitments, for the Bodhisattva commits himself to a central focus of thought in action for life and for lifetimes. The Bodhisattva has understood the full meaning of the first verse of the *Dhammapada*, "All that we are is the result of what we have thought: it is founded on our thoughts," and he has taken on, in making such a vow or pledge, the highest ideal conceivable to an individuated entity. For him, then, such ideal thoughts are more real than the *maya* of what we call everyday facts. Herein we find a paradox or mystery. The Bodhisattva sets for himself an ideal which cannot ever be fully attained and yet he throws his whole being into its achievement with a focus of interest, concern and total commitment unknown to the average man. The taproot of reality, then, is a plane of ideation so refined that it can never fully incarnate in this world.

But we also must notice that the Bodhisattva takes a pledge. A pledge must be taken to someone or something. The Bodhisattva, however, cannot take this pledge to human beings, for although they benefit greatly from the Bodhisattva's activity, the Bodhisattva works for them whether or not they realize, understand or even care. So, since the pledge must be taken to something or someone that can hold the pledge-taker accountable, we must rule out human beings. While the Mahayana is full of the most marvelous celestial and transcendental beings, it does not identify any sovereign God, does not teach any ultimate external source of accountability. Therefore, the Bodhisattva must take the pledge to something within himself, and yet to something higher than whatever set of forms he currently occupies or anything which he can fully manifest. Remaining true to the doctrine, 'Work out your own salvation with diligence,' the Bodhisattva holds himself accountable to the highest in him for what he is pledged to do on the plane of thought in some form or *rupa*.

Just what is it the Bodhisattva wishes to do for all beings? While it is clear that he cannot save another, we might give the defining characteristic of the Bodhisattva in any level of spiritual attainment as constant attention to the true self-interest of another. Thus the Bodhisattva sees that his own true self-interest is bound up in serving others to the utmost. While, except for the psychic selfishness and blockage of the personality, it is easy to serve the apparent self-interest of others, the Bodhisattva must have the supreme wisdom to know at any given time, in any particular context, what the true self-interest of another is. This is perhaps why some *sutras*, such as the *Gandavyuha*, maintain that to arouse fully the desire for enlightenment is to have already gone a long way toward achieving it. Or, when applied to the Bodhisattva, we might say that to be truly able to take the pledge of Bodhisattvahood, the Bodhisattva must already have achieved a high state of spiritual knowledge, self-control, devotion and illumination.

The Bodhisattva, then, is much more than a human being with an exceptionally generous heart. In fact, in striving to achieve an ideal himself, the Bodhisattva becomes an ideal for us, since his life can be reflected in our lives. If, indeed, the Buddha-nature is to be found in every man and universal brotherhood is thus a reality, then the Bodhisattva's help is not simply a matter of abstract good will or localized assistance, but comes in part through his standing as a model or archetype for all human activities and relations. Perhaps this is why the Mahayana has portrayed the Arhat ideal as being ultimately selfish and divisive, and not directly contributory to the spiritual evolution of mankind.

In D.T.Suzuki's commentary on the *Gandavyuha Sutra*, we find remarks made about what assists one in becoming a Bodhisattvic being. One element that is taken as important is the cultivation of good friends *(kalyanamitra)*. Suzuki implicitly recognizes that we must ask the question, "What constitutes a good friend?" Those who are our friends because they can use us and exploit us for their own purposes cannot be counted as good friends; neither can those who are friends with us because of a kind of neurotic dependence and who attach themselves to us because they find a lack in themselves and need us to fill it. While this characterization is of course crude, it is clear that most interpersonal relations are of this kind. Plato, in his dialogue *The Symposium,* has Aristophanes say that at some time in man's past, he was slit in half so that each one of us is only half a whole human being. Thus it is that we rush about the world desperately clinging to various people whom we hope to see as our other half. This mythic characterization captures very well the substance of most human relationships. There is a desperation about them, a fulfilling of needs, which suggests that neither party is a whole independent being, a true individual on his own. To put it in the strongest possible terms, this kind of friendship is a mutual vampirization of one another. And good friends cannot engage in that.

Because the good friend cannot be an exploiter nor solely moved by needs, he must, then, be one who can benefit and uplift his friend. The good friend leaves each one he meets with a little clearer intimation, a little stronger feeling of the essential nobility, the germ of Buddhahood within himself, and of the possibility of transcending himself. Hence two or more good friends working together may generate a powerful current elevating both towards enlightenment. The good friend can do this only by recognizing the higher within himself and thereby recognizing the higher within others. Perhaps this is the meaning of the Christian assertion: "Where two or three are gathered together in my name, there am I in the midst of them" (*Matthew* 18:20). Perhaps it lies behind Krishna's words in the *Bhagavad Gita* (Chapter 9): "Unto thee who findeth no fault, I will now make known this most mysterious knowledge."

The good friend is one who always sees so much good in others, who sees so many possibilities for the good, that he is capable of handling judgments of the limitations of others – an ideal completely inverted in *Kali Yuga* where we are all capable of analyzing in great detail one another's faults, but are almost blind to the Buddha-nature in ourselves and hence in others. Our judgmental excesses are naturally the result of forgetting our true heritage, our real nature and, thus, of succumbing to the pressures of corrupt social relationships. The good friend constitutes an emulation of the Bodhisattva on the terrestrial plane. Good friends working together form an earthly reflection of the Brotherhood of Bodhisattvas who work for all beings.

But the *Diamond Sutra* tells us that while the Bodhisattva vows to save every being, the Bodhisattva at the same time recognizes that there are no beings to be saved. Because of this kind of statement, and because of our discussion of the appeal to the higher in the Bodhisattva, we must ask the question, "What kind of view of the universe must the Bodhisattva have?" The Bodhisattva must have a profound realization of the essential unity of all things and must see that unity reflected on every plane of existence. Hence, while we see fragmented consciousness on the worldly plane, due to the fragmentation of our own consciousness, the Bodhisattva sees the thread that unites all consciousness, and hence all beings, into one. Where consciousness is fragmented, it may be united by law. The Bodhisattva therefore sees Karma not as an obstacle or a burden, but as the factual unity of all agents in *maya*. But further, the Bodhisattva has a reverential intimation of the one source of all differentiations, of all the worlds. This has been called divine or universal mind, the highest *Ishwara*, *Alaya*, undifferentiated consciousness.

From *Alaya* the Bodhisattva gets his sustaining compassion, for he sees that, "Compassion is no attribute. It is the Law of Laws," in the words of *The Voice of the Silence*. In the *Bhagavad Gita* the Krishna who says, "I established this whole Universe with a single portion of myself, and remain separate," (Chapter 10) is also the Krishna who says:

> I am the sacrifice and sacrificial rite; I am the libation
> offered to ancestors, and the spices; I am the sacred

> formula and the fire; I am the food and the sacrificial
> butter. . . (Chapter 9)

This suggests that all manifestation is a sacrifice, beginning with universal mind and ending with the smallest element of existence. Properly understood, sacrifice and compassion are the same thing. Hence the Bodhisattva sees the justice of Karma, for Karma is but sacrifice-compassion reflected in *maya*.

Thus we are finally led to the question of the agony or suffering of the Bodhisattva. Since the full Bodhisattva has the option of entering into Nirvana and renounces it, we are inclined to think that he suffers. But he sees Nirvana as a flight from mankind. The desire for it may be the subtlest form of that very sense of separateness that he believes is the origin of suffering in the universe. On the other hand, in renouncing Nirvana, he definitely takes on limited forms of embodiment and action on the human plane. Even if he chooses to remain disembodied, he nevertheless must occupy some vehicles, no matter how refined, and thereby limit his own modes of operation. Thus the Bodhisattva's primordial sacrifice is that of impelling his consciousness into some level of incarnation, a vehicle, which is necessarily more limited than the full range of his consciousness. That is only part of the suffering of the Bodhisattva. In fact, it is probably presumptuous of us to call this suffering at all. For while the Bodhisattva is operating under limiting conditions, as are all beings who have Buddha-nature, the Bodhisattva has voluntarily and with full self-awareness engaged in this activity, in his return to Plato's cave. Since he knows why he is limited, whereas we do not, his suffering is not the suffering of ignorance. Hence, insofar as we suffer because we do not understand the conditions in which we must operate, or because we cannot get what we want, or because others do not do what we desire, we are not suffering the suffering of the Bodhisattva.

There is another kind of suffering, both more tragic and more noble, the suffering of others which we must helplessly observe, in the knowledge that people must learn for themselves and that vicarious learning is impossible. This is akin to the suffering of the Bodhisattva who must stand by, without interfering with Karma, and watch countless humans destroy themselves and one another, committing useless acts of physical and psychological violence, only to be swept away in the first great psychic vortex, incarnation after incarnation. He who would find no fault, who would usher every being into Buddhalands, must stand and watch this, and that surely is Bodhisattvic suffering. Yet the Bodhisattva is not caught up in psychic pressures and whirls as we are.

While he must see all this, he has a larger picture, a cosmic perspective, and he knows that all beings, suffering and to be saved, are, in the largest cosmic perspective, somewhat 'unreal' – so he may appreciate the dance of Siva, the regenerator. He may in his perception transcend good and evil and see the fitness of all things in the Great Dance which has a nature and a value of its own, independent of any incarnated consciousness or limited conceptions of what right and wrong must be. He stands as witness to seemingly perpetual personal degradation and yet sees the untouched purity of our Buddha-nature. Such a being can throw himself into the world, seeking the true self-interest of every sentient creature, remaining Krishna-like in utter detachment from the world. To dwell on such an exalted conception, and to seek ceaselessly to embody it in daily living, is doubtless the noblest endeavor conceivable for any human being anywhere on earth. As *The Voice of the Silence,* dedicated by H.P. Blavatsky to the few, teaches:

> In Northern Buddhist countries, where the doctrine of *Nirmanakayas* – those *Bodhisattvas* who renounce well-earned Nirvana or the *Dharmakaya* vesture (both of which shut them out forever from the world of men) in order to invisibly assist mankind and lead it finally to Paranirvana – is taught, every new *Bodhisattva,* or initiated great Adept, is called the "liberator of mankind."

## THE BODHISATTVA ORDINATION

*Just as the earth and the other three elements, together with space, eternally nourish and sustain all beings, so may I become that source of nourishment and sustenance which maintains all beings situated throughout space, so long as all have not attained to Peace. When the Sugatas of former times committed themselves to the Bodhichitta, they gradually established themselves in the practice of a Bodhisattva. So, I too commit myself to the Bodhichitta for the welfare of all beings and will gradually establish myself in the practice of a Bodhisattva. Today my birth has become fruitful; my birth as a human being is justified. Today I am born in the Buddha Family; I am now a son of the Buddha. Now I am determined to perform those acts appropriate to my Family; I will not violate the purity of this faultless, noble Family.*

Shantideva

*Hermes,* May 1975
Elton Hall

# ASHOKA

*King Priyardarshi says:*

*I commanded this edict on Dharma to be engraved twenty-six years after my coronation.*

*It is difficult to achieve happiness, either in this world or in the next, except by intense love of Dharma, intense self-examination, intense obedience, intense fear of evil and intense enthusiasm. Yet as a result of my instruction, regard for Dharma and love of Dharma have increased day by day and will continue to increase.*

*My officials of all ranks – high, low and intermediate – act in accordance with the precepts of my instruction, and by their example and influence they are able to recall fickle-minded people to their duty. The officials of the border districts enforce my injunctions in the same way. For these are their rules: to govern according to Dharma, to administer justice according to Dharma, to advance the people's happiness according to Dharma and to protect them according to Dharma.*

Ashoka
*Pillar Edict I*

Shakyamuni Buddha taught and guided his followers for fifty years after his Enlightenment under the Bodhi Tree. His fundamental message was simply expressed in his first sermon, but the Four Noble Truths and the Noble Eightfold Path were of such spiritual simplicity that monks and laymen alike found them difficult to practise. The reality of *dukha*, suffering due to *avidya*, ignorance, and the possibility of its removal required nothing less than a total, if gradual, self-transformation. Though the goal was clear, the way was beset by every obstacle that ignorance, passion and confusion could engender in mind, body and the psychic nature. Knowing this, the Buddha did not outline a creed, choosing rather to encourage and correct his disciples through dialogues focussed on the practical problems of spiritual striving. His answers, including his steadfast refusal to explore questions which "tend not to edification", turned his followers back upon their own resources even while providing them with everything they could use to be lamps unto themselves. In addition, he established the Sangha, the order which includes all humanity as spiritual aspirants but which sets apart those who have taken vows to achieve Enlightenment and to centre all their energies upon doing so. His teachings provided the wisdom needed, and his Sangha the method required, to assure continuity of effort after his death.

Within a year of the Buddha's *Parinirvana,* the Sangha gathered together its members and attempted to set down the public teachings of the Enlightened One. Ananda was requested to recite all he knew, since he had been the constant companion and personal attendant of the Buddha. His words, supplemented by the recollections of others, engendered the earliest form of the *Tripitaka,* the three baskets of doctrine, discipline and exegesis, though probably the first two baskets alone were established at this time. Many monks had received private instructions which were not included in the public teachings, and these constituted the sources of the Mahayana tradition. About a century after this first council, a second was called to resolve numerous questions regarding doctrine and practice, and though the gathering resolved them, seeds of schism were planted. In time, eighteen schools would arise, not counting Mahayana viewpoints.

Within three years of the *Parinirvana,* Ajatashatru of Magadha conquered the neighbouring republic of Vriji, whose constitution the Buddha had approved, and soon afterward Koshala also came under his rule. His son established his capital at Pataliputra (modern Patna). Around 410 B.C. the populace of the nascent empire revolted and placed Shaishunaga, a Vriji aristocrat, on the throne. He and his descendants extended the scope of their rule, established a rudimentary bureaucracy and made Pataliputra a major city. During the reign of his son Kalashoka (Ashoka the Black), the second Buddhist council convened at Vaishali, and he was persuaded to support the more orthodox standpoint in the deliberations. The dynasty ended when Nanda, a minister close to the last king, assassinated him and seized the throne. The Nandas developed an integrated monarchy, expanded the empire of Magadha, encouraged agriculture, established a sound administrative system and accumulated vast resources of men and money. Alexander of Macedon's invasion of northwestern India, coupled with the increasing unpopularity of Nanda rulers, led to their downfall. Tradition holds that in 326 B.C. a young man named Chandragupta Maurya met Alexander, who recognized in him the potential for a great destiny, for Chandragupta alone understood the full meaning of the *Chakravartin*, the universal ruler who mirrors on earth the *Mahapurusha.*

While still a young man, Chandragupta overthrew the Nandas and assumed the throne with the help of Kautilya, who wrote a treatise on statecraft. After fighting Seleucus, Alexander's general and successor in Persia, he concluded a treaty which relieved the empire from Graeco-Persian threats and unwittingly assured himself a respected place in subsequent Greek and Roman histories. He took advantage of the administrative system nurtured by the Nandas, and used his status in the Hellenic world to establish close and amiable contacts with Babylon and lands farther west. Recognized as a brilliant general with command of an army of well over half a million soldiers, he was revered as an equally brilliant king, who matched his genius in uniting India with wise restraint in not pushing beyond the subcontinent. Pataliputra became a cosmopolitan centre of such enormous proportions that Chandragupta created a special section of municipal officials to look after its welfare, and special courts were established to meet its judicial needs. Aelian wrote that Chandragupta's palace exhibited an unequalled aesthetic refinement with which "neither Memnonian Susa with all its costly splendour, nor Ekbatana with all its magnificence, can vie". And Arrian indicated the exceptional character of the Mauryan empire when he noted that "the Indians do not use aliens as slaves".

Though the Greeks knew Chandragupta as a devotee of Brahmanical Hinduism, Indian tradition suggests that he restrained Brahmin power by favouring other religions. Jain records aver that he became a Jain in later life and even that he abdicated after a reign of twenty-four years, placed his son on the throne, retired and fasted to death in ascetic Jain fashion. Bindusara followed his father's foreign policy, retained his chief ministers, including Kautilya, and ruled for at least a quarter of a century. He expanded the empire and consolidated the machinery of government. He was fortunate in having a number of able sons, for he found himself in the awkward position of being personally popular even amongst peoples on the verge of revolt. Provincial ministers sometimes oppressed the populace, and in time they reacted strongly. Rather than suppress such outbreaks through the deployment of his enormous army, he dispatched his sons to act as viceroys in troubled areas. His son Ashoka first demonstrated his kingly skills as viceroy in Taxila. Though Bindusara followed the precepts of Vedic religion, he favoured the ascetic Ajivaka community, using Ajivaka sages as counsellors in the way his father had availed himself of Jain advisors. Though he could not secure an orderly succession to the throne, he guaranteed a continuity in effective government which survived a four-year interregnum and contest for kingship.

The legends and traditions from India, Greece, Tibet, China and Sri Lanka which becloud Ashoka's life also testify to the lustre of his rule and to his remarkable character. Although Ashoka left carved rocks and pillars throughout his empire, they were inscribed in the Brahmi script and in local dialects. The script was abandoned within three centuries, and the dialects were forgotten as well. Ashoka's edicts remained unread until James Prinsep successfully deciphered an inscription in 1837. Stories of Ashoka flourished from the time of his death and grew more fanciful with the passing centuries. Even though the legends do not always agree with one another or with the edicts, together they afford considerable insight into his reign.

Thus saith His Sacred and Gracious Majesty the King: On the high roads, I caused banyan trees to be planted by me to shade cattle and men. I caused mango gardens to be planted and wells to be dug at two-mile intervals, rest-houses were constructed, many watering-stations were established here and there, for the comfort of cattle and men. Slight comfort, indeed, is this. People have been made happy through various kinds of facilities for comfort by previous kings as well as myself. But this was done by me so that people might strictly follow the path laid down by Dharma.

*Delhi-Topra Pillar Edict*

Ashoka, whose name means 'free from sorrow', was born about 304 B.C., in the last years of Chandragupta's rule. His childhood is unknown, though he must have been a brilliant child amongst remarkable siblings, for Bindusara strengthened his reign and the empire by dispatching his sons to serve as viceroys in distant provinces. Ashoka was sent to Taxila (Takshashila) to pacify a rebellion that Crown Prince Susima had been unable to quell. After successfully restoring order and gaining the good will of the people, Ashoka became viceroy of Ujjain. Though Buddhist legends tend to blacken Ashoka before his conversion and to depict him as a saint afterwards – extremes not justified by other evidence, including the inscriptions – doubtless his resolve and strength of will manifested themselves distinctively in different phases of his life. Tradition avers that Ashoka was given to pleasures and enjoyments as a young man, and earned the semi-derisive name Kamashoka. Nonetheless, the Taxila experience left a strong impression on Ashoka, convincing him that he alone would be able to govern the Mauryan empire. When Bindusara fell ill, Ashoka assumed effective government from Ujjain, in part because Susima was again in difficulties at Taxila. Ashoka seized the throne upon Bindusara's death, but his brother and designated heir to the throne enforced his claim with his army. A violent struggle ensued, involving perhaps a number of brothers – though the legendary claim that Ashoka slew ninety-nine male siblings is probably an exaggeration – and four years passed before Ashoka emerged as the undisputed ruler of the Mauryan empire.

Ashoka became emperor in about 272 B.C., but he postponed his coronation *(abhisheka)* until he had consolidated power. Then he took the throne-name of Devanampriya Priyadarshin and the title *raja.* Devanampriya means 'dear to the gods' and Priyadarshin can be rendered 'he who looks benevolently'. He had inherited an empire which stretched from modern Afghanistan across Kashmir and included Nepal, subsumed the whole Gangetic plain and extended into Bengal. It crossed the whole of the Indian subcontinent and encompassed all of it save for the modern states of Tamil Nadu and Kerala. The years of internecine struggle encouraged laxity and perhaps rebellion, and it appears that Ashoka worked to restore order in the empire. The Kalinga empire to the south, sufficiently famous for Megasthenes, the Greek ambassador to the Mauryan court, to describe its military prowess, may have made incursions into Mauryan domains. Ashoka realized that the future of Indian civilization lay with one or the other of these two mighty empires, and in the eighth year of his reign he determined to conquer Kalinga. The firmness of his rule and the harshness of the Kalinga war earned him the epithet Chandashoka (Ashoka the Fierce). Within two years Kalinga was reduced to submission, but only at the cost of a hundred thousand deaths in battle, the slaughter of civilians, untold numbers of wounded and the deportation of another one hundred and fifty thousand men.

Though his singular victory secured the Mauryan empire peace on all sides and assured it of lasting influence in India – indeed, India was united for the first time in recorded history – Ashoka was horrified by the carnage. His nominal adherence to Vedic religion and his tolerant support of Jains and Ajivakas had not prepared him to confront and understand human suffering on such a vast scale.

> Devanampriya, the conqueror of the Kalingas, is remorseful
> now, for this conquest is no conquest, since there was killing,
> death and banishment of the people. Devanampriya keenly feels

all this with profound sorrow and regret. But, what is worse than this, there dwell in that country Brahmanas, Shramanas and followers of other religions and householders who have the duty of rendering due service to elders, to mother and father, and to *gurus*, of showing proper courtesy to friends, comrades, companions and relatives, as well as to slaves and servants, and firm devotion to Dharma. To these, injury, death or deportation may have happened. And the friends, comrades, companions and relatives who still retain undiminished affection for those affected by the war are terribly pained by this calamity. To Devanampriya, *Dharmavijaya* – conquest by Dharma – is the most important victory.

*Rock Edict* XIII

Whether Ashoka was transformed all at once, or whether the impact of his conquest affected him over time, it had two radical consequences. Spiritually, he became a follower of the *Buddhadharma*, the Teachings of the Buddha. Politically, he renounced war and conquest as acceptable methods for preserving the empire and sought to replace them with the inculcation of Dharma. He synthesized these two commitments in a threefold devotion to *dharmapalana*, *dharmakarma* and *dharmanushishti*, protection of Dharma, action according to Dharma and instruction in Dharma. Rather than follow in the footsteps of his grandfather and renounce the world, his understanding of Dharma held him responsible for the welfare of all his subjects, and he translated this general duty into an attempt to exemplify *dharmarajya*, the rule of Dharma. Long after his specific policies and works were forgotten, Buddhist tradition revered him as the first and ideal *Dharmaraja* – the Buddhist counterpart of the Hindu idea of the *Chakravartin* – and bestowed upon him the name of Dharmashoka.

Ashoka was less concerned with the details of Buddhist doctrine than with translating Buddhist standpoints into individual exemplification and government policy. For him, this effort was compatible with cosmopolitan civility and religious tolerance. His court maintained friendly relations with the *yavana* (foreign, specifically Greek) king of Persia, with Ptolemy II Philadelphus of Egypt, Antigonus II Gonatas of Macedonia, Magas of Cyrene and Alexander of Epirus (or perhaps Corinth). Eventually, he sent Buddhist teachers – some of them from his own family – to those centres, though without lasting influence. More importantly, he formed a close and lasting friendship with Devanampiya Tissa, King of Sri Lanka. Tissa sent a mission to Ashoka, who in turn sent his favourite son, Mahendra, and grandson Sumana, both monks, to Sri Lanka. Tissa was converted to the Buddha's Teaching, and soon Ashoka's daughter, Sanghamitra, joined the mission to instruct the women of the royal household. She bore with her a branch of the Bodhi Tree, which took root and survives in Sri Lanka to the present day.

*Dharmarajya,* as Ashoka understood it, permitted him to be devoted to the Buddha's Teaching and to revere and support the Sangha, but it required him as monarch to nurture and support all religious traditions in his realm. To this end, he inscribed edicts throughout the empire exhorting the people to practise Dharma, but kept the explicit content of that concept sufficiently universal to include Hindu, Jain, Ajivaka and other interpretations of it. Though he gave land, food and money to the Buddhist Sangha, he similarly supported the other spiritual traditions. Thus the Pillar Edicts mention gifts to the Sangha, and the Cave Inscriptions deed sites to the Ajivakas. Legend maintains that a third Buddhist council was convened in his reign and that he laboured intensely to preserve the unity of the Sangha – an effort that ultimately failed – but the Edicts speak only of purifying the order. Scholars tend to believe that no third council took place, or that Ashoka had little to do with it, but the absence of detailed testimony in the Edicts may only show that he saw no value in recounting publicly his role in the inner affairs of the Sangha.

Ashoka did not neglect public works or administration. Though he retained capital punishment for extreme offences, he devised a system of appeals to give every chance for a revised judgement that might replace execution with a fine. He reformed the tax system so that each region and village could appeal for relief when harvests and commerce had declined, reorganized the bureaucracy so that individuals could not wield power arbitrarily, and devised a new class of official. The *mahamatras*, literally 'great in measure', were established to monitor the operations of government. They travelled throughout the empire to ensure that officers and officials performed their duties efficiently, fairly and non-violently. Some were assigned to look after the welfare of the Sangha, and they even journeyed outside the realm to do so. Others saw to the well-being of other religious sects. Some reviewed the judicial administration, taxation department operations, municipal government and public works. They reported directly to Ashoka, who took interest in the details of his empire. Ashoka established rest-houses, dug wells, planted trees and founded hospitals along major roads. It seems that he even inaugurated a rudimentary social security system. He promulgated rules for the protection of cows, forbade animal sacrifices and abolished hunting for sport. He replaced the royal hunt with the royal pilgrimage and visited Bodh Gaya and many other sacred sites.

Both tradition and the Edicts suggest that Ashoka sent many of his trusted intimates on extended missions, and a large proportion of his family entered the Sangha. When his chief queen, Asandhimitra, died, he was bereft of his strongest support. Karuvaki, always less interested in Ashoka's aims, assumed this powerful position, and though she supported the Sangha, she insisted on proclaiming it in the *Queen's Edict*. The last chief queen, Tishyarakshita, is said to have grown so jealous of Ashoka's devotion that she attempted to destroy the Bodhi Tree, which Ashoka personally nurtured back to health. Whether or not the ageing emperor was held a virtual prisoner in his own palace, as tradition states, it seems that his last years were sad and lonely. When he died about 232 B.C. after forty years of illustrious rule, the light went out of the Mauryan empire. Neither legend nor the scanty records which survive can agree on who succeeded him, or when or in what order. Apparently several kings ruled in fairly rapid succession, and then the Mauryan line disappeared into oblivion.

Ashoka's empire soon passed out of memory. But the ideal he upheld as *aryaputra* (prince) and *dharmaputra* (son of the Dharma) increased in lustre with each passing epoch. Generations which could not recollect the Mauryans, nor point out the boundaries of their realm, nor even read the Edicts, nonetheless remembered the great king, "beloved of gods", who taught Dharma and lived what he espoused, who had set the standard against which subsequent rulers were measured and often found wanting, and who had promulgated a simple yet fundamental doctrine of tolerance and civility based upon respect for the spiritual aspirations of all people to adhere to the Dharma. They recalled that there had been a minor golden age, and knew that it was possible for human beings to experience a golden age again.

> *There is no gift that can equal the gift of Dharma, the establishment of human relations on Dharma, the distribution of wealth through Dharma, or kinship in Dharma.*
>
> *Rock Edict XI*

*Hermes*, January 1985
Elton Hall

# NAGASENA

*The good man, O King, perfect in uprightness, is like a medicine to men and gods, an antidote to the poison of evil. He is like water to men in laying the dust and impurities of evil dispositions. He is like a treasure of jewels to men in bestowing upon them all attainments in righteousness. He is like a boat to men in conveying them to the further shore of the four swollen streams – of lust, egotism, delusion and ignorance. He is like a caravan owner to men in that he guides them beyond the sandy desert of rebirths. He is like a mighty rain cloud in that he fills their hearts with satisfaction. He is like a teacher to men in that he trains them in every good. He is like a skilled guide to men in that he points out the path of peace to them.*

Nagasena
*Milindapanha IV 4, 14*

With the death of Ashoka, the ideal of *dharmarajya* – the rule of Dharma – passed quickly from Mauryan rule. Though the descendants of Ashoka managed to retain the throne for another half a century, their internecine rivalries and periodic divisions and reunifications of the empire assured a precipitous decline in their fortunes. The last Mauryan emperor, Brihadratha, was deposed by his commander-in-chief, Pushyamitra, who ruled under the title 'general'. At about the time of Pushyamitra's ascension, Bactrian Greeks seized Gandhara and conquered Vahika (the Punjab). Although the succession of Greek kings was as confused as that of the later Mauryans, one monarch, Menandros (Menander to Western historians and Milinda in Buddhist texts), earned a permanent place in the annals of history. As Pushyamitra aged, he supported Brahminical religion and ancient rituals, thereby effectively ending the pervasive influence of Ashoka's magnanimous concept of Dharma. Menandros occupied much of his territory and even marched as far as Pataliputra, where he remained long enough to build a great stupa. When he returned to his capital at Sakala (commonly assumed to be Sialkot in the Punjab), he took the ideal of *dharmarajya* with him. Buddhist principles became international, spreading from Bactria and the original capital of Menandros at Taxila to central Asia and beyond.

Menandros was admired by both his Greek and Indian subjects for his military genius, his ability to govern fairly, his even-handed support of Greek, Buddhist, Hindu and Zoroastrian traditions, his preservation of economic prosperity and his devotion to the life of the mind. Known to the Greeks as *basileus* and the Indians as *maharaja*, he was acknowledged by both as *Dharmaraja*, the king of justice. His government was Hellenistic in structure, but even while he increased the prominence of the Greek cities originally founded by Alexander the Great, he ensured that the older Indian cities joined them in importance. In later life he cultivated a deep interest in philosophical discussion and reflection, frequently debating thinkers from different traditions and often confounding them with his urbane wit and penetrating insight. Menandros met Nagasena in the course of these debates, was convinced by him, and joined the Buddhist Sangha. He encouraged the dissemination of Buddhist thought throughout his kingdom and built a monastery – the Milindavihara for Nagasena. According to the *Milindapanha* (*The Questions of King Menandros*), Menandros renounced his kingdom in favour of his son, entered the monastic community and died an Arhat, having achieved *nirvana.* Plutarch wrote that he died in camp during a war, but both sources agree that he became a Buddhist. Near the end of his reign he sent a large delegation of monks from Caucasian Alexandria, his birthplace, to attend the consecration of the great stupa at Anuradhapura in Sri Lanka.

According to the *Milindapanha*, Nagasena was the disciple of Dharmarakshita, the Greek disciple dispatched by Ashoka to Aparanta in western India. Only Nagasena was able to banish the king's doubts and win him over to the Sangha. He was, however, no ordinary monk, for he had been called from transcendental realms to perform this task. The *Milindapanha* recounts how the king confounded monks and laymen alike and how his words fell upon the mystic ear of Assagutta, an Arhat who dwelt high in the Himalayas. Assagutta convened an assembly of Arhats on the summit of Mount Yugandhara to see if any could match wits with Menandros. When all demurred, Assagutta proposed that they prevail upon the god Mahasena in the heaven of the Thirty-Three. By meditation, the Arhats vanished from Yugandhara and appeared in Sakka's celestial kingdom, and the king of the gods conveyed them to Mahasena's dwelling. Although he initially resisted the request to incarnate in human form, he agreed to do so when it became clear that the principles of religion would be furthered through his Bodhisattvic sacrifice.

When the Arhats returned to their Himalayan abode, they chose one of their number, Rohana, who had been lost in meditation and unaware of the crisis, to act as their agent amongst men. Following their instructions, he journeyed to the village of Kajangala, wherein the wife of the Brahmin Sonuttara had conceived a child. The god Mahasena was born as the boy Nagasena ten lunar months later. Each day for seven years and ten months Rohana begged for food at Sonuttara's house, only to be turned away. Finally the family relented – not knowing that doing so brought an end to Rohana's penance for being lost in meditation when the crisis caused by Menandros' wit had to be met – and the monk received a portion of food each day. At exactly this time Nagasena reached the age of seven and began to study the three Vedas. He penetrated their arcane meanings almost upon hearing them, mastered them and turned to meditation. When he discovered that he had not found the root of reality in his knowledge, Rohana "felt in his mind what was passing in the heart of Nagasena".

Rohana met Nagasena and promised him the secret of reality. Obtaining his parents' consent, Nagasena began instruction under Rohana as a member of the Sangha. Rohana deliberately set the *Suttanta* (discourses) aside and took up the *Abhidhamma* (deeper meanings of the faith). When he mastered it in seven months, he was admitted into full membership in the Sangha. But Nagasena doubted the wisdom of his teacher in setting aside the *Suttanta,* and

Rohana at once picked up the thought, which he derided in a thought sent back to the surprised Nagasena. He asked forgiveness, but his teacher withheld it, pending a confrontation with Menandros. Instead, he sent Nagasena to Assagutta for further instruction. Assagutta accepted Nagasena as an attendant and tested him by having him instruct others in the *Abhidhamma*. Both he and his hearers attained insight as he taught, and Assagutta knew it was time for him to fulfil his destiny. He sent Nagasena to the Ashoka Park in Pataliputra to meet Dharmarakshita.

Dharmarakshita taught Nagasena the outer and inner meanings of the *Tripitaka* – the three baskets of Buddha's teaching – in six months. The last night of this period witnessed Nagasena's enlightenment, and the earth thundered joyously while the heavens rained sandal dust and mandarava flowers upon the new Arhat. Immediately the Arhats of the Himalayas summoned Nagasena, who vanished from Ashoka Park and appeared before them. They asked him to face Menandros, then they all set out for Sakala, their yellow robes shimmering like lamps and drawing the scented zephyrs of the Himalayan heights along with them.

Nagasena and his illustrious retinue took up lodgings in the Sankheyya hermitage near Sakala, and he was made the chief of the Sangha there.

> Learned, with varied eloquence, sagacious, bold,
> Master of views, in exposition sound,
> The brethren – wise themselves in holy writ,
> Repeaters of the fivefold sacred word –
> Put Nagasena as their leader and their chief.
> Him, Nagasena of clear mind and wisdom deep,
> Who knew which was the right path, which the false,
> And had himself attained *nirvana's* heights.

Soon Menandros sent word that he would visit the Sankheyya grove and debate with Nagasena. When the king arrived, he immediately recognized Nagasena by his serene confidence.

> At the sight of Nagasena, wise and pure,
> Subdued in all that is the best subjection,
> Milinda uttered this foreboding word –
> "Many the talkers I have visited,
> Many the conversations I have had,
> But never yet, till now, today, has fear,
> So strange, so terrible, o'erpowered my heart."

Menandros did not fear for his safety, but he had a premonition that he had met his match. Since he took his philosophical discussions seriously, he sensed that he would be compelled to accept Nagasena's conclusions, a change of heart that would alter his life.

As soon as polite salutations had been exchanged, Menandros asked how the Thera (Elder) was known. "I am known as Nagasena, O King. . .yet this is only a generally understood term, a designation in common use, for there is no permanent individuality involved in the matter." This answer brought a flood of questions from Menandros.

> If, most reverend Nagasena, there be no permanent individuality involved, who is it, pray, who gives to you members of the Sangha your robes and food and lodgings and necessaries for the sick? Who is it who enjoys such things when given? Who is it who lives a life of righteousness? Who is it who devotes himself to meditation? Who is it who attains to the goal of the Excellent Way, to the *nirvana* of the Arhat? And who is it who destroys living creatures? Who is it who takes what is not his own? Who is it who lives an evil life of worldly lusts, who utters lies, who drinks strong drink, who commits the five sins which work out their bitter fruit even in this life? If there be no permanent individuality, there is neither merit nor demerit, neither doer nor causer of good or evil deeds; there is neither fruit nor result of good or evil karma. If a man were to kill you, there would be no murder. It follows that there are no real teachers or masters in your Sangha and that your ordinations are void.

Thus began a discussion which covered every aspect of Buddhist teaching, replete with rich examples and insights. The discourse as it has been preserved in the *Milindapanha* is doubtless a crafted compendium of Hinayana doctrine. Nonetheless, the logic of the dialogue and the nature of many of the illustrations suggest that the text may reflect the essence of an historic event, for Menandros is depicted as a skilled dialectician and Nagasena is portrayed as a master of Buddhist thought.

When Nagasena asked if the axle or the pole, the wheels or the frame, the ropes or the yoke, was the king's chariot, he answered that it was none of these things nor all of them together. "It is on account of having all these things that it comes under the generally understood term 'chariot'." "Just so", Nagasena explained, "do I come under the generally understood term 'Nagasena'." Generally expressed, a thing or individual is a temporary matrix of *skandhas* – aggregates of elements – and therefore there is no metaphysical difference between general and proper nouns. Nagasena elaborated the doctrine of dependent origination, using the example of the king and his shadow, to show that everything depends on something else for its existence. Having won the king's undivided attention, he laid down a requirement for further discussion. The king must discuss as a pandit, or scholar, and not as a king, for monarchs simply reject those who do not agree with them, whereas scholars acknowledge errors and accede to superior reasoning. Menandros agreed, and Nagasena undertook to come to Sakala regularly for discussions.

"Let our discussion be about the truth", Menandros proposed, and then asked about the aim of the Sangha. "Our renunciation is to the end that sorrow may perish and that no further sorrow may arise", Nagasena explained, pointing out that not all monks joined the order with such lofty motives. Reincarnation could be avoided, he taught, only by reasoning and by wisdom, for "reasoning has comprehension as its mark, but wisdom has cutting off.... The recluse by his thinking grasps his mind and by his wisdom cuts off his failings." In addition, five other qualities have to be acquired:

good conduct *(shila)*, faith *(shraddha)*, perseverance *(virya)*, mindfulness *(sati)* and meditation *(samadhi)*. Nagasena quoted Buddha to show that *shila* was the basis of the whole of the Path:

> Virtue's the base on which the man who's wise
> Can train his heart and make his wisdom grow.
> Thus shall the strenuous *bhikku*, undeceived,
> Unravel all the tangled skein of life.

If the mark of virtue is the presence of all good qualities, the mark of faith is tranquillity and that of perseverance is rendering support; that of mindfulness is recollection and presence of mind; that of meditation is being the leader which marshals the other qualities to one end or goal; and that of wisdom is both cutting off and enlightenment.

> When wisdom springs up, O King, it dispels the darkness of ignorance; it causes the radiance of knowledge to arise; it makes the light of intelligence shine forth; and it makes the Noble Truths plain.

For Nagasena, intelligence is the same as wisdom, and so an individual who will not reincarnate again invariably knows it because he is aware of the cessation of the causes of rebirth, for only *namarupa*, name and form, suffers rebirth and the Arhat no longer identifies with either. *Rupa* includes everything that is gross and *nama* all that is subtle and mental. They arise together, and where they are found, time appears, and with time, reincarnation. The Arhat, free of rebirth, does not experience time, whose root is *avidya*, ignorance.

> By reason of ignorance came the *samskaras* (forces or potentialities), by reason of the *samskaras* consciousness, by reason of consciousness *namarupa*, by reason of *namarupa* the six organs of touch (eye, ear, nose, tongue, body and sensory mind), by reason of them contact, by reason of contact sensation, by reason of sensation thirst, by reason of thirst craving, by reason of craving becoming, by reason of becoming birth, and by reason of birth old age and death, grief, lamentation, sorrow, pain and despair.

In setting out the twelve *nidanas*, or links in the circular chain of dependent origination, Nagasena showed that there was no apparent beginning or ending to the sequence. He used the example of the hen and the egg to illustrate his point. Since the chain cannot be exhausted, there is no immortal soul to be found within it. The chain must be broken by appeal to the ground in which it arises, and that is enlightenment.

Having been introduced to the Buddhist standpoint, Menandros retired to study the scriptures and to ponder what he had been taught. His skill in and fondness for debate impelled him to test Nagasena by confronting him with apparently contradictory doctrines and injunctions from the sacred texts. Nagasena responded to some of these dilemmas by explication, some by argumentation, and some by showing that the statements had to be understood in their context. Since Nagasena readily admitted a gap between the ideals of the Sangha and the practices of many of its members, Menandros refrained from formulating the chasm between ideal and reality as a dilemma. On one occasion, Menandros confronted Nagasena with a text from the *Jataka* which enjoined non-violence and another text which exhorted: "Punish him who deserves punishment, favour him who is worthy of favour." Nagasena patiently explained that the maxim of non-violence is derived from the nature of the Dharma, whereas the second passage has a specific application.

> The proud heart, great King, is to be subdued, and the lowly heart cultivated; the wicked heart is to be subdued, and the good heart to be favoured; carelessness of thought is to be subdued, and exactness of thought to be nurtured.

Menandros was troubled by the Buddhist emphasis on feeling love for all beings, because he could think of numerous instances where love had resulted in tragedy for either the lover or the beloved. Nagasena explained that love which was focussed on an object could result in a variety of consequences – good, bad or indifferent – but that love without an object is universal and not the attribute of any individual.

The virtues of love are not attached to the personality of the one who loves, but to the actual presence of the love that one has invoked in his heart. . . . At the moment in which an individual has realized this sense of love, neither fire nor poison nor sword can do him harm.

Menandros posed eighty-two dilemmas to Nagasena, who responded to each to the satisfaction of the king. No longer did Menandros wish to debate for argument's sake, nor to test Nagasena's skill and knowledge. Rather, he wished to learn from a teacher whose wisdom was proven, and his questions became those of a disciple who was open and receptive to understanding.

Nagasena developed an elaborate metaphor for the Sangha – Buddha's City of Righteousness.

The Blessed One's City of Righteousness, O King, has righteousness for its rampart, fear of wrongdoing for its moat, knowledge for its battlement, zeal for its watchtower, faith for its pillars, mindfulness for the watchman at the gate, wisdom for the terrace above, the Suttantas for its market-place, the Abhidhamma for its crossways, the Vinaya (law) for its judgement hall, and constant self-possession for its chief street.

Its flower bazaar consists of the subjects for meditation, and its perfume bazaar is the virtues. Its fruit bazaar is composed of the results of each stage of its Path, whilst its antidote bazaar contains the medicaments of the Four Noble Truths. Its medicine bazaar holds the means of mindfulness and the powers of morality and wisdom; its ambrosia bazaar is meditation upon the Real. Its jewel bazaar contains the seven priceless gems of right conduct, meditation, knowledge, emancipation, insight, discrimination and the sevenfold wisdom of the Arhats. The City can be seen by those who have cultivated eyes to see; it is both the foundation of the Sangha and the proof of the reality of Buddha.

Having shown the nature and meaning of Buddha, the Dharma and the Sangha, Nagasena offered one hundred and five similes of the ideal monk and Arhat. For example, the *bhikshu* should be like the earth in remaining the same, being self-perfumed, standing firm, never wearying, and being free of ill-will towards others. Like water, he should be pure, refreshing, free from offence, much desired by the world and harmless. Like fire, he should burn away everything unnecessary and undesirable, show no pity towards his inclinations, light up his heart into a purifying blaze, benefit all beings and dispel darkness. Like the wind, he should penetrate the groves of meditation, bend everything before his examination, be above all earthly concerns, bear good qualities along with himself and yet remain homeless in the world. Just as space cannot be grasped, so too the *bhikshu* should elude the grasp of every desire; like space, the effort of the *bhikshu* should know no limit; and like space, he should depend on nothing outside himself.

According to the *Milindapanha*, Menandros asked Nagasena three hundred and four different questions, which resulted in his complete acceptance of the Teachings of Buddha. Whether he became a monk near the end of his life, as the *Milindapanha* declares, or remained a lay disciple, as Plutarch implies, he ruled with a wisdom and detachment that earned him a unique place in Greek and Indian history. Nothing is known of Nagasena after his lengthy encounter with the king. This seems altogether appropriate, for he had been called into mortal existence for the sake of the Dharma, and, having performed his task, he vanished from the attention of history. Yet he left behind a method of explicating the Teaching of Buddha which became the archetype of subsequent elucidation. His subtle blend of metaphysics and ethics, argument and example, produced a model of useful discourse and an encouragement to practice. The *Milindapanha* is unique in being revered by Hinayana and Mahayana alike. Its depictions of the Path and the Goal have been relevant to every succeeding generation, for it is above all a portrait of the Arhat.

*He strives with might and main along the Path, searches it out, accustoms himself to it; to that end does he make firm his self-possession, to that end does he hold fast in effort, to that end does he remain steadfast in love towards all beings in all worlds; and still to that does he direct his mind again and again, until gone far beyond the transitory, he gains the Real, the highest fruit. And when he has gained that, the man who has ordered his life aright has realized nirvana.*

*Milindapanha IV* 8, 84

*Hermes,* February 1985
Elton A Hall

# ASHVAGHOSHA

*Whilst the essence of mind is eternally clean and pure, the influence of ignorance makes possible the existence of a conditioned mind. But in spite of the conditioned mind, the mind itself is eternal, pellucid, pure and not subject to change. Since its original nature is free from particularization, it knows in itself no change whatever, though it produces everywhere the various modes of existence. When the oneness of the totality of things (Dharmadhatu) is not recognized, then ignorance along with particularization arises, and all phases of the conditioned mind are thus developed. But the significance of this doctrine is so profound and unfathomable that it can be fully understood by none save the Buddhas.*

Ashvaghosha
*Mahayana Shraddhotpada Shastra*

When Kanishka, great Buddhist emperor of the Kushana dynasty, rode out of the northwest and across central India, he conquered everything in his path. The ideal of Ashoka had inspired the religious and social policies of a succession of western Indian kingdoms, and his exemplary statecraft impelled them to seek a new Indian unity. Kanishka came to the gates of Pataliputra, and though its king resisted furiously, the city fell. Legend holds that Kanishka demanded nine hundred million gold pieces as indemnity for the war. The king could not provide even a small fraction of that sum, but he went before the emperor like a defeated monarch prepared to come to terms. He offered Kanishka three treasures, each of which was worth a third of the amount demanded. The first was a fowl which was said to embody compassion. The second was a begging bowl which had belonged to the Buddha. The third was Bhikshu Ashvaghosha, a renowned playwright and master of Buddhist philosophy. Kanishka accepted the three as full payment, and Ashvaghosha joined him in

Purushapura (Peshawar) and became the spiritual counsellor for the court.

Ancient chroniclers differ on the details of Ashvaghosha's birth and life. He is said to have been born in eastern, western or southern India – but not in the north – into a Brahmin family. His exceptional intelligence manifested almost from the beginning, for he excelled in every department of knowledge even as a young student. Fiercely Brahminical in his convictions, he enthusiastically and readily defeated the simple Buddhists he encountered in debate. Longing for more challenging confrontations, he journeyed to Magadha in central India, where he could dispute Buddhists in one of their strongholds. His dialectical eloquence is said to have silenced a bell in a *vihara*, and he sent a shock wave through the Buddhist world. His notoriety brought him to the attention of Parshva, the northern Buddhist thinker whom the Chinese call the eleventh Indian patriarch. Parshva decided not only to debate Ashvaghosha but to convert him. He travelled to Magadha, where Ashvaghosha enthusiastically accepted the challenge. Parshva proposed that the defeated individual should become the disciple of the victor, and Ashvaghosha accepted. He also deferred to the patriarch's age and permitted him to speak first.

To the surprise of the large assembly, Parshva did not burst into metaphysical discourse or an elaborate line of argumentation. Rather, he asked just one question: "What shall we have to do in order to keep the kingdom in perfect peace, to have the king live long, to let the people enjoy abundance and prosperity, all free from evils and catastrophes?" To their even greater surprise, Ashvaghosha remained silent for a time, then bowed his head in submission to the patriarch. Thus, he became a *shramana* and began to study the Sutras. He was not immediately convinced of Parshva's wisdom, of course, but when he demonstrated his integrity by submitting to the conditions of the debate without cant or conditionality, Parshva manifested himself in several luminous transformations. Then Ashvaghosha knew that his new Teacher was no ordinary human being, and he joyfully undertook the life of the disciple. Parshva returned to the north, leaving his closest disciple, Punyayashas, to instruct Ashvaghosha. According to Taranatha, however, Ashvaghosha was defeated by Aryadeva in a battle of mantramic magic. While wrestling with his bitter defeat, he happened to read a Buddhist text in which his conversion and destiny were prophesied by the Buddha, and he joined the Sangha at once.

Ashvaghosha's genius shone in many directions. He wrote plays on Buddhist themes, though only the *Shariputra-prakarana (Play about Shariputra)* survives save for scattered fragments. He developed the *kavya* style of Sanskrit poetry and became the father of Sanskrit drama, remaining its undisputed master until the advent of Kalidasa three centuries later. He composed epics, at least two of which survive, including the *Buddhacarita,* the first complete life of the Buddha. Chinese records tell of seven philosophical works attributed to him, including works which foreshadow the standpoint of Nagarjuna. Two of these are time-honoured spiritual classics – the *Mahalankarasutrashastra (Book of Great Glory),* consisting of stories illustrative of retributive karma, and the *Mahayanashraddhotpadashastra (The Awakening of Faith in the Mahayana),* a text fundamental to most schools of Mahayana thought. There is also a tradition that claims Ashvaghosha composed a musical score for voice and instruments around the theme of *shunyata* and the emptiness of worldly delusions. It is said that so many people, including a number of princes of Pataliputra, were moved by the piece to join the Sangha that the king forbade its performance out of fear that his kingdom might otherwise be depopulated.

Little is known of Ashvaghosha's later life. After the death of Parshva, Punyayashas became patriarch, and upon his demise, Ashvaghosha received the title. During the reign of Kanishka, a fourth Buddhist council was organized by Ashvaghosha. He used his remarkable rhetorical skills to elucidate the arcane concepts and subtle logic of Mahayana metaphysics and ethics, winning northern Buddhist acceptance of them. This congregation did not have the universal representation found in earlier councils, however, and southern Indian and Sinhalese monks did not attend. *The Awakening of Faith* may have been written for this occasion as an affirmation of the utterly transcendental nature of ultimate reality, which is both the goal and the means for reaching it. When Ashvaghosha disappeared from human history about A.D. 150, he left a sacred legacy which has served as the fountainhead of Buddhist schools and doctrines from Gandhara and Central Asia to China, Korea and Japan.

In *The Awakening of Faith*, Ashvaghosha sought to free the receptive mind from every form of bias, ism and particularized viewpoint by using a few abstract and universal concepts in a philosophical dialectic to unfold spiritual consciousness. His clear rejection of philosophical dualism, pluralism, materialism and nihilism gives his teaching the superficial appearance of monism, though a thoughtful reading will show that his concepts are transcendental and open-textured, perhaps more akin to spiritual therapeutics than epistemology. His text opens with an invocation and closes with a promissory exhortation and benediction. The sections between these two move from above below, beginning with the absolute unity of the One Mind, its two fundamental aspects and its three great features – essence, attributes and influences – then applies the teaching in terms of faith and, finally, efficacious practice. The text is traditionally mnemonically summarized as a discourse on "One Mind, Two Aspects, Three Greatnesses, Four Faiths and Five Practices".

Beginning with an invocation of the Buddhas in the ten directions, the Dharma and the Sangha, Ashvaghosha outlined the contents of his text and indicated its purpose: to arouse faith in the Mahayana, banish doubts and nurture the seed of *bodhichitta*, the Buddha-consciousness. For Ashvaghosha, 'Mahayana' did not refer to a body of doctrine and practice distinct from that of the Hinayana or Theravada, but rather to the essence of reality – *bhutatathata* – without attribute or quality in itself and the ground of being as the One Mind. As *bhutatathata*, it is inconceivable and indescribable suchness, but it manifests as *samsara,* the round of birth and death, in three aspects. The first is its quintessential nature, the second comprises its attributes, which are collectively *Tathagatagarbha,* the womb or matrix of the Tathagata, and the third is its activity, the impulse towards good which makes it Mahayana, the Great Vehicle. It is a vehicle – *yana* – because the Buddhas ride it, and Bodhisattvas who ride it will become Buddhas. It can be called the One Mind because it is the *hridaya* and *chitta,* the heart and mind, of all sentient beings, the "soul of things".

The One Mind is the Absolute, *bhutatathata,* expressed in the temporal order, *samsara.* As the Absolute, it is transcendental, but as the round of birth and death, it is phenomenal. *Bhutatathata* should not be conceived of as outside the temporal order like a rather abstract extra-cosmic god, for it is coextensive with the kaleidoscope of phenomena. *Bhutatathata* and *samsara* are two dimensions of one reality, differing epistemologically but not ontologically. Meditation and right conduct constitute the raft which carries one across the sea of *samsara* to the infinite shore of reality, or, in an alchemical metaphor, the Alkahest or universal solvent which resolves sentient consciousness into its ultimate ground, the Absolute. Each human being lives at the nexus of these two dimensions, being essentially inseparable from the Absolute, yet through ignorance – *avidya* – an exile in the phenomenal realm. *Tathagatagarbha* is the connecting point, the embryo of Tathagata, which is *bhutatathata* in man. It is the seed of the *Dharmakaya* – the body of Pellucid Truth or Pure Reality – which is the plank of salvation for human beings lost in the fickle currents of *samsara.* Thus *Tathagatagarbha* is *chittaprakriti,* the essence of Mind, both *parishuddha* and *prabhasvara,* pure and radiant. The two aspects of the One Mind cannot be said to be identical, yet there is no duality involved. The Absolute suffuses the relative world of phenomenal consciousness as *Alayavijnana,* the universal treasury of mind, containing the seeds of ignorance as well as of Enlightenment.

Enlightenment is like *Akasha,* space, for it is *Dharmadhatu,* universal unity, and is therefore the *Dharmakaya* of the Tathagatas, who are said to abide in it eternally. Because human beings are unenlightened, it is necessary to speak of Enlightenment as if it occurred at some time. Yet, since Enlightenment is not an event in the temporal order, but rather its timeless transcendence, such language is only a heuristic device. Ordinary people advance towards Enlightenment by renouncing the tendency to draw conclusions. When *shravakas*, Pratyeka Buddhas and novice Bodhisattvas recognize personal perceptions for what they are, they free themselves from the snares of gross particularization and gain Enlightenment in appearance. Bodhisattvas who recognize the *Dharmakaya* but are not yet one with it achieve approximate Enlightenment. When they merge with the source of consciousness, they attain true Enlightenment, and they realize that it appears in two aspects, pure wisdom *(prajna)* and incomprehensible activity (karma). *Alayavijnana* dissolves for them, and they realize that there is no Enlightenment in time.

Non-enlightenment arose in Mind because of a disturbance – ignorant action, *avidyakarma* – which resulted in a distinction between subject and object, and this distinction produced the pervasive condition of *dukha,* misery. Consciousness of a perceiver led to awareness of an external world – ego-produced environment – and six kinds of phenomena resulted: sensation, memory, attachment, ideas or names, deeds which produce a sense of individuality, and suffering that expresses the loss of freedom in consciousness. Ashvaghosha analysed this process in meta-psychological detail and pointed to the process which sustains ignorance.

> Ignorance becomes the *raison d'être* of all forms of defilement (impermanence). And this ignorance perfumes suchness, and by perfuming suchness, it produces *smriti,* subjectivity. This subjectivity in its turn perfumes ignorance. Because of this reciprocity, the truth is misunderstood. Because it is misunderstood, the subjective world of particulars appears. And because of the perfuming power of subjectivity, modes of

individuation are produced. By clinging to them, deeds are done, and we suffer as a result both mental and bodily miseries.

This spiritually soporific process can be reversed through discipline and effort which lead to *nirvana*, the condition of action without an actor.

> As ignorance is annihilated, *Alayavijnana* is no more disturbed so as to be subject to individuation. As the mind is no more disturbed, the particularization of the surrounding world is annihilated. When in this way the principle and condition of defilement, their products, and the mental disturbances are all annihilated, it is said that we attain *nirvana* and that spontaneous activity is achieved.

Buddhas and Bodhisattvas incarnate in myriad guises to bring about the entrance of all beings into *nirvana*. They may use four methods of 'entertainment' – *dana*, giving; *priyavacana*, endearing speech; *arthacarya*, beneficial action; and *samanartha*, cooperation – the six *paramitas* or any mode that aids in perfecting *bodhi*, wisdom. Out of their boundless compassion, *Mahakaruna*, they do whatever is necessary to induce beings to tread the path to Enlightenment, whether by sudden or gradual means.

Ashvaghosha saw in the personalized concept of the *Atman* the single greatest block to Enlightenment. Whilst he affirmed the reality of the Mahayana, he argued that the aspirant must realize that there is neither a permanent personal self nor any permanent particular thing, that individuals and objects are neither *rupa* (form) nor *chitta* (mind), neither *prajna* (intelligence) nor *vijnana* (consciousness), neither *abhava* (non-being) nor *bhava* (being). Strictly speaking, they are inexplicable, although the Tathagata teaches by means of words and definitions as part of his skilfulness *(upaya)* in coaxing people to abandon delusion for *tattvajnana*, real knowledge. The Bodhisattva, who has renounced gross illusions yet still strives to merge with the Absolute through serving all beings, cultivates this skilfulness through practising truth, nurturing true repentance, strengthening the roots of merit *(kushalamula)* by reverencing the Buddha, the Dharma and the Sangha, and through *mahapranidhana*, great vows.

Buddhas and Bodhisattvas, despite their innumerable virtues, powers and skilful means, cannot help human beings who do not make themselves receptive to Dharma.

> Tathagatas are only waiting to reveal Themselves to all beings as soon as the latter can purify their own minds. When a mirror is covered with dust, it cannot reflect images. It can do so only when it is free from stain. It is ever the same with all beings. If their minds are not clear of stain, the *Dharmakaya* cannot reveal itself in them. But if they be freed from stain, then it will reveal itself.

Human beings prepare their minds by arousing faith, *shraddha*, in themselves. This faith is ultimately in *bhutatathata*, and specifically in the Buddha, the Dharma and the Sangha. It is perfected through five kinds of action: *dana* (giving), *shila* (right conduct), *kshanti* (patience), *virya* (constant energy), *shamatha* (tranquillity) and *vidarshana* (insight). The first three deal with compassionate action and self-restraint, which are nurtured by dauntless energy motivated by compassion. *Shamatha* is initially practised by withdrawal and meditation upon *bhutatathata* as *alakshana*, devoid of all attributes, uncreate and eternal. In time their consciousness will come to practise *shamatha* in all states of activity and withdrawal.

> When the practiser by virtue of his *samadhi* (mental equilibrium) attains an immediate insight into the nature of the universe *(Dharmadhatu)*, he will recognize that the *Dharmakaya* of all Tathagatas and the body of all beings are one and the same and *ekalakshana* (consubstantial). This is called *ekalakshanasamadhi*, the *samadhi* of oneness. By disciplining oneself in this *samadhi*, one attains infinite *samadhis*, because *bhutatathata* is the source of all *samadhis*.

Many individuals cannot readily sustain meditation upon *bhutatathata*, attributeless reality, because they have insufficiently cultivated the root of merit over lives. They will be distracted by visions both horrible and alluring, including visions of Bodhisattvas and Buddhas, by the crowd of memories or restless anticipation of the future. If the practitioner gains some facility in meditation, beings may appear to teach him supernormal powers, including clairvoyance, clairaudience, telepathy, memory of previous lives, miraculous abilities and the destruction of passions. He or she may drift into some state of static abstraction or enter a supercelestial realm of idealized pleasures. Although these marvellous powers come naturally to the enlightened Arhat, they are the poisonous serpents hidden under Mara's delusive flowers for those who have not attained perfect wisdom. The aspirant should remind himself or herself that all the things of the world are nothing in themselves, and are in essence *nirvana*. Thus one should reject them as tempting mental hallucinations and turn towards the transcendent essence of Mind.

Meditation alone will not lead to the highest reality. Without clear intellectual insight, *vidarshana*, one will be estranged from compassion and seek the subtle selfishness of spiritual indolence. To avoid this error, one should contemplate seven truths. First of all, one should think of the transience of all things.

> One should contemplate that all things in the past are like a dream, those in the present are like the lightning, and those in the future are like clouds that spontaneously come into existence.

Thirdly, one should recognize that whatever has a body is impure, the lodging place of false views. One should see that ignorant minds take the unreal for the real. Whatever comes into existence should be thought of as a chimera, without reality. Sixthly, one should realize that absolute truth, *Paramarthasatya*, is not a product of the individuated mind and that no reasoning or analogy can encompass it. Finally, one should dwell on the fact of suffering as the invariable result of ignorance. In addition to meditation and contemplation, the aspirant should take the great vow to renounce the whole process of *samsara*, should nourish in himself or herself the seeds of compassion for all beings.

Those who follow this course of thought and action will be drawn inexorably, if gradually, to the *Buddhakshetra*, the Buddha-realm, wherein they may behold the World-Honoured One and gain immeasurable spiritual benefit. Their feet will be securely placed on the path that leads to an Enlightenment which, however distant it may seem in the future, is wholly out of time and therefore eternally present.

> By practising this doctrine all Buddhas have attained the most excellent knowledge. . . . By practising this doctrine, Bodhisattvas in the past consummated, and Bodhisattvas in the future will consummate, pure and spotless faith in the Mahayana.

––––––

*The world is overcome – aye! even here!*
*By such as fix their faith on Unity.*

Shri Krishna

**OM**

*Hermes,* March 1985

Elton A Hall

# NAGARJUNA

*Those who speak with discretion*
*Are respected by humanity,*
*Like the sun, gleaming through the shadows,*
*Engenders warmth by its rays.*

*Though you suffer in the practice of Dharma*
*Let not your mind be anxious.*
*When the moon has been eclipsed,*
*Will it not shine freely again?*

*To garland the altar*
*Only full blossoms are gathered;*
*A gardener does not*
*Uproot the plant too soon.*

*Careless speech will get you caught*
*Like the parrot, the songster and the water-hen*
*Man fails to catch the water-duck,*
*Whose skill is his silence.*

*It is easy to live shouldering others' loads,*
*And easy to don tree-bark in the forest.*
*It is easier for men to die,*
*Than to pass their days in quarrelling.*

*Moral conduct, self-restraint,*
*And total control of the mind –*
*What else does one ever need*
*Who perseveres in these?*

Nagarjuna
*The Staff of Wisdom*

Ashvaghosha's efforts to demonstrate the underlying unity of diverse schools of Buddhist thought left a precious legacy in *The Awakening of Faith*. It did not, however, turn the tide of dogmatic sectarianism. The eighteen schools drifted ominously towards exclusivity, each claiming to have the only complete and correct formulation of the truth. Monks of differing persuasions continued to live together, and the gradual emergence of Nalanda as a centre of Buddhist studies encouraged this custom. Nonetheless, sectarian attitudes undermined the heart of the Buddha's teaching and saddened those who had tread the Path of the Tathagatas. Since the philosophical basis for unity within divergence in respect to details had been laid, a method was needed to give the foundation vitality. Nagarjuna provided a philosophical, psychological and magical method which could lead individuals to see far beyond their divergent perspectives to the universal horizon of Buddhadharma.

Mystery and legend surround every aspect of the life of Nagarjuna, and even the oldest sources disagree about his birth, the time during which he lived and exactly what he wrote. There is universal agreement, however, that he was born in south India outside the highly developed Buddhist centres. Most likely, he was born into a Brahmin family sometime in the latter quarter of the second century A.D. According to many traditions, including Taranatha's history, astrologers determined that Nagarjuna would die at the age of seven. When the fateful year approached, Nagarjuna's parents could not bear to watch their remarkable son die, and so they sent him to a small Buddhist monastery whose monks were known for their compassion. His diligent study of Buddhist texts overcame his fate, and he survived by gaining the *vajra* or 'diamond body'. Some sources add that the Buddha Aparimitayuh aided him by encouraging him to revere the *Aparimitayurdharani* in his devotions. Kumarajiva, however, wrote that Nagarjuna grew up as a Brahmin who learnt the secret of invisibility. With three companions, he would enter the royal palace and have his way with the women there. Even though invisible, the guards discovered their indiscretion and managed to kill Nagarjuna's friends. Though he escaped, he saw that lust leads to sorrow, and he entered a monastery to discover the path to enlightenment and freedom from all desires.

Nagarjuna became the friend of kings, repaired monasteries and stupas, and spread the teachings of the Buddha. His skill as an exponent of Dharma made him famous throughout India, and it attracted the Nagas, the guardians of wisdom who dwell in Nagaloka outside of Jambudvipa. They attended his discourses in the guise of young boys and were so deeply moved that the king of the Nagas invited him to visit their realm. This tradition holds that the Nagas were guardians of the Mahayana sutras, the arcane teachings of the Buddha, and scholars generally agree that these texts came out of south India, though their ultimate origin remains unknown. Nagarjuna persuaded the Naga king to allow him to take some of the scriptures back to Jambudvipa, where he placed them before the world. Another account avers that Nagarjuna was given the Mahayana sutras by a sage who dwelt in the secret fastnesses of the Himalayas. Given the rich symbolism surrounding the Nagas, who are sometimes said to be high spiritual Initiates, both stories may tell the truth. Until this time, Nagarjuna had been known as Arjuna because his mother had given birth to him under an *arjuna* tree, thus recalling the birth of the Buddha, and 'Naga' was prefixed to it because of his intimate friendship with the Nagas.

According to some accounts, Nagarjuna taught for a number of years at Nalanda, and though he personally did much to restore and maintain the sacred sites at Bodhgaya, the centre of Buddhist teaching gradually shifted to Nagarjuna's seat. Later in life he returned to southern India where he spread the Dharma in every direction. Having mastered the deepest teachings of the Mahayana, he acquired *siddhi, riddhi* and *abhijna* – psychic powers, magic and spiritual clairvoyance. Once, during a severe famine, he created gold out of base material and exchanged it for foreign grain, thereby sustaining the Sangha. It was said that he enlisted the aid of Yakshas and Nagas to build stupas and monasteries. He did not use his remarkable powers for himself, however, and employed them only when ordinary means were unable to accomplish a necessary task.

Some biographers said that he lived for a hundred years, basing their assertion on the relative dates of kings and teachers whom he knew. Others, however, told a more remarkable tale. On his way to visit several classes of invisible beings, he saw some children playing together and predicted that one of them would become a king. When he returned twelve years later, he found that the boy had indeed become King Udayana. The two became close friends, and Nagarjuna taught him the secret of the elixir of life so that the king would not die before Nagarjuna renounced his *vajra* body. Many years later, Sushakti, the king's youngest son, discovered the reason for his father's longevity. Already mature and desiring the throne, he despaired because he knew that Nagarjuna could not be killed and showed no inclination to leave his work. Nonetheless, Sushakti went to the Bodhisattva and explained his plight. Nagarjuna remarked that he had once beheaded a man in a previous incarnation, and told Sushakti to cut off his head with a blade of *kusha* grass. He added that he would eventually return to use the *vajra* body again. Sushakti beheaded Nagarjuna and his father died soon afterward, but fearing that the Bodhisattva would return quickly, he interred the head and body in shrines placed four miles apart. The head split open, revealing five stone images of Avalokiteshvara, and the two shrines began moving gradually towards one another. It is said that they are now within hearing distance of each other and that Nagarjuna will return when they meet. In this account, Nagarjuna lived about four hundred years.

The impact of Nagarjuna's teaching is as awesome as the story of his life. He was hailed as the father – and perhaps founder – of the Madhyamika or 'Middle Way' school of Buddhist thought. He made accessible the great Mahayana scriptures, and especially the Prajnaparamita sutras, and wrote commentaries and explanations. In addition, he composed verses which distilled the teaching of the Buddha in a way that disciples of every school could appreciate, and he wrote letters which set forth practical rules which kings could follow even while fulfilling their duties. He was one of "the four suns which illumined the world", the other three being Ashvaghosha, Kumaralabdha and Aryadeva. In Tibet, Nagarjuna is revered as an incarnation of Manjushri. Nagarjuna is honoured wherever Mahayana Buddhist thought prevails, and his works survive in Sanskrit, Tibetan and Chinese. When Buddhist thought was threatened by the delusion of sectarianism, the *Indian Chronicle* recorded, "Who but the two master-workmen – Ashvaghosha and Nagarjuna – could set it right?"

Building on the metaphysical doctrines delineated by Ashvaghosha, Nagarjuna sought to abolish contention amongst the schools by showing that assertions arising out of relative truth lead invariably to absurdity. Since absolute truth cannot be formulated, Nagarjuna could say, "I have no *pratijna* – proposition or position – to defend." His fourfold negative dialectic reduced any standpoint to incoherence insofar as it claimed to embody the truth. But Nagarjuna did not aim to turn monks into sceptics, but rather to make them sceptical of the images and formulations of truth which they were tempted to convert into dogmas. Once stripped of the insidious belief that one's deepest insights are somehow the absolute truth itself, one is open to authentic wisdom. Nagarjuna responded to the desire for spiritual knowledge by expounding the meaning of the *Prajnaparamitasutra* in its different forms. For those who were sufficiently grounded in their understanding of the arcane teachings, he provided methods of practice in his strict monastic disciplines, advice on living the spiritual life through his verses, and secret instruction in magic for those who were ready and could make spiritual use of such knowledge.

Nagarjuna insisted that all understanding must be rooted in a clear recognition that there are two levels of truth, relative truths which may be useful in a limited context but are illusory from a more inclusive standpoint, and absolute truth which is concealed by all relativities.

> Those who do not understand the distinction between these two truths, do not understand the deep significance of the Buddha's teaching.

If the distinction between the two kinds of truth is grasped, one will recognize that ultimate truth can be neither conceptualized nor formulated. In addition, however, every relative truth falls short of absolute truth by reifying entities and objects when, in fact, they are empty of independent reality.

> One of the profoundest teachings of Mahayana is called *shunyata*. If one can understand this doctrine, one can understand Mahayana and possess the six *paramitas* without hindrance.

Given the centrality of these doctrines, how could different schools dogmatize the teachings of the Buddha? For Nagarjuna, *anupalambha*, non-contentiousness, was the heart of the Buddha's message, and the tendency to make exclusive or absolute claims was a sad example of *graha*, clinging, a manifestation of *tanha*, the thirst for embodied existence. Thus, the very doctrine which could emancipate humanity had become yet another means of bondage. Nonetheless, this unfortunate misapplication demonstrated the thirst in human beings for the Real, but without *dharmanam bhutapratyaveka* – right understanding – spiritual aspiration is inverted and becomes craving for concretion and form.

This error is the root of all conflict and suffering, and the first step towards its removal is a comprehension of *pratityasamutpada*, conditioned origination. If everything subject to name and form is dependent on something else for its existence – that is, if everything is caused by something else – no thing can have an independent reality or self-nature. But the cause of everything is likewise dependent on something else for its existence, and in manifestation there is an infinite regression of dependencies. Therefore nothing subject to name and form is real in itself, and so no thing can in itself aid one in discerning Reality. Clinging to name and form distances one from Truth. Put in another way, the congeries of qualities and characteristics which constitute manifest objects of every kind is determinate, whilst ultimate reality is forever indeterminate. The indeterminate is the ground of the determinate, but, Nagarjuna insisted, it is not a separate entity but rather the ultimate nature of everything.

Each human being is determinate, conditioned, and as limited by name and form as anything else. Yet, like everything manifest, man is not merely grounded in the Real, for his essential nature is the Real. The lack which human beings experience as aspiration arises from their essential nature. The ignorant imagination, however, mistakes the relative duality of man's determinate and indeterminate nature for an absolute separation, and this gives rise to clinging and, eventually, to despair. The mind imprisoned in its own *avidya,* ignorance, is therefore its own enemy. Realization of this error – and, in time, of the truth – is possible because the mind can come to see the contradictions inherent in its false viewpoint. Nagarjuna's analysis of categories, the elements of existence and of the understanding aimed to reveal the *shunyata* or void ness of conditioned existence and the voidness of *shunyata* itself. Through the reversal of clinging to form by cleaving to *shunyata,* it is possible to awaken the Real, to see the voidness of the seeming full and the fullness of the seeming void.

Nagarjuna's dialectic was not simply apophatic, because his negation of every standpoint did not simply prove them false but appreciated their relative truth without confining one to any particular formulation. "Everything holds good in the case of one who is in agreement with *shunyata",* Nagarjuna taught. *Prajna,* the capacity to discern the degree and level of truth in every standpoint while recognizing the relative nature of them all, is the key to the Madhyamika or Middle Way. As the principle of comprehension, it is that Way.

> Ultimate truth cannot be taught except in the context of mundane truth, and unless the ultimate truth is comprehended, *nirvana* cannot be realized.

As one's understanding increases through garnering the truth present in limited perspectives, the dualism which alienates the individual from himself gradually gives way before a dawning metapsychological integration that also reveals a harmony with the whole of Nature through a recognition of its divine ground, *shunyata*. As sectarian dogmas fall away, the aspirant discovers that Truth is no view yet underpins all views, just as they each reflect some aspect of it to a degree. The aim and purpose of the Madhyamika is to instil a sense of the Real through recognition that conditioned reality is based upon, rooted in and nothing but *shunyata*.

In the *Dvadasadvarashastra (The Treatise of Twelve Portals)* Nagarjuna delineated twelve portals through which one could pass to understanding without residues of doubt. The first portal concerns causal conditions.

> Things are produced from diverse conditions,and
>> therefore have no self-nature *(svabhava)*.
>
> If they have no self-nature, how can there be such
>> things?

A careful analysis of causation discloses that things which are caused – and all manifestation is caused – have no independent reality. In terms of what they seem to be, they are *shunyata*, empty. The second portal addresses the problem of production.

> If an effect is already present in a cause,
>> there can be no production.
>
> If an effect is at the outset unreal in
>> respect to a cause, there likewise can be
>> no production.
>
> If an effect is both real and unreal, there
>> can be no production.
>
> How then can there be production?

Further, the third portal attests,

> Briefly and broadly, conditions do not
> contain effects.

> If there are no effects within conditions,
> how can they come from conditions?

The first three portals teach that no ontological meaning can be given to the concept of causality. The fourth portal shows that the same analysis applies to characteristics or qualities of things, whilst the fifth portal demonstrates that the three universal characteristics of all things – origination, persistence and destruction – are themselves unreal, that is, empty. In the sixth portal, Nagarjuna holds one cannot prove either that an object is identical with its characteristics or that it is different from them. Since both standpoints are true in part and untrue in part, it is possible to move towards Truth through mundane truths so long as one adheres to this Middle Way.

The seventh portal attacks the seemingly fundamental distinction between being and non-being.

> There cannot be being with non-being, nor can
> there be being without non-being.

> If there can be being with non-being, then being
> should always be non-being.

Origination and persistence are characteristics of being, whilst decay and destruction belong to non-being. Thus being and non-being can neither exist together nor separately. The eighth portal applies the argument regarding being and non-being to Nature to show that since all things are in a condition of ceaseless change, there is no self-nature in them. The ninth portal adds that since things cannot be understood in terms of their essential nature or from the process of causation, they are *shunyata.*

Since there can be no creation without cause and effect, as the tenth portal teaches, and since causality is empty, there is no creation. Nagarjuna applies this conclusion to the idea of suffering to show that even suffering has no real existence. The eleventh portal examines creation from the standpoint of time to demonstrate that it cannot occur in the past, present or future, and so cannot occur at all.

> 'Earlier than', 'later than' and 'simultaneous with' –
> such events are impossible.
>
> How then can events be produced by causes?

The twelfth portal uses the argument from time to show that nothing can be produced.

> The effect already produced is not to be produced; that not yet produced is not produced.
> Without that which is already produced and that which is not yet produced, that which is being produced is not produced.

Although Nagarjuna's fame is due in large measure to his stunning dialectical paradoxes, he did not devise them for idle amusement. He was convinced that anyone who assiduously meditated upon *shunyata* would possess the alchemical key which, when used to unlock the portals on the Middle Way, would lead one to the elixir of life. He gave a talisman for all aspirants in the *Mahaprajnaparamitashastra*:

> *There is realization of Reality, but not as it is imagined in any extremes. Neither anything nor nothing, devoid of all prapanca – conceptualization and elaboration – this is what is called realization of the Way. If one were free from extremes, then prapanca itself would be the Way. Bodhi is itself the Way, the Way is itself bodhi.*

*Hermes*, April 1985
Elton Hall

# ARYADEVA

Even though Nagarjuna's Herculean effort to provide a methodological foundation and philosophical basis for drawing together diverse Buddhist standpoints failed to achieve its aim, he gave an impulse for spiritual renewal that ramified in many directions. He founded the Madhyamika – the Middle Way – school which worked to preserve a sense of fraternity amidst diversity. With the emergence of the Madhyamika, the meta-psychological and metaphysical power of the Mahayana made an enduring impression on every aspect of Buddhist tradition. Those who resisted the suggestion that Gautama Buddha had imparted an arcane teaching to his most advanced disciples nonetheless freely borrowed Madhyamika methods and analogies to elucidate their own views. The tradition that Nagarjuna was head of the great university-monastery of Nalanda testifies to the pervasive influence of his thought. Madhyamika nurtured itself in India and then spread to China and Japan, where it flourished in conditions quite different from those of its birthplace. It came to have its own offspring – the Yogacharya school of idealism – and eventually divided into two distinct emphases. In the fifth century Bhavaviveka held that Madhyamika had a positive content of its own, whilst Buddhapalita sought to reduce all philosophical positions to absurdity in the belief that this would lead to the intuitive realization of Reality beyond all possible cognition.

Long before the Madhyamika expansion, however, Nagarjuna's vision was consolidated with consummate dialectical skill by his chief disciple, Aryadeva, one of "the four suns which illumined the world". Like his illustrious teacher, Aryadeva's life is thoroughly immersed in legend and hagiography. Biographers report that Aryadeva, born in the heart of a lotus, became the foster-son of Panchashringa, King of Sinhala, which is generally believed to be the modern Sri Lanka. His natural grace and brilliance so impressed his father that he was declared Crown prince and enthroned as heir apparent. He had already studied the Theravadin Buddhist doctrines in depth, and the prospect of becoming king saddened him. Eventually he renounced the throne for the life of a monk, but the delicate political complications arising from the presence of a former Crown prince near the throne of another successor impelled him to travel to India. Having already learnt the arts and sciences in addition to Ceylonese Buddhist thought, he sought for a teacher who could guide him to the core of the Dharma.

In time Aryadeva met Nagarjuna and became his devoted disciple for life. According to Hsuan Tsang, Aryadeva found Nagarjuna's dwelling and had himself announced. Rather than inviting Aryadeva to enter, Nagarjuna ordered that his begging bowl should be filled with clear water and taken to Aryadeva. Upon receiving the bowl, Aryadeva dropped a needle into it and sent it back. Nagarjuna welcomed the newcomer, saying to his astonished pupils that the bowl filled with water represented his knowledge, and the needle signified that Aryadeva had penetrated to its very bottom. Aryadeva was appointed the spiritual successor of Nagarjuna and eventually became head of Nalanda. He wrote a number of texts, the most famous of which is *Chatuhshataka (The Hundred Treatise)*, which survives in the Tibetan translation and in Sanskrit fragments. Taranatha related stories that Aryadeva established monasteries and performed a number of remarkable magical feats, though he added that he could not vouch for these traditions.

Aryadeva was sometimes called Nilanetra, 'blue-eyed', because of unique markings on his face, but the name may be associated with his attainment of the 'rainbow body'. He was also called Kanadeva, 'one-eyed *deva*', owing to a mysterious encounter with Shiva in his aspect as Maheshvara. While disputing with theistic Shaivites, he argued that a golden statue of Maheshvara was not the god himself, and to prove the point, he tore out the left eye of the image. When Maheshvara visited Aryadeva the next day, the monk tore out his own eye to show that he was not prideful, for the statue is not the god, and the body is not the perceiver within it. Though Aryadeva's works suggest that he debated Jain philosophers, theistic Vaishnavas and Shaivites, and the followers of numerous diverse Buddhist standpoints, his concern was to remove error rather than to compel every individual to adhere to exactly the same doctrine and practice. He marshalled his sublime dialectic with special enthusiasm in critical analyses of theistic traditions in which Deity was first personalized and then absolutized. He launched equally strong critiques against Theravadin systems which emphasized practice to the exclusion of understanding.

Above all, Aryadeva wished to alter the Theravadin tendency to base spiritual practices and ethical norms on a psychological understanding of suffering, replacing it with ethical insight rooted in abstruse metaphysics. He saw that ethics without a firm grasp of metaphysics premised upon the doctrine of two truths – *paramarthasatya* and *samvritisatya*, absolute and conditional – strengthened practice while neglecting meditation. Mahayana metaphysics, on the other hand, required the marriage of meditation and ethical action like two sides of a coin. Despite the stringency of the path of emancipation, Aryadeva applied the standpoint of the Two Truths to include all receptive beings in the Dharma.

> Love for the religion is prescribed by the Tathagatas for those who long for heaven; the highest truth, however, is prescribed for those seeking deliverance. One who desires religious merit cannot always speak of *shunyata*. Does not medicine turn to poison when wrongly used? Just as one can make a thing clear to a mleccha only by using his language, so one cannot explain anything to the common people save by using the common language.

Nonetheless, relativistic explanations are useful only to the degree that they guide one towards meditation on the fullness of the seeming Void, *shunyata*.

Tradition holds that Aryadeva's most challenging and triumphant debate was with Matricheta, a great devotee of Maheshvara. He travelled as he taught and in time he came to

Nalanda. Nagarjuna and Aryadeva were on retreat at Sri Parvata, and the monks were discomfitted by Matricheta's powerful argumentation. A message was sent to Nagarjuna, who tested his disciple and sent him to confront the threat. The four debates were conducted on two levels, dialectical and magical. Aryadeva won each dialectical exchange, but only by demonstrating his superior ability in magic through blocking Matricheta's attempts to invoke invisible assistance. Matricheta's disciples immediately entered the Sangha, but Matricheta himself held back until he had completed a profound meditation on his errors. Then he repented without reserve and eventually became a renowned Buddhist teacher. Subsequently, Aryadeva retired to South India, where he continued to teach until his death. Some sources maintained that Aryadeva was stabbed by the angry disciple of a vanquished Tirthika, yet even as he lay dying he refused to allow his followers to pursue his assailant. "Everything is unreal", he said. "Reflect upon the true meaning of all things in the world of phenomena. Who is pierced or murdered? Who is a friend and who a foe? There is neither murdered nor murderer." Thus restraining his disciples, he afforded his attacker the opportunity to escape and perhaps repent and set his feet upon the path of emancipation.

Buddhist tradition reveres Aryadeva not only as a superlative exponent of Madhyamika teachings but even more as a Bodhisattva who gave his life for the sake of humanity. He balanced uncompromisingly incisive analysis of mental confusion with positive guidance for the reorientation of consciousness towards the Bodhisattva Path. This dialectical equilibrium underlies the *Chatuhshataka,* Aryadeva's most honoured work. It opens with arguments for the elimination of erroneous preconceptions, namely that things are permanent, pleasant, pure or the self. The relativity of phenomenal existence and the First Noble Truth show that nothing in experience can be permanent, pleasant or truly pure. If this is understood, it is clear that there can be no self at this level. Once spiritual reliance on the mundane world is abandoned through realization of its inherent impermanence, one is ready to contemplate those Bodhisattvic practices which lead to

Buddhahood. Thus one needs to eliminate the *kleshas*, defilements which hinder spiritual growth. To achieve this, one must seek out their cause in the many levels of enjoyment that arise from seemingly desirable objects of the senses. Only then is one ready to take up discipleship. Having made clear the requirements of the path of emancipation, Aryadeva added a vigorous analysis of the insubstantiality of all *dharmas*, constituents of existence, which are shown to be nothing but ciphers of *shunyata*. Beginning with the idea of a self, and including time, dogmatic opinions, the faculties of sense and their objects, doctrinal extremes (such as existence and non-existence, identity and difference) and conditional reality, Aryadeva subjected the elements of phenomenal existence to the negation of the *Shunyavada*, the way of emptiness. He concluded with a discussion of the epistemological and logical problems involved in the teaching of *shunyata*.

Aryadeva also composed treatises which would appeal to a wide audience of serious students. His *Skhalitapramathana-yukt-hetu-siddhi (The Dialectic Which Refutes Errors Establishing Logical Reasons)* sets forth a variety of erroneous views and summarizes those doctrines which will aid the disciple in overcoming them and progressing towards Enlightenment. By coming to understand the depth and tenacity of psychic structures, one prepares oneself to consider the Dharma without blindness, bias or prejudice. The metaphysical expressions of the highest truths can then be used to break up the matrices of ignorance and delusion and transform consciousness. Thus Aryadeva wrote the *Dialectic* to offer aid in "this world of the five degeneracies" – degenerations of life span, of understanding correct views, of afflictive emotions (greed, anger, ignorance, pride and their kin), of psychological stability of sentient beings and degeneration of this age of strife. Curiously, Aryadeva does not begin with denying the putative existence of the non-existent; rather, he affirms the existence of that which some deny. Rejecting the argument that all things come to an end and therefore need no care today, he insists that whilst all things perish, they leave seeds for future growth. Nothing just happens, but is invariably caused. Thus, only by cultivating those virtues which attack the roots of dependent causation can one achieve freedom from an endless round of involuntary rebirths.

> If our migration to high and low states
> Were unrestricted and as free
> As a bird flying without impediment,
> Then no obstructions could exist.
> But by virtue or through wrongdoing,
> Our path is made for weal or woe.
> These have the power for joy or sorrow,
> Here gods' power counts for nothing.

Having affirmed the efficacy of right action because of the impermanence of all things – and not because anything can be said to remain the same – Aryadeva then denies that any conceivable notion of an individual self can be valid.

> It is like, for example,
> The oft-made mistake
> Of beholding a rope as a snake.
> The phenomenon of the rope
> Is not seen for what it is,
> But is seen as possessed of a self.
> Yet as the rope a snake can never be,
> So phenomena are never self.

Similarly, those who are tempted to reduce the phenomenal world to some permanent material substratum are equally in error.

> These elemental things – fire and water,
> Earth and wind – cannot exist in themselves,
> For they are compounded of smaller things,
> Subatomic parts (*p'a-ra-rab dul*), and so
> Even the most minute particle
> Can be divided six ways.
> Thus 'smallest part' cannot exist,
> And likewise every substance

Can never permanent be
And threefold its destruction is.

To those who see in the present order of things the lineaments of permanence, believing that one is naturally reborn in the same race or gender, social position or personality, Aryadeva warns:

Just as gold or silver will to the moulds conform–
Be they lions, horses or bulls –
Just so does the spirit – the mental continuum –
Conform through the impulsion of desire
In colour and form and structure of consciousness
Like figures that are moulded in the fire.

When one begins to realize the deceptive nature of all phenomena, however, a tendency can arise through which one believes that if one only understands the nature of all the kinds of phenomena that appear, one will somehow discern the Real within them. This is the subtle error of confusing exact classification with spiritual insight.

If high states are attained
By knowing this way
Of making enumeration,
Then things like precious gold
Should be compelled to appear
By the counting of sticks and stones.
Thus we must in fairness say
That this kind of logic
Is by common sense refuted,
Not to mention by ultimate truth.
It is as if a hungry man
Said that he was full
After listing all his favourite foods.

For Aryadeva, the fundamental error in the misperception of Reality arises from a failure to recognize the egolessness or lack of inherent nature of all things. When some inherent substantiality or reality is granted to phenomena, one then fails to grasp the truth of dependent origination at its root. This misunderstanding is the direct cause of the five afflictions – desire, hatred, ignorance, arrogance and doubt – and these five ensure the relevance of the First Noble Truth. Metaphysically, the error can be explained with relative ease, but it cannot be understood without great effort. To grasp the voidness of the seeming full and the reality of the seeming void, one has to penetrate and break up the patterns of misperception and misunderstanding that pervade every level of embodied consciousness. Thus the pure metaphysics of the *Shunyavada* – way of the Void – must be translated into the Madhyamika, the Middle Way, which avoids all extremes and excess. The Bodhisattva Path, along which one journeys by stages through progressive awakenings to the real nature of things and the gradual stripping away of false conceptions of the self, is the only way to perfect knowledge and full Enlightenment. The Middle Way, which has been characterized as 'zerology' – the study and practice of *shunya* – is trod by penetrating learning and also reducing oneself to a zero while joining oneself to the whole – *shunyata* – through selfless service and meditation on fundamentals. Aryadeva is called a Bodhisattva because he fused clarity of insight with compassionate action in the unwavering conviction that all could tread the path of emancipation.

> *Arjuna! if a man sees everywhere –*
> *Taught by his own similitude –one Life,*
> *One Essence in the Evil and the Good,*
> *Hold him a Yogi, yea! well-perfected!*

> Shri Krishna

**OM**

*Hermes*, May 1985
Elton Hall

# ASANGA

*Whoever thoroughly experiences Samsara as it really is, circles in Samsara with an undefiled mind. And whoever has a mind which is unwearied by the aspects of impermanence, suffering and egolessness of Samsara, such a one does not quickly enter Nirvana. And whoever has a mind which is unfrightened by Nirvana stores up equipment for it, and though beholding the good qualities and benefits in Nirvana, nonetheless does not yearn for it, and so does not quickly enter Nirvana. This is the bodhisattva's great means for attaining perfect Enlightenment. This means is well grounded in that firm conviction in supreme shunyata. Therefore, for the bodhisattva who has well taken hold of shiksha marga, the Path of Instruction, cultivating conviction in supreme shunyata, is said to be the Mahan Upaya, the Great Means, for reaching knowledge of the Tathagata.*

Asanga
*Bodhisattvabhumi*

Tradition teaches that there have been three revolutions of the wheel of Dharma. The first was inaugurated by Gautama Buddha's public Teachings, enshrined in the doctrines of eighteen schools collectively called Hinayana or Lesser Vehicle, and surviving today in the Theravada, the way of the elders. The second was initiated by Buddha's esoteric doctrines, emerging as the Mahayana or Great Vehicle, which is the source of the diverse schools of Tibet, Mongolia, Korea, China and Japan. The third revolution commenced with Asanga and the Yogacara school, a branch of the Madhyamika which emphasized meditation as a fundamental aspect of Buddhist practice. H.P. Blavatsky suggested that this complex history contains a deep mystery. Asanga, also known as Arya Asanga or Aryasanga, has been confused with another teacher, Aryasangha, a direct disciple of Buddha, who is the true founder of the first and ever secret Yogacharya school. In conflating the earlier teachings of the arcane Yogacharya school with elements of tantric and magical practices, Asanga compromised his exceptional brilliance and insight. Since the pure Yogacharya books – *Narjol chodpa* in Tibetan – have never been made public, one must cautiously examine Asanga's encyclopaedic *Yogacarabhumi*, of which the *Bodhisattvabhumi* is a part, for it contains "a great deal from the older system", according to H.P. Blavatsky.

Asanga's birth is shrouded in legend. Taranatha wrote that Asanga's mother had been in a previous life a monk with a mastery of the *Tripitaka*, the Three Baskets of the Theravadin canon. Once, when arguing with a monk, he deeply hurt the feelings of his opponent by accusing him of having a female brain. Avalokiteshvara, to whom the offender was pledged, predicted that he would live a number of lives as a woman to understand the utter injustice of the remark. Sometime in the fourth century this monk was born as Prakashashila in the city of Purushapura (modern Peshawar) in Gandhara. Though a Brahmin, she first married a Kshatriya and gave birth to Asanga. Sometime later she married a Brahmin and had two other sons, Vasubandhu and Virinchivatsa. Though Asanga was considerably older than his half-brothers and would be expected to take up the duties of a warrior and leader, Prakashashila told him that he was destined for other service and encouraged him to enter the Sangha.

Asanga entered the Sangha and spent a year serving the *upadhyaya*, the *acharya* and the Sangha, and then he studied the sacred texts, including the *Tripitaka* and the Mahayana sutras, for five years. As a blue-robed Mahishasaka monk, he learnt advanced methods of meditation. When his understanding equalled that of his teacher, he received a secret initiation and withdrew to a cave on a mountain called variously Kukkutapada, Gurpaparvata and Gurupada. There he meditated upon Maitreya, to whom he dedicated himself. After three years, however, he had failed to behold his celestial preceptor and made ready to leave his rocky abode. As he stepped outside the cave, he saw that the wings of birds had gradually worn down the rocks around their nests, and thinking, "I have lost assiduity", he returned to his meditations. Disappointed after another three years, he again made ready to leave, but he noticed the effect dripping water had had on the stones on which it fell, and he returned to his contemplation. A third time he left his cave and came across an old man rubbing a piece of iron with a fine cloth to make needles out of it, and he returned to his meditation. But in the twelfth year he gave up all hope and left his mountain fastness.

Heavy-hearted, he made his way towards the city of Achintya, where he saw a dog infested with worms. Realizing that the poor creature would die of the infestation, but not wishing to destroy the worms, he determined to give them flesh cut from his own body. No sooner had he made the sacrifice of his physical form than the dog vanished and in its place stood Maitreya, resplendent in a halo of *lakshanas*, divine graces. Asanga could not contain himself. Weeping, he asked why the vision had not occurred before, but only now when he was in too much physical pain to have wished for it. Maitreya explained that he had always been present, but that Asanga's own blindness had prevented him from seeing. Once his great insight – *prajna* – had been matched by compassion – *karuna* – his eyes became clear. Maitreya asked what Asanga truly desired, and he replied, "To spread the Mahayana." Thereupon Maitreya took Asanga into the Tushita realm, Maitreya's celestial abode. There he was taught the deepest meanings of the *Prajnaparamita* sutras and was instructed in the five works of Maitreya. When Asanga returned to terrestrial existence six months – some say twenty-five years – later, he began an energetic career in rejuvenating Buddhist thought and practice in India.

The Tibetans call this form of history *rnam thar*, sacred biography, which is essential for understanding the path to Enlightenment and is therefore less concerned with the exact details of external events than with the inner significance of the life recounted. Asanga began by founding *viharas*, monastic communities, and since he had mastered the *abhijnas*, supernormal powers, he could travel as far in one day as the average monk could cover in nothing less than a month. Since he could read the minds of others, he matched his teachings to the understanding of his hearers. Eventually his great erudition brought him to the attention of King Gambhirapaksha, who became his patron and generously financed much of Asanga's work. In time Asanga wrote down the five books of Maitreya and wrote commentaries on them, including the *Uttaratantra,* a work which Tsong-Kha-Pa said was not a Yogacara but a Madhyamika text. In addition, Asanga wrote commentaries on the *Prajnaparamita* sutras as well as his own expositions, including his enormous *Yogacarabhumi (Stages of Yoga Practice).* Late in life he persuaded his brother Vasubandhu to join the Yogacara school, and Vasubandhu successfully laboured to make Asanga's doctrines accessible to the general population. Asanga, his work thus secured by his brother, retired to Rajagriha – the site of the First Council after the Buddha's *Parinirvana* – and died. His disciples built a *chaitya,* a reliquary, in his honour.

Despite the tremendous spiritual impulse Nagarjuna had imparted to the Mahayana, his sheer dialectical brilliance had frightened many followers. He had steered a middle course between the tendencies to take the world of phenomena as real in itself and to reject all existence as unreal. Between naive realism and nihilism, Nagarjuna placed the doctrine of *shunyata* as *Tathata,* the Void, as the essential nature of all things. Recognizing the meta-psychological proclivity to hypostasize *shunyata* itself as a 'thing' alongside other phenomena, he taught the principle of *shunyatashunyata,* the emptiness of the Void. At the same time, he insisted that *shunyata* was not a mere nothing, for "if all this were not *shunyata,* there would be no creation and no destruction". *Shunyata* is not another category of phenomena, and yet it is the *sine qua non* of all phenomena. Nonetheless, many who followed the Madhyamika found this doctrine too subtle and drifted into a depressing nihilism, whilst those of other schools found their doctrines shaken by Nagarjuna's devastating dialectic.

Asanga attempted to counter these tendencies, while remaining loyal to the spirit of Nagarjuna's teachings, through a variety of *upaya* or methods. He modified the ancient formula of "two truths", *Paramarthasatya* and *samvritisatya,* absolute and relative truth, into the *trilakshana* or "three natures" standpoint. In this view, phenomena have three natures: *parikalpita,* which is a mental construct and in that sense imaginary and corresponding to *samvritisatya; paratantra,* a nature independent of the mind yet subject to dependent origination; and *parinishpanna,* absolute nature corresponding to *Paramarthasatya.* This perspective is not so much a denial of the ancient doctrine of two truths as a practical means to avoid nihilism on the path towards Enlightenment. As the mind frees itself from its self-imposed constructs, it does not drop into an abyss of nothingness, but rather discovers that things-in-themselves exist, though dependent for their existence on other things and therefore not absolutely real. The root of this intermediate existence is *shunyata,* the Void. The schema fills the gap between the mind's freedom from its own delusions and the supreme realization of *Paramarthasatya.*

In conjunction with the threefold doctrine of truth, Asanga also posited an eightfold classification of consciousness. Consciousness, *vijnana,* under the impulsion of karma, hypostasizes the duality of appearances, though such duality has no real existence. Consciousness evolves eight aspects to present the world as the ordinary individual experiences it. Five of these aspects correspond to the five sense-organs, and the sixth is mental perception. Seventh is the defiled mind, that is, the mind deluded by the notion of a self as a real entity. The eighth aspect of consciousness is *alayavijnana,* the universal storehouse of all impermanent experience. Over time it gathers the seeds of karma and thus reflects both all that has been done and all that will unfold in the fruition of karma. *Alayavijnana* is not, however, ultimate reality: it is *chitta,* mind, in its most universal sense, and as such it is part of the *skandhas,* aggregates out of which a *persona* is formed. The *skandhas* are *anitya, dukha* and *anatma,* impermanent, suffering and without self. Just as *alayavijnana* draws upon the mind's experience of the world, so the mind is affected by *alayavijnana.* What arises out of *alayavijnana,* therefore, is not *shunyata.*

For Asanga, the world is *chittamatra*, 'mind-only', but not in the absolute sense suggested by some scholars and even by late Yogacara writers. Asanga borrowed the term from the practice of meditation wherein any image which comes into the mind is said to be *chittamatra*, 'mind-only'. Such images, however splendiferous, are entirely creations of the mind and do not constitute a direct transcendental experience of *shunyata*. Similarly, Asanga argued, the famous passage in the *Dashabhumika Sutra*, *"chittamatram idam yad idam traidhatukam"* ("these three realms are nothing but mind"), means that the experiences one has of the three realms, *kamaloka*, *rupaloka* and *arupaloka* – the worlds of desires, forms and formlessness – are all like the images held in meditation. They are creations of the mind and are not the lineaments of reality. Though the *Lankavatara Sutra* identifies *alayavijnana* with the *Tathagatagarbha*, the world of the Tathagata, Asanga rejects the equation. Tsong-Kha-Pa later wrote that the doctrines of the *Lankavatara* were provisional, that is, suitable as medicine for most minds but requiring inner interpretation for those ready to achieve insight. Hinting at a deep mystery in regard to *Tathagatagarbha*, Tsong-Kha-Pa supported Asanga's view that *alayavijnana* is not ultimate reality. Once one achieves such purity of consciousness in meditation that any sense of subject and object utterly vanishes, one witnesses *shunyata* and then recognizes the true meaning of calling the world 'mind-only'. But in that indescribable exaltation one is not other than *shunyata.*

That is called reality which is the sphere of cognition completely purified of the obscuring force of defilement. What is that reality? The Four Noble Truths – suffering, its origin, the cessation and the path leading to its cessation. It is that knowledge which arises in those having clear comprehension who, after thorough investigation, arrive at the understanding of the Four Noble Truths.

What is the reality which is the sphere of cognition completely purified of the obscurations to the knowable? . . . It is the domain and the sphere of cognition that belongs to the Buddha-Bhagavans and *bodhisattvas* who, having penetrated *dharmanairatmya*, the non-self of *dharmas*, and having realized, because of that pure understanding, the inexpressible nature of all *dharmas*, know the sameness of the essential nature of verbal designation and the non-discursively knowable. That is the supreme *Tathata*, real nature, there being none higher, which is the supreme limit of the knowable and for which all analyses of the *dharmas* are undertaken, and which they do not surpass.

Since *Tathata*, 'suchness' or 'real nature', is *shunyata*, the Void, the nature of names or designations of things and the things themselves have the same nature, for sameness, *samata*, is also equivalent to *shunyata*. Thus the neophyte on *shiksha marga*, the Path of Instruction, comes to realize that *dharmanairatmya*, the non-self of all *dharmas*, and knows that no *dhamma* or element of existence has any independent nature or self, that it has no expressible nature, and therefore that it cannot allow attribution. Thus *dhammas* do not exist as they are generally thought or expressed. For Asanga, this explains the meaning of Buddha when he taught that he came for the redemption of all beings although he knew that there are no beings to be redeemed. Reality, for the Enlightened Ones, transcends both being and non-being, but Reality is not somehow a third thing apart from them. Rather, Reality is both being and non-being simultaneously. *Dharmas* exist, but not as they are thought or designated, and yet both the phenomenal and noumenal aspects of *dhamma* have the same essence, for the essential nature *(svabhava)* of all *dharmas* is *shunyata*.

Freedom from the delusion of discursive thinking necessarily comes in stages, for the eight aspects of consciousness, though a functional unity, are not all one. Each aspect has to be understood for what it is, emptied of its false claims to an independent nature, and put in its place. For example, the three *kleshas* or defilements of consciousness – lust, hatred and delusion – are often depicted at the centre of the Wheel of *Samsara* on Tibetan banners. From a psychological and ethical standpoint they can be considered the basis of *dukha*, suffering. From a metaphysical viewpoint, however, the three *ashravas* would be thought of as the 'gates to hell'. They are 'outflows' associated with sense-desire, love of existence and ignorance. For Asanga, unlike most Buddhist thinkers, these perspectives are deliberately conflated, so that the *ashravas* are the *kleshas,* the same forces present in different aspects of eightfold consciousness. If one truly eradicated the *kleshas,* Asanga held, one would have removed the *ashravas* as well. The *bodhisattva* who reaches that lofty plane of knowledge where mental defilements are purged and Reality is understood has freed himself from every vestige of discursive thought. But this means that the various modes of delusion are as deeply rooted as consciousness itself when conceived apart from *shunyata.* The *kleshas* have to be removed at every level right up to *alayavijnana.*

Thus that one, with such mastery, is the best of and incomparable amongst all beings. And you should understand that the *bodhisattva* has five superior benefits which govern all circumstances. They are that he attains supreme peace of mind, having gained the tranquil stations and not through pacifying defilement; that his knowledge and vision with respect to all the sciences are unimpeded, utterly pure; and perfectly clear; that he is unwearied by his circling in *Samsara* for the sake of all beings; that he understands all speech of the Tathagatas that has veiled meanings; and that, because he is self-reliant and does not depend on others, he is not led away from his zealous devotion to the Mahayana.

Such a sublime accomplishment does not allow the *bodhisattva* to retire from the world of anguish and ignorance, however, for the *bodhisattva* cultivates a profound compassion commensurate with his wisdom and insight. Each benefit he has garnered from his journey along the Path of Instruction is matched by concomitant action undertaken on behalf of all living beings. Since his mind is truly tranquil, he dwells always in a state of happiness, a state appropriate to a *bodhisattva* who knows the way to Enlightenment and the yoga that removes the weariness of mental and physical exertion. His supreme knowledge of the sciences impels him to nurture the *Buddhadharmas* – the knowledge, attainment, method and teaching of Buddha – amongst all beings. His freedom from weariness in circling through *Samsara* allows him ceaselessly to nurture and encourage the evolution of beings, each at its own level and each within the karmic limits of its incarnation and mode of existence. His ability to understand the speech used with veiled meaning by the Tathagatas permits him to remove the doubts and difficulties of serious disciples who want to follow the Path he has trodden. It also gives him the power to discern *saddharma*, the true Dharma, from its subtle but fictitious resemblances, so that he can uphold the Teaching which is otherwise undermined by shadowy inversions. Finally, his complete self-reliance guarantees that he will never fall into error and thus mislead others and that he will remain faithful to his vow and thereby be a worthy example.

The five activities appropriate to a *bodhisattva* strengthen him even as they help others. They are called *karaniyas* or *bodhisattva* duties, because in them the distinction between *prajna* and *karuna* dissolves, as does the distinction between self and others, and even that between *Nirvana* and *Samsara*.

According to Taranatha, the Mahayana had suffered great decline before Asanga came to spread its teachings. During his long lifetime he vigorously disseminated the Dharma to tens of thousands of individuals who entered the Sangha. He came to be called Arya, 'noble', and Maitreyanatha, 'one devoted to Maitreya', and it is said that though he taught for well over ninety years, he never looked a day older than he did on the day he beheld Maitreya near Achintya. Though all his works were eventually translated into Chinese, the sage Dharmakshema was so moved by the *Bodhisattvabhumi* that he translated it immediately after its composition. It became one of the six basic texts of Atisha's school in Tibet (which was later reformed as the Gelukpa order by Tsong-Kha-Pa), where it remains an essential part of Mahayana studies. Traditional sources agree that Asanga attained the third of the ten stages associated with the Bodhisattva Path, that of *Prabhakari*, the 'Light-giving', where the *bodhisattva* "diffuses the great light of the Teaching amongst all living beings". Asanga the Light-Giver is revered as the perfected practitioner of meditation and an exemplar of selfless service to humanity.

> *The subtle Soul sits everywhere, unstained:*
> *Like to the light of the all-piercing sun*
> *Which is not changed by aught it shines upon*
> *The Soul's light shineth pure in every place;*
> *And they who, by such eye of wisdom, see*
> *How Matter, and what deals with it, divide;*
> *And how the Spirit and the flesh have strife,*
> *Those wise ones go the way which leads to Life!*

Shri Krishna

## OM

*Hermes*, June 1985
Elton Hall

# DIGNAGA

*I salute him who is Logic personified,*

*Who attends to the welfare of living beings,*

*The Guru, the Blessed One, the Protector,*

*And to demonstrate the ways of Logical Proof,*

*I shall draw together under one head*

*The different fragments from my other writings.*

Dignaga

*Pramanasamuccaya*

*When Dignaga had written this on a rock with a piece of chalk, the earth shook, a light blazed forth and a thunderous sound was heard.*

Taranatha

*History of Buddhism in India*

The philosophical traditions of India have always honoured logic, the art of reasoning. Hindu, Buddhist and Jain sages alike look beyond the limits of reason and conceptualization, but they insist upon the crucial role played by clarity of thinking in self-transcendence and spiritual realization. Like Plato and unlike Aristotle, Indian thinkers paid more attention to the logic of concepts and principles of inference than to the topology of categories. Nagarjuna raised logic to the recondite level of compelling dialectic, and those who came after him refined various aspects of his crucial work. Vasubandhu in particular addressed the need for precise dialectic, because debate was neither a mere intellectual game nor an occasion for mutual hostilities. The spiritual seriousness of argumentation is evidenced by the fact that an individual defeated in a thorough and exhaustive exchange was honour-bound to accept the victor's standpoint, even if this meant changing religious allegiances. Whilst logic had been a dominant concern of many thinkers and teachers, Dignaga turned his whole mind to the topic and refounded the art of reasoning in the service of Truth.

Sometime in the early years of the fifth century, Dignaga (also known as Dinnaga) was born into a Brahmin family in Simhavakta near Kanchi (Kanchipuram). Nothing is known of his early years except that he took as his *Upadhyaya*, spiritual preceptor, Nagadatta of the Vatsiputriya school. This branch of Buddhist thought espoused the view that there existed a kind of real personality independent of the elements or aggregates composing it. Though Dignaga learnt the whole of the *Tripitaka*, the Three Baskets of non-Mahayana Buddhist wisdom, he was not satisfied with Vatsiputriyan attempts to deny the eternality of self whilst affirming its continuity through a series of lives. When his preceptor enjoined him to search for the "indescribable self", the principle of 'I' which is neither identical with nor different from the *skandhas*, he opened all the windows of his dwelling by day and filled every corner of it with lamps by night. Stripping himself naked, he repeatedly examined himself from every angle. Soon other monks noticed his bizarre behaviour and reported it to Nagadatta. When asked why he carried on in this way, he replied that he failed to understand what he had been instructed to seek and so had bared himself to see if it might be uncovered. Recognizing a challenge to his doctrine, Nagadatta grew angry and ordered Dignaga to leave his *vihara* or monastic community.

Dignaga left in silence. He knew that he could demonstrate the untenability of Nagadatta's doctrines, but he was profoundly aware of the wrongness of attacking the teachings of one's *Upadhyaya*. His efforts to indicate a fundamental problem indirectly had only angered Nagadatta, and Dignaga departed with a heavy heart. In time, however, he encountered Vasubandhu, who fully understood Dignaga's insights, and willingly undertook to teach him Yogachara thought. Vasubandhu explained five hundred *sutras* to Dignaga, including all those belonging to the Mahayana and Hinayana traditions, as well as the mysterious *dharani sutras.* He mastered the science of *vidya mantra* and refined the art of debate. Nonetheless, he felt that he was a worthless student because of his inability to persuade his first teacher to reconsider his doctrines. Once when he was in a state of spiritual depression, Manjushri, the sword-wielding Bodhisattva of supernal wisdom, appeared to him in a vision, brought him to his senses and instructed him at great length in the Dharma. Dignaga was spiritually regenerated and took up his work with a zeal that never waned for the rest of his life. He retired to a cave in the Bhotashela hill near Odivisha (Orissa), where his intense meditation bore the inexpressible fruit of *samadhi.*

A few years later, a great debate was arranged at Nalanda. As in most monastic communities, Buddhists of diverse schools dwelt peacefully together. Even while they vigorously debated the merits of their differing doctrines, they were bound together in the brotherhood of the Dharma. Nalanda not only hosted every shade and hue of Buddhist thought, but also housed numerous non-Buddhist teachers and students. Dignaga was invited to debate a group of remarkable *tirthikas,* non-Buddhist instructors, renowned for their dialectical agility. Dignaga defeated each one in turn so decisively that they all joined the Sangha. He tarried for some time at Nalanda, where he taught the *sutras* and wrote many volumes on Yogachara doctrine and on logic. Eventually he returned to his cave near Odivisha and devoted himself to meditation. While there, he resolved to compose the *Pramanasamuccaya,* aphorisms on *pramana,* valid knowledge.

According to Taranatha, he wrote the beginning lines of this great treatise with a piece of chalk on a rock. When he took his begging bowl and went out for his morning round, a Brahmin called Krishnamuniraja came upon these words, realized their portentous significance, and erased them. The next morning Dignaga began again, but once more the words were eradicated in his absence. On the third morning Dignaga wrote the same words, but added the sentence "Know this to be extremely important" and challenged the defacer to a debate. Reading this challenge, Krishnamuniraja sat down and waited for Dignaga to return from gathering alms. When Dignaga came back to his dwelling, the two engaged in a ferocious debate. When Dignaga emerged victorious, he invited the *tirthika* to accept the Dharma, but Krishnamuniraja threw a magic powder which ignited the belongings of Dignaga, and then fled. Once again, Dignaga fell into a spiritual depression, blaming himself for failing to convert his opponent. But Manjushri appeared to him and remonstrated with him, warning that "wrong ideas result from evil company". Assuring him that no one would bring harm to his treatise, Manjushri promised to remain Dignaga's *kalyana-mitra*, true spiritual friend, until he attained full enlightenment.

Dignaga composed his treatise in peace and returned to his meditations. Once he grew ill. After his mendicant rounds, he returned to the forest and fell fast asleep. While he slept, he had visions of numerous glorious Buddhas who instructed him. Meanwhile, the king, out in the forest for recreation, came across the sleeping monk. Celestial deities were raining flowers upon Dignaga, the forest plants were bowing in his direction, and elephants stood quietly over him to afford him shade. When the king awoke him with the sweet sounds of musical instruments, he asked, "Are you Dignaga?" "So I am called", the monk replied. And the king prostrated before his feet. Tradition records that Dignaga journeyed south and restored damaged *viharas*. The king of Odivisha and the royal treasurer helped build monasteries, and Dignaga continued to draw opponents into the embrace of the Dharma. He performed a number of wondrous feats, including restoring a precious tree to life by chanting over it. Though he had many followers, he refused to have attendants, preferring to live alone. He died alone in the verdant forests of Odivisha, having lived a life dedicated to meditation and teaching others to clarify consciousness for the sake of Truth.

Dignaga set himself a monumental task. He sought on the one hand to produce a definitive treatise on the principles of logic which could be used to understand the fundamental meaning of ideas and ideals. On the other hand, he wanted to show that diverse standpoints could be understood, communicated, assessed and reconciled. Some resisted his teaching, for it demanded rigorous mental training, the renunciation of bias and a desire to bring all one's mental faculties to peak awareness. Some thought he was a quibbler and a hair-splitter, but such judgements confuse the careful, even ponderous, quality of his work with the fiery spirit which infuses it. Despite the stringent dialectical requirements of the *Pramanasamuccaya,* it rapidly assumed importance for Buddhists of every school, and Hindus, Jains and Zoroastrians alike felt the need to grasp its contents not only for debates like those held at Nalanda but also as an aid in understanding their own spiritual inheritance. It was translated into Chinese in the second half of the sixth century, and it remains the foundation stone of the 'new logic', fulfilling the prophecy of Manjushri that "in later times this Shastra will become the sole eye of all the Shastras".

The first chapter of the *Pramanasamuccaya* takes up the question of *pramana,* valid knowledge. A number of dialecticians treated perception, logical inference, the testimony of others, authority and scripture as independent means to truth and implicitly endowed them with equal epistemological status. Dignaga did not question the value of these sources of knowledge and opinions, but he clarified their relationship to one another and delineated their ranges of application. For him there are only two means to knowledge – *pratyaksha* and *anumana,* perception and inference. Dignaga offered no definition of perception, in part because it is common knowledge and in part because it cannot be defined save through itself. Pure perception is free from preconception of any kind and is therefore unconnected with name, genus, species and conceptualization. This suggests that most of what is ordinarily called perception is in fact tainted by the mental constructs and habits which mediate and obscure the function of the senses. Thus, when one mistakes a rope for a snake, the error does not occur because of misperception but rather because of preconception based on fear, previous experience or memories of frightening encounters recounted by others in the past. Given this characterization of perception, it is possible for the man of meditation to perceive supramundane realms of objects and planes of being inaccessible to untrained consciousness victimized by the *kleshas* and *caittas* enumerated by Vasubandhu.

Perception, never susceptible to categorization, is in every case unique. Thus perception is invariably of individual characteristics or "infinite peculiarities". In attempting to convey to another what one has perceived, one invokes class descriptions, communicating a generalized phenomenon – a cow, book or whatever – rather than the unique perception one experienced. Inference, however, is quite another matter, for inferential knowledge is general and can be expressed by name, genus, species and all the categories of thought and language. Dignaga cannot say that perception involves the interaction of senses with their objects, because such a claim could be established only by invoking the elements of inference. Thus, Dignaga's conception of perception is the epistemological correlate of *chittamatra,* Mind-only. Those pairs of opposites which give value and tone to perceptions – pleasure and pain, for example – are not objects of knowledge but rather colorations of consciousness.

*Anumana,* inference, is of two kinds: *svarthanumana* and *pararthanumana,* inference for oneself and inference for another. Inference for oneself is knowledge of a thing derived from its distinctive marks or characteristics. The mark might be the effect of the thing inferred, as one infers fire from smoke which is its effect. It might be essential identity, as an acacia is identical with a tree. And it might be absence of perception signifying the non-existence of what is not perceived. Non-perception of a pot, for instance, permits the inference that no pot exists here where one is looking. *Pararthanumana,* inference for the sake of others, is more complex, for it is concerned with what one can demonstrate to another on the basis of what one can infer for oneself. In addition to the inference, one must show its validity by some parallel example to another. For instance, in the assertion that

> This sound is non-eternal,
> Because it is a product of effort
> Like a pot, unlike *akasha*

the reason for the non-eternality of this sound is that it is the result of effort. The parallel example or homologue is a pot, which is also the product of effort, and the non-parallel example or heterologue is *Akasha,* which is not the product of effort.

Dignaga devised a list of nine reasons which can link subject and predicate, centering on non-eternality, being produced or a product of something else, audibility and tangibility. Depending on whether the reason is wholly present in, partially present in or absent from the homologue and the heterologue, Dignaga created a table of validity, which was the first attempt of its kind to systematize logical inferences. Though its structure is logical, the nature of his reasons requires basic knowledge of the world in order to determine the truth of arguments. As in Aristotelian syllogisms and in modern propositional logic, the conclusions are true if and only if the premisses are true *and* the logical form is valid. The reason *(hetu)* can be either affirmative or negative. It is affirmative when it is always accompanied by whatever is given in the predicate: the hill is fiery because it is smoky, smoke being the reason. It is negative when what is declared absent in the reason is absent in the predicate: the hill is not smoky because it is not fiery. Dignaga's "law of extension" requires that one who wishes to convince another of his own conclusion has to state both subject and predicate as well as the reason which connects them, along with suitable examples which illustrate the linkage between the reason and the predicate.

For Dignaga, comparison is not an independent source of knowledge, because recognizing the similarity between two objects is an act of perception. Similarly, the testimony of others depends upon either the credibility of the individual or the credibility of the fact itself. In the first case, inference is involved, whilst the second is a case of perception. Even though Dignaga reduced the means to knowledge to only two, he showed that the traditionally accepted sources of understanding do not have to be rejected, since they can be understood as special instances of perception and inference. He also discussed the importance of the use of analogy and sought to distinguish between acceptable and far-fetched analogues. The basic schema of Dignaga's system of logic left a variety of issues unresolved, many of which he took up in other treatises. In addition to extensive discussions of subjects and predicates (minor and major terms) and the use of example, he compiled illustrated collections of fallacies. He also warned against theses or propositions which one must reject out of hand because they are incompatible with perception, contradict inference, reject overwhelming public opinion, deny one's belief, are self-contradictory (e.g., "My mother has always been barren"), or use terms incomprehensible to the system of thought under discussion. He added that one cannot prove a thesis which is universally accepted (for example, "Fire is warm") precisely because of its universal acceptability.

Demonstration and refutation together with their fallacies are useful in arguing with others; and perception and inference together with their fallacies are useful for self-understanding.

Dignaga established a three-step method of proof when one reasons with oneself, and a five-step method for convincing others. Since all that one experiences short of Enlightenment is *chittamatra*, merely consciousness, clarity of thought is crucial at every stage of the Bodhisattva Path. For Dignaga, logic is not an end in itself but rather an invaluable aid in transforming the processes of consciousness. He elevated debate out of the murky plane of polemic into the realm of dispassionate discourse and became the founder of medieval Buddhist logic. In later centuries he was given the name Tarkapungava, Fighting Bull, for his formidable dialectical skills. Unfortunately, subsequent generations lost something of the sacred vision that brought Dignaga face to face with Manjushri and retained only the logic. Thus his pioneering work became the backbone of an uninspiring scholasticism and the tool of those who take greater delight in quibbling than in meditation. Nonetheless, his work was a valuable aid not just for the Yogachara school, but for all Buddhists and numerous Hindu traditions as well. His efforts have been honoured by the fact that all who have known them have used them freely.

> *Life is – of moving things, or things unmoved,*
> *Plant or still seed – know, what is there hath grown*
> *By bond of Matter and of Spirit: Know*
> *He sees indeed who sees in all alike*
> *The living, lordly Soul; the Soul Supreme,*
> *Imperishable amid the Perishing:*
> *For, whoso thus beholds, in every place,*
> *In every form, the same, one, Living Lord,*
> *Doth no more wrongfulness unto himself*
> *But goes the highest road which brings to bliss.*

Shri Krishna

## OM

*Hermes*, September 1985
Elton Hall

# VASUBANDHU

*The Supreme Truth of all dharmas*
*Is nothing save tathata,*
*Forever true to its own nature.*
*The sole truth of chittamatra, Mind-only.*

*When the root of conditionality is removed,*
*Along with all limiting conceptions,*
*The plane of chittamatra is reached,*
*As the six sense-organs and objects are voided.*

*Without grasping and beyond all thought,*
*Abides the transcendental Wisdom,*
*And when the fruits of karma and the senses are*
*renounced,*
*Relative knowledge recedes before perfect Wisdom.*

*This is the realm of passionless purity,*
*Indescribable, yet fruitful and enduring,*
*Wherein one resides in freedom, serenity and joy.*
*This is the Law of the Great Buddha.*

Vasubandhu
*Trimshika*

Some years after the birth of Asanga, his remarkable mother, Prakashashila, married a learned Brahmin and gave birth to two sons. The eldest, Vasubandhu, was born around the time of Asanga's ordination as a Buddhist monk. Unlike Asanga, whose father was a Kshattriya, Vasubandhu was raised a Brahmin and instructed in the three Vedas, but when he attained maturity he decided to become a Buddhist monk. By then his brother Asanga was far away, already formulating and teaching the Mahayana doctrines that came to be known as the Yogachara. When

Vasubandhu received his own ordination at Nalanda, he studied the *Tripitaka*, the Three Baskets of teachings of the non-Mahayana schools, of which the Theravada is the only surviving representative. Whilst his remarkable brilliance and penetrating insight rivalled those of his brother, he did not follow Asanga's path of intense solitary meditation.

Instead, he journeyed to Kashmir, where he came under the beneficent influence of Samghabhadra, who encouraged him to master the teachings of the eighteen non-Mahayana schools as well as all the branches of exoteric knowledge. Taranatha wrote that Vasubandhu also extensively studied the six systems of Hindu philosophy and mastered its methods of debate. Upon completing his studies he returned to Nalanda, according to Bu-ston. Taranatha adds that he lived for a number of years in Magadha, the literary home of the Pali tongue. While residing in Magadha, Vasubandhu read his brother's *Yogacharabhumi* but found the Mahayana doctrines too recondite. He doubted the widespread belief that Asanga had actually received instruction from the Bodhisattva Maitreya, and tradition holds that he exclaimed: "Alas! Asanga meditated for twelve years in the forest, but instead of attaining success he has composed a work fit to be an elephant's load." His sardonic remarks came to the ears of Asanga, who was not offended, but simply said, "It is time to convert him."

Asanga devised a thoughtful strategy and trained two monks, having each one memorize a specially chosen Mahayana *sutra*. Then he sent both to call upon Vasubandhu. In the evening the first monk recited his *sutra*, outlining the Mahayana standpoint. Vasubandhu saw the logic of the system but wondered if it might not encourage indolence. In the morning, however, the second monk recited the *Dashabhumisutra*, which sets forth the ten stages of the Bodhisattva path as the fusion of theory and practice. Vasubandhu was overwhelmed. Great sadness and regret came upon him for the disrespect he had previously shown for his brother's path. He contemplated cutting out his tongue in penance for his disparaging remarks, but the surrounding monks restrained him from rash self-injury and insisted that he seek his brother's advice on how best to atone for his wrong. Vasubandhu went to Asanga, embraced the Mahayana and recanted his discourteous remarks. Asanga instructed Vasubandhu to refrain from harming himself and to do penance by applying his formidable skills and eloquence to learning and teaching the Mahayana doctrine. Asanga taught Vasubandhu *sutra* and *mantra,* and his willing disciple soon mastered the sacred texts and became proficient in meditation. When debating with his brother, Vasubandhu was quick-tongued but Asanga usually won. Others saw this as a paradox, but Asanga explained that he was slower because he borrowed his ideas from Maitreya, whereas Vasubandhu worked them out on his own. It is said that Vasubandhu thoroughly learnt each *sutra* by heart after listening to Asanga recite it only once. When Vasubandhu entered the Mahayana, a great number of monks joined him. He assisted Asanga for a number of years and helped spread Yogachara Teachings.

Upon the death of Asanga, Vasubandhu is said to have become the *Upadhyaya,* chief preceptor, of Nalanda. He spent most of the remainder of his life at Nalanda, where he performed his duties with vigour and precision. He produced more than fifty commentaries on Mahayana and other *sutras,* composed expositions of Asanga's works and wrote a number of original treatises. He was an effective dialectician and eloquent expositor of *Buddhadharma,* and he conscientiously performed the daily duties of a teacher at Nalanda. Every morning he would recite an appropriate text and expound its meaning. Throughout the day he would advise and counsel younger monks, guiding them by his own example in discharging with great care the duties of a monk. In the evenings he would listen to debates and resolve differences of standpoint by clearly summarizing the essence of the doctrine. Taranatha declared that he was visited by his deity in deep sleep and thus received instruction in arcane spiritual wisdom.

Once he accepted an invitation to discourse in Gauda, east of Nalanda, and while he explained the *sutras* there, deities showered golden flowers upon the attentive citizenry. On another occasion he visited Odivisha, and during a short period of relaxation he revealed no less than five separate clusters of precious gems. When people showered him with gifts, wise monks noticed that *nagas, yakshas* and other non-human intelligences joined them in paying homage to him. On one occasion, when an uncontrollable fire broke out in Rajagriha, Vasubandhu extinguished it with an invocation, just as he once brought a plague in Janantapura under control through a *mantram.* It is also said that his vast *vidyamantra,* knowledge of sacred syllables, allowed him to control ageing and determine the time of his own death. Late in life he was called to Nepal to restore the purity of the teaching. After reorganizing the Buddhist community there, he bade farewell to his disciples, uttered a particular *mantram* thrice backwards, and died. A *caitya* was erected in his memory in Nepal. He had lived between eighty to a hundred years, the majority of them spent in disseminating Yogachara teaching. According to Taranatha, his death was "the setting of the sun of the Dharma for the time being", and Paramartha added that "all who study the Mahayana and the Hinayana in India use the productions of Vasubandhu as their text-books".

Vasubandhu laboured to make Asanga's teaching accessible to a wide range of minds. Perhaps his finest surviving work is the *Trimshikakarikaprakarna (Treatise of Thirty Verses),* a succinct digest of Yogachara thought. Vasubandhu announced the root perspective of Yogachara in the first verse of the text: conceptions of self *(Atman)* and conceptions of elements of reality *(dharmas)* do not entail that either exist. Rather, their inherently fictitious character gives rise to the whole phenomenal world. As mere phenomena, they arise as the manifestation of ceaselessly changing states of consciousness. The kinds of consciousness capable of manifestation fall naturally into three types distinguishable by function: *Alayavijnana* is the universal storehouse of ideation, characterized by the maturation of its activity over time; *Manas* is that consciousness which is capable of cognition and deliberation; *Manovijnana* is the coordinating centre of the five senses, each of which involves a kind of consciousness commensurate with sensation. There are in sum three types and eight kinds of consciousness.

*Alayavijnana,* the eighth and highest consciousness, is sometimes called *vipakavijnana,* or retributive consciousness, because its fruits (karma) ripen at different times. It is also called *sarvabijakavijnana* because it carries within itself all the *bijas* or seeds which will sprout as karmic effects. *Alayavijnana* is, therefore, the repository of the results of action, the treasury of karma yet to be expended. *Alayavijnana* cannot be fully defined because its basis – and therefore its contents – cannot be entirely known. Nor can it be assigned place or location since it is the basis of all other kinds of consciousness. Its root powers of perception and discrimination must remain forever a mystery. It can, however, be associated with the five *caittas* or attributes: *sparsa* (mental contact), *manaskara* (attention), *vedana* (sensation), *samjna* (conception) and *chetana* (volition). It is always associated with *upeksa,* the sense of indifference. Manifesting itself like a relentless torrent, it is renounced only by the Arhat who attains *Nirvana.*

*Manas,* the seventh consciousness, evolves from *Alayavijnana,* which it takes as its basis and support because the universal storehouse is the true object of manasic consciousness. *Manas* is characterized by cognition and intellection, and is invariably accompanied by the four *kleshas* or sources of affliction and delusion: *atmamoha* (self-delusion), *atmadrishti* (belief in a self), *atmamana* (self-conceit) and *atmasneha* (love of self) – as well as by the five *caittas.* Since *Manas* operates in the realm in which beings are born, it ceases in the Arhat. It is paralysed in the higher states of meditation on the transcendental path. If *Alayavijnana* is thought of as neither defiled, obscured nor defined, *Manas* is undefined but defiled. Neither 'good' nor 'bad' can be predicated of either of them, as they can of the remaining six forms of consciousness.

Together, these remaining kinds of consciousness constitute *Manovijnana,* the third evolute of mind, distinguished by perception and discrimination of objects. In addition to their association with the *caittas* and the *kleshas,* they are also involved with special and secondary forms of both. These special *caittas* include *chanda* (desire), *adhimoksha* (resolve), *smriti* (memory), *samadhi* (meditation) and *prajna* (discernment). Beneficial *caittas* encompass *shraddha* (belief), *hri* (shame) and *apatrapa* (integrity), as well as *alobha* (non-covetousness), *advesa* (non-anger), *amoha* (non-delusion), *virya* (diligence), *prashrabdi* (mental composure), *apramada* (watchfulness), *upeksa* (equanimity) and *avihimsa* (harmlessness). The *kleshas* appear in *Manovijnana* and the five forms of sense-consciousness as covetousness, anger, delusion, conceit, doubt and false views, as well as the twenty secondary troublesome mental qualities: fury, enmity, hypocrisy, vexation, envy, stinginess, deception, fraudulence, harmfulness, pride, shamelessness, lack of integrity, restlessness, torpor, unbelief, indolence, idleness, forgetfulness, distraction and thoughtlessness. Remorse and drowsiness are indeterminate mental qualities because they carry no moral valence, and *vitarka* and *vicara*, reflection and investigation, can be beneficent or maleficent, depending upon the way they are used. Whilst the five sense-consciousnesses manifest in various ways determined by cause and condition, *Manovijnana* is always active except in beings who have no objective thoughts, either because they have transcended them because they are deep in meditation beyond thought, or they are mindless.

Once Vasubandhu had shown that consciousness manifests in two ways – as perception or as the object of perception – he drew the unavoidable conclusion that neither *Atman* (a separate and permanent self) nor *dharmas* (independent elements of reality) exist. Thus, the whole of manifestation is *chittamatra*, merely consciousness. Vasubandhu did not absolutize this fundamental formulation any more than his brother Asanga did, since he understood that rigid judgements arise too readily from restrictive and dogmatic conceptions of consciousness. Vasubandhu denied the independent reality of the external world but just as vigorously rejected views which made the universe the subjective fantasy of individuated objective mind. As an objective idealist, he explained how mind gives rise to the kaleidoscope of manifestation.

Since *Alayavijnana* contains all *bijas* or seeds, from time to time different kinds of transformation occur, and since *dharmas* intersect and conjoin, distinctions are engendered which can be perceived, recognized and sorted in diverse ways. The seeds of previous deeds manifest as karma, that aspect of apprehension in which results are the objects of perception. At the same time, the capacity for further conception is brought to what is already thus conceived. Like all other action, both conceiving and conceived leave *bijas* which will sprout in the future. Even as previous seeds come to fruition, new seeds are deposited which will eventually bear fruit of their own. The inertial process of reduplication is reflected in *parikalpitasvabhava*, the self-reproductive imagination. What is imagined has no inherent nature of its own. The nature of all things is either *paratantra*, dependent on others, or *parinishpanna*, ultimate reality. Dependent nature consists of discriminations and conceptions which are themselves the result of causality and conditionality. Ultimate reality is forever free from any degree of dependence, and therefore it is free of the operations of the objectivizing imagination. The nature of ultimate reality cannot be said to be either the same as or different from the nature of dependence on others, just as impermanence is neither the same as nor different from impermanent *dharmas.* This means that one who has not directly perceived the nature of ultimate reality cannot perceive the nature of dependent origination.

Vasubandhu used his terse discussion of the nature of existence as the basis for an explanation of the triple aspects of *nihsvabhava*, non-existence, a teaching intimated by the Buddha in his statement that *dharmas* have no self-nature. The first aspect is *lakshananihsvabhava*, non-existence in respect to appearances, for all distinguishable characteristics are dependent products of the imagination and have no existence independent of it. The second is *utpattinihsvabhava*, non-existence in respect to innate nature or origination, since even origins are the products of mental discrimination. The third is *paramarthanihsvabhava*, non-existence in respect to absolute truth. This is far removed from anything based on objectivizing imagination, where the conceptions of *Atman* and *dharmas* arise. *Dharmaparamartha,* the supreme truth about all *dharmas,* is *bhutatathata,* absolute reality, ever immutable and therefore always abiding in its own nature. And this is *vijnaptimatrata,* the true nature of consciousness itself, the state sometimes referred to as 'Mind-only'. Consciousness transcends even the subtlest distinction of subject and object, perceiver and perceived. Patanjali spoke of the Spectator without a spectacle.

*Vijnaptimatrata* is the highest consciousness, beyond the scale of individuation, differentiation and degree, where consciousness knowingly abides in itself. It sows no seeds and therefore has no harvest to reap. In itself consciousness dwells outside of time and events, free of action and reaction. But until consciousness abides in its true nature, the dual power of apprehension – conceiving and being conceived – will exert itself and mind will be ensnared by attachment and drowsiness. So long as an individual perceives any object as an object (even if he believes that it is *chittamatra,* only consciousness), he is not really residing in *vijnaptimatrata,* for the eight forms of consciousness are still active. If, however, he surveys the realm of objects without even conceiving the idea of an object, his wisdom is that of *vijnaptimatrata,* because both object and its apprehension are absent.

Without perception, inconceivable and incomprehensible,
This is transcendental supramundane wisdom.

Because of the abandonment of the dross of these two barriers,
Inner transformation into perfect wisdom is achieved.

This is pure *dhatu,* undefiled, without obscuration, devoid of parameters, inconceivable and incomprehensible, yet both intrinsically good and enduring. This transcendental ground of consciousness and being is undivided by distinctions or degrees, and having no internal or external relations, it is called bliss. In that holy unconditioned ground, the enlightened being abides in *vimuktikaya,* the body of emancipation.

This is the Law of Great Silence, Mahamuni, the Dharmakaya,
Realized by the great Buddha, Shakyamuni.

Asanga and Vasubandhu were always considered together, not just because they were brothers and equally articulate spokesmen for Yogachara thought, but owing to their remarkable complementarity. Asanga turned inward through rigorous meditation and expounded what he had discovered and verified by direct inner experience. Vasubandhu saturated himself in the philosophies of the eighteen non-Mahayana schools and in his brother's own teaching. He turned outward, seeking to explain to others in comprehensible terms the heart of Yogachara doctrine. He wrote careful analyses of differing viewpoints within and outside the Buddhist tradition, and taught and debated wherever and whenever he was needed. Taranatha wrote that there were sixty thousand Mahayana monks in India at the time of his death, a tremendous increase from the time of Asanga just a few years before. Bu-ston reported that Asanga confided to Vasubandhu that he had been drawn to the philosophical life in all his five hundred immediately previous incarnations. Not surprisingly, when these luminous dialecticians of the divine departed from the earth, it was said that the sun of the Dharma had set for the time being.

*Hermes,* August 1985
Elton Hall

# BUDDHAGHOSA

The spectacular rise of the Great Vehicle after the dissemination of the *Mahayana Sutras* overshadowed the evolution of other schools. Buddhists who focussed on non-Mahayana texts remained active and produced an enormous literature in Pali, the literary and textual language of non-Mahayana Buddhist thought. They did not, however, produce a teacher of comparable stature to Nagarjuna, Aryadeva or Asanga. Consequently, their numbers waned and many texts were lost in India before the Mahayana crossed the Himalayas into Tibet. Yet one man stood out, in part because he chose to go to Sri Lanka and preserve the work begun there by Mahendra, the son of King Ashoka. The response to his efforts invigorated the Theravada, which is the only non-Mahayana school which has survived to the present day and which spread throughout Southeast Asia. Bhadantacariya Buddhaghosa gathered all the sources he could find and composed definitive expositions of Theravadin doctrine and practice, deliberately subordinating his considerable originality to faithfulness to his revered tradition.

Though a modern edition of Buddhaghosa's works fills thirty volumes, little is known of his life and activities. The first great impulse of Buddhist thought, initiated by Buddha and culminating in the formation of the *Tripitaka*, the Three Baskets of teachings, spread to Sri Lanka with the arrival of Mahendra and a cutting from the original Bodhi Tree under which Buddha achieved Enlightenment. There the sacred texts were preserved in Pali but elucidated in Sinhalese, though Buddhist thought drifted towards stagnation in the first centuries of the common era. The Great Monastery (Mahavihara), founded in Mahendra's time, flourished under royal patronage, but the Mahayana tendencies of the rival Abhayagiri Monastery produced a reaction that resulted in a stultifying concern for orthodoxy. Meanwhile, Indian Buddhists eventually embraced the Great Vehicle and left Sri Lanka virtually isolated, the preserver of texts and materials neglected by the rest of the Buddhist world. Buddhaghosa was born during this period of Theravadin decline around A.D. 400 in Ghosa near Bodh Gaya, according to a very late and perhaps imaginary legend. Amongst the sparse details that he gives about himself, he declared that he once lived in Kanchipuram and in Morandacetaka, which some historians identify with Mylapore near Madras.

According to the *Mahavamsa,* the chronicle of Sri Lanka, Buddhaghosa was born a Brahmin and became a devoted student of Patanjali's *Yoga Sutras.* Once in the course of reciting the *Sutras* aloud, he was overheard by a Buddhist monk named Revata, who proceeded to explain each passage fully. When Buddhaghosa asked after the source of the monk's wisdom, he pointed to the Enlightened One, and Buddhaghosa joined the Sangha. Because his speech – *ghosa* – was deep and resonant, carrying far like the word of Buddha, he received the name by which history knows him. After a serious study of the *Tripitaka,* he sought insightful commentaries on its treatises, but Revata told him that only Sri Lanka had kept them pure. Upon his teacher's suggestion, Buddhaghosa journeyed to Anuradhapura, the royal capital of Sri Lanka, and established himself in the Great Monastery within sight of the sapling of the Bodhi Tree. When he announced his intention to translate the Sinhalese commentaries into Pali for the benefit of his Indian co-disciples, the elders tested him by giving him two verses for a complete commentary. The result was the *Visuddhimagga (The Path of Purification).* No sooner had he completed it, however, than a group of deities hid the work, and he had to undertake the task again. These deities repeated the theft, but Buddhaghosa compiled a third commentary. When the elders came to view the finished treatise, the deities produced the first two versions, and when everyone saw that the three were identical in every respect, an elder said, "surely this is the *bodhisattva metteyya.*"

Buddhaghosa was entrusted with all the revered literature of the Great Monastery, and rather than simply translating it into Pali, he created a number of compendia which gathered all the relevant literature under a schematized list of subjects. He thus produced a kind of encyclopaedia of Sinhalese Buddhist thought. Since almost all the sources he used have been lost to history, his selfless effort saved for posterity the efflorescence of Ashoka's great missionary undertaking. His labours also inspired a renewal of Theravadin creativity both in Sri Lanka and in South India. This renaissance continued until it blossomed yet again in Burma, which helped Sri Lanka keep Buddha's message alive after it had disappeared from its original home. Though nothing is known about the length of Buddhaghosa's stay in Anuradhapura, history suggests that he eventually returned to India and probably took part in the resurgence of Pali Buddhist thought there. His last years and death are secrets of silent time.

The *Visuddhimagga* is perhaps Buddhaghosa's greatest work. Beginning with a description of *sila*, virtue, and its purpose, fruition and benefits, it passes on to an extensive discussion of *samadhi*, concentration or meditation, leading to *vipassana*, insight, and a full understanding of the Four Noble Truths. After a lengthy theoretical exposition of *panna*, understanding, practical applications are brought to bear on meditation experiences. Finally, advanced stages of realization leading to *nibbana* are delineated. For Buddhaghosa, the four stages of the spiritual Path are marked by distinct perfections. One who has "entered the stream" as well as one who has but one life remaining before Enlightenment is marked by perfection in *sila*. An individual who will not be subject to involuntary incarnations in the future exhibits perfection in *samadhi*, and one who has become an *arahant* and experienced the supreme culmination of realization is perfect in *vipassana*. Virtue involves the volition of one who follows the path of purification, for it requires both the fulfilment of duty and deliberate self-restraint. Virtue *(sila)* composes *(silana)* the individual through consistent self-coordination and through upholding edifying thoughts and intentions, and so virtue is like the head *(siras)* of the body, directing all its members, and it is cool *(sitala)*, calming every impulse.

> Who would dare to circumscribe
> The benefits that virtue brings,
> Without which clansmen
> Find no footing in the Teaching?
> No Ganges, no Yamuna,
> No Sarabhu or Sarassati,
> Nor flowing Aciravati
> Nor noble Maul River,
> Can wash away the stain of things
> That breathe in this world.
> Only *sila's* waters
> Cleanse the stain in living things.

In addition to virtue as a positive force generated through practice and restraint, it forms the basis of *dhutanga,* ascetic practice, which purifies motives and the powers of character. The thirteen forms of withdrawal are not to be understood as ways of escaping from the temptations of worldly involvements. Although retiring from the teeming thoroughfares of daily life can reduce external distractions, an individual takes his world – the tropism of consciousness – wherever he goes. *Dhutanga* aims to simplify one's desires and redirect one's motives, producing a contentment of mind and blamelessness of deed which allows one to take delight in treading the path of purification. *Sila* and *dhutanga* together provide the ethical and psycho-physical foundations for meditation. For Buddhaghosa, concentration and meditation can take myriad forms, but those which aim towards realization and *nibbana* are those which nurture *cittass, ekaggata,* unification and one-pointedness of mind. In his careful survey of Pali texts, Buddhaghosa discerned forty subjects suitable to this kind of meditation.

Ten *kasinas*, totalities, can be used: earth, water, fire and air, blue, yellow, red and white, light and local space. Ten kinds of foulness can also be helpful, including the bloated, the livid, the festering, the cut, the scattered and the bleeding. There are ten kinds of recollection – of Buddha, Dhamma and Sangha; of virtue, generosity, the deities and death; of mindfulness in respect to the body, mindfulness in respect to breathing, and recollection of peace. One can also take as a subject for meditation one of the four *brahma-viharas,* sublime abodes – *metta, karuna, mudita* and *upekkha,* love, compassion, joy and equanimity – providing that one extends these to include all beings. Four immaterial states can be used for meditation: boundless space, limitless consciousness, nothingness and the state of neither perception nor non-perception. Finally, one perception, the repulsiveness of food, and one analysis, that of the four elements, can be employed. These forty subjects for meditation constitute a pharmacopoeia for diverse temperaments, in which an individual can use what he needs to achieve the basic plane of concentration required to undertake the stages of meditation. Those stages are reached in two ways, access and absorption, for an individual may touch a higher degree of unified consciousness long before being able to maintain continuity in it.

When the mind is fully concentrated and free from distractions, it is capable of entering the first stages of meditation, known as the *rupa jhanas,* or meditative states cognizant of form. In the initial *rupa jhana* one experiences *vitakka* and *vicara, samadhi, sukha* and *piti* – reasoning, investigation, inner seclusion, pleasure and joy. Here the mind is active in every respect, though focussed upon a single ideal subject of meditation. Passage to the second *rupa jhana* occurs when both reasoning and investigation are stripped away and one experiences the pleasure and joy of inner seclusion. As one ceases to be bound by the cruder forms of pleasure and pain, one reaches the third *rupa jhana,* characterized by joy and inner seclusion. When the root polarity that gives rise to the pairs of opposites (including pleasure and pain) is removed, one dwells in the fourth *rupa jhana,* inner seclusion and equanimity. Once this highest of the states which admit of form has been attained, one is prepared to look deeply into the *brahma-viharas,* the sublime abodes, beginning with *metta.*

> He should first pervade himself with love. He can recollect such
> gifts, kindly words, and so on, as inspire love and endearment,

and such virtue and learning as inspire respect and reverence met with in a teacher or preceptor, developing love towards him in the way beginning, 'May this good man be happy and free from suffering.' With such a person, of course, he attains absorption.

*Karuna* cannot be readily aroused by concentrating on those one likes, dislikes or is indifferent to.

> First of all, on seeing a wretched man, unlucky, unfortunate, in every way a fit object for compassion, unsightly, reduced to utter misery. . .compassion should be felt for him in this way: This being has indeed been reduced to misery; if only he could be freed from this suffering! . . . Having aroused compassion in this way, compassion can be aroused for a person dear to one, indifferent to one, and hostile to one, respectively.

Contrary to the method for nurturing compassion, *mudita* or joy can be engendered on behalf of the good fortune of one closest to oneself, a boon companion. Then that joy can be extended to those who are emotionally and psychologically neutral in respect to oneself, and finally, towards those who are hostile. *Upekka*, or equanimity, is best aroused initially towards a neutral party, then extended to include those dear to one, those hostile to one, and, lastly, towards oneself. Insight is the product of realizing the four sublime abodes, but one must be careful not to succumb to the near enemy or come to fear the far enemy of each. The simulacrum of love is greed, since, like love, it appreciates virtues, and the far enemy is ill will, frighteningly alien to love. The near enemy of compassion is grief, for both witness human failure, and its opposite is cruelty. Joy rooted in the settled and comfortable life of the home is the near enemy of universal joy, and aversion or boredom is its distant foe. The 'bliss' of ignorance is the near enemy of equanimity, since both overlook faults, and it is opposed by greed and resentment.

> These ways of abiding are best in being the right attitude towards beings. And just as Brahma-gods abide with pure and

pristine minds, so the meditators who associate themselves with these *brahma-viharas* dwell on an equal footing with these deities.

Each distinct plane of consciousness is correlated with a level of being or matter, and just as there are immaterial and transcendental levels of being, so there are transcendent states of consciousness. From the terrace of the highest *rupa Jhana*, the man of meditation may gain access to the four *arupa* or formless *jhanas*. By ignoring the material realms and dwelling upon the infinitude of space, the *yogin* achieves *akasanancayatana*, the formless realm of infinite space, space without limits, qualities or objects of any kind. Meditation upon infinite space leads consciousness to realize its own infinitude (for it can entertain infinite space and not just some abstract conception of it as an object of meditation), and the realm of *vinnanancayatana*, infinite consciousness, is attained. This realization leads naturally to the recognition that nothing is present to the awakened consciousness, and the third formless realm, that of *akincannayatana*, or nothingness, is reached. The meditator can now step to the limit of mundane existence with the realization of *sanna-n'asannayatana*, neither perception nor non-perception. The fourfold stages of both the *rupa* and *arupa jhanas* unfold naturally to the persistent practitioner of meditation. Tradition holds that Buddha was taught how to attain the last two degrees by two of his teachers, Alara Kalama and Uddaka Ramaputta. For Buddha, however, discovering the outermost limits of terrestrial consciousness was not enough, just as it was not the end of Buddhaghosa's commentary.

The cultivation of meditation opens the way for the unfoldment of supernormal capacities which nonetheless belong to the highest development of mundane consciousness. These *abhinnas* or higher forms of knowledge begin with the *iddhis* or supernormal powers. An individual may learn to project numerous non-physical doubles of his body and thus appear simultaneously in more than one place. This mind-formed body can pass through walls, levitate, walk on water and perform marvellous feats. Though the *manomaya* form is not the physical body, it marks a perfect control of the constituents of the body, elements of which can be used for the benefit of the world by Bodhisattvas. The second *abhinna* is *dibba-sota* or divine ear, which is the perfection of clairaudience. The third, *parassa cetopariya-nana* or knowledge of other minds, includes telepathy in all its forms, including the instantaneous understanding of each human heart. *Pubbe-nivas anu-sati* is the detailed and deliberate remembrance of former births, a capacity which can safely be used only by those who have attained a high degree of self-knowledge and detachment. The fifth *abhinna, dibba-cakkhu* or divine eye, is more than clairvoyance, for it allows its possessor to witness the continuity of individual consciousness through the destruction and rebirth of different forms. The sixth *abhinna* is not mundane, but transcendental, because it involves the destruction of the *asavas,* cravings for sensuous pleasure, for embodied existence and ignorance – the 'three gates of hell'.

Some aspirants attain the transcendental path, *lokuttara magga,* by passing through the various *jhanas* and destroying the *asavas.* Unfortunately, many get caught in one superconscious state or another and fail to gain the insight that emancipates one from involuntary incarnation in the ocean of *samsara.* Others follow the safer way of Buddha, using the full concentration achieved to contemplate *dukkha, anicca* or *anatta,* the painful, the transitory or the egoless. If the fundamental condition of differentiated existence is suffering, then meditation upon this condition will reveal the aimlessness of the world, that is, its incapacity for exhibiting eternal truths. If everything in the universe is impermanent, meditation upon transitoriness will show that the world is signless, unable to sustain the meaning of reality in its appearances. And if everything in the world is without essential nature, meditation upon egolessness will demonstrate that appearances cannot delineate reality. If any one of these three lines of meditation is pursued to its end, realization of transcendental wisdom is inevitable. This is the way of direct insight. Thus the process which had its source in *sila,* virtue, and flowed together into the mighty stream of *samadhi,* meditation, eventually reaches the boundless ocean of *panna,* wisdom.

The power of concentration brought to the precise focus implicit in the art of meditation yields knowledge of *samsara* and realization of *nibbana*. The enlightened man, *arahant,* knows the world of relative truth as well as the indescribable truth of reality. He has fully developed *panna,* understanding.

> With dreadful thump the thunderbolt
> Annihilates the boulder.
> The driven, fire-whipped wind
> Annihilates the wood.
> The radiant orb of solar flame
> Annihilates the darkness.
> And developed understanding, too,
> Annihilates the tangled overgrowth
> Of inveterate defilements,
> The source of every woe.
> Yet its blessing even in this life
> A man himself may know.

Buddhaghosa collated Theravadin wisdom in ways which made it accessible and readily transmitted. Though meditation waned as a central practice in Sri Lanka and South Asia, his work was preserved and revered. In the twentieth century, however, monks have awakened to the lasting importance of his message, and once again concentration is becoming the beacon-light of the Theravadin path.

> *I will declare to thee that utmost lore,*
> *Whole and particular, which, when thou knowest,*
> *Leaveth no more to know here in this world.*

Shri Krishna

**OM**

*Hermes,* July 1985
Elton Hall

# DHARMAKIRTI

*The general run of mankind is addicted to platitudes and has no interest in subtlety. Not caring for profound sayings, they are filled with hatred and the filth of envy. So I do not write for them, for my heart has found satisfaction in my work and through it my love for deep continuous meditation over every well-spoken word has been fulfilled.*

*None in this world will easily grasp the deep utterances in this work. It will be absorbed by and perish in myself just as a river is absorbed and lost in the ocean. Even those endowed with a tremendous power of reason cannot fathom the depths. Even those with exceptional intrepidity of thought cannot perceive its highest truth.*

Dharmakirti
*Pramanavartika*

Eighth century India witnessed the final efflorescence of Buddhist insight and creativity on the subcontinent. Although Nalanda continued as the pre-eminent Indian Buddhist centre for another four centuries, before being destroyed in the Muslim invasions, it became increasingly isolated. India turned to its multivalent Hindu roots, whereby devotional and theistic modes won over the populace and Vedanta attracted philosophical thinkers. Nalanda along with lesser Buddhist schools became scholastic and defensive, and by the time of Dharmakirti an amorphous but pervasive pessimism had begun seriously to affect Indian Buddhists. At the same time, the message of Buddha began to penetrate Tibet and flowed along the ocean trade routes to South Asia. It had already entered China, where a host of translators laboured to render Mahayana *sutras* and philosophical writings into Chinese, and the first translations into Tibetan were attempted. By the time the Buddhist tradition was virtually forgotten in India, the works of Nagarjuna, Asanga, Vasubandhu, Dignaga, Chandrakirti, Shantideva and Dharmakirti had become foundation stones of a Buddhist renaissance and expansion in strange and alien lands, where it has remained vital until the present.

Dharmakirti was born into a Brahmin family in Trimalaya (perhaps Tirumalla) and from early childhood was recognized as a boy of exceptional intellect. He studied the arts and sciences, was deeply immersed in the Vedas, and by the age of sixteen was accepted as a mature scholar. Then, when he took up some Buddhist texts and studied them thoroughly, to the surprise and distress of the orthodox community he decided to don the yellow robe. After resisting the persuasive arguments of local Hindu scholars, he was forced to leave his home. Making his way to Nalanda, he was brought into the Sangha by Dharmapala and formally made a pupil of Vasubandhu, who was, however, too old to undertake the strain of conducting Dharmakirti's spiritual education. Eventually he came under the guidance of Ishvarasena, a pupil of Dignaga, who saw to his training and read him Dignaga's works on logic and dialectic. On his first reading of Dignaga's famous *Pramanasamuccaya,* Dharmakirti understood it. On his second reading he assessed its inadequacies, and on his third he boldly proclaimed his critique. Many would have held this to be irreverent, but Ishvarasena was delighted and instructed Dharmakirti to compose a commentary on his mentor's great work. After deep meditation he had a vision of Heruka, the fierce protective emanation of the Buddha Akshobhya, who blessed him with three mystic sounds. Then Dharmakirti began to write, producing the greatest works in the history of Buddhist logic.

Owing to his vast knowledge of non-Buddhist doctrines, he willingly restricted his debating activities to *tirthikas.* Though his dialectical skills and impeccable fairness were deeply appreciated at Nalanda, his writings were received with indifference because none could fully understand them. Eventually he travelled to debate in courts and scholarly centres throughout the land. When he came to Kalinga, he built a monastery and remained there, teaching a large group of disciples until he died. Gradually his greatness as a thinker became clear to the spiritual descendants of his own disciples. In time he was seen as perhaps the only Buddhist dialectician who equalled even Shankaracharya, and an apocryphal legend arose that he had actually vanquished the philosopher in debate. It is possible, given scanty evidence, that he debated and converted the son of Bhatta Acharya, who was believed to be a reincarnation of Shankara. According to Taranatha, after Dharmakirti died, a shower of flowers fell during the cremation ceremony and sweet celestial music was heard for seven days thereafter. His bones spontaneously formed into a crystal orb, which was preserved at Kalinga for many years.

Dharmakirti composed seven works which came to be known as the "Seven Treatises", the quintessential survey of logic for Tibetan Buddhists. His philosophical neutrality made his views compatible with a variety of doctrines, and they were readily inserted into the teachings of Chandrakirti and Shantideva. Dharmakirti's self-engendered conversion convinced him that Buddha is the ultimate source of all knowledge, leading him to try to unravel the inner logic of the Teachings. His methodological scepticism compelled him to reject the authority of Buddhist scriptures except when they withstood the same rigorous dialectical examination to which he subjected non-Buddhist texts. Though he accepted Dignaga's view that perception is a form of knowledge, he added that it had to be unerring. For him, the transience of the external world did not mean that it was simply unreal, but rather that one had to understand the nature of its reality. Perception is of fleeting moments, instants in time and space, and the seeming continuity given to objects of perception is produced by the mind. Pure perception itself is of reality and is instantaneous, but what is perceived is necessarily thought of and expressed in terms of cognitive relationships, which are an illusion. Only inference can deal with universals, and thus the objects of perception and inference are quite different from one another. Logic cannot be wholly separated from epistemology, and so logic leads naturally into a dialectic which, as Nagarjuna taught, inevitably undermines positive beliefs and formulations. Without meditation and discipline, dialectic tends towards sceptical pessimism, but with them, it provides a purifying way of life not dependent on false claims to know.

His *Pramanavartikakarika* is a sweeping commentary on Dignaga's great text, and it is condensed in his *Nyayabindu (The Drop of Logic),* long preserved in Tibetan but recently recovered in a Sanskrit manuscript found in a Jain temple. In the first chapter Dharmakirti held that all the ends sought by human beings are attained through knowledge, which must not only be valid but also perfect. Such knowledge is gained through *pratyaksha* and *anumana,* perception and inference. Perception, however, must be free from preconception and error. For Dharmakirti, preconception is not merely the crude surcharge of perspectives and conclusions imposed upon what one perceives. These have to be purged before one can even begin to speak of perceiving. Rather, preconception is in essence the throwing up of false images which are then erroneously thought to be objects of perception, as when one mistakes the shadow of a tree for the tree itself or a rope for a snake. Error tends to occur when the context of perception is not sufficiently taken into account. For instance, one will not see clearly in darkness, or, when one travels downstream on a boat, the trees on the river banks will appear to be moving upstream.

Although examples drawn from sight are the most accessible illustrations of perception and preconception, Dharmakirti insisted that perception through the five senses is only one kind of perception, and not the most important. There is also perception by the mind, encompassing the objects of dreams and contemplation. Perhaps the most readily recognized but most difficult to describe mode of perception is that of self-consciousness. Finally there is the noetic perception of the accomplished meditator. It is incommunicable to one who has no commensurate experience save by analogy and correspondence, for it reflects the perceptive mysteries. Perception differs from inference, for the object of inference is like any other object in its class *(samanyalakshana),* whilst the object of perception is only like itself *(svalakshana).* A cow which is seen is unique and cannot be replaced by another cow without altering the perception. The cow that is inferred, however, belongs to a class, and any member of that class can be substituted by any other. Perceptual knowledge is, therefore, of particulars and inferential knowledge is general. Objects of perception consist of instantaneous moments given seeming duration through an act of the mind which blurs perceptions together. Similarly, the false sense of self is formed by assuming continuity on the basis of a contiguity of moments. When objects of perception are stripped of these superadded mental accretions, so that they remain purely *svalakshana,* they are *paramarthasat,* absolutely real. From this standpoint the highest Enlightenment is pure perception. Negative perception, perceiving that something is not, has some epistemological relevance but played no logical role in Dharmakirti's system. Enlightenment involves *shunyata,* the Void, but it is in no sense negative perception.

Dharmakirti, like Dignaga, distinguished between inference for oneself *(svarthanumana)* and inference for the sake of others *(pararthanumana),* for though both involve the middle term or reason, inference for others requires that the reason be stated in convincing words. Inference for oneself involves a kind of syllogism in which the reason must meet three requirements. In the example

> The hill has fire,
> Because it has smoke,
> Like a kitchen, but unlike a lake

the middle term ('smoke') must abide in the minor term ('hill'), that is, there must indeed be smoke on the hill. Secondly, the middle term ('smoke') has to abide only in cases which are homologous with the major term ('fire'). Thus, smoke is in a kitchen, and a kitchen is homologous with things that contain fire. Thirdly, the middle term ('smoke') must never abide in cases which are heterologous with the major term ('fire'). Smoke never occurs in a lake, which is heterologous with things that contain fire.

Besides having to meet these three conditions, the middle term has to be one of three kinds. It could bear a relation of identity to the major term, including what modern logic would call being a subset, as in the statement "This is a tree, because it is a *shimshapa*", since the *shimshapa* is a kind of tree. The minor term could be an effect, as in "There is fire, because there is smoke", since smoke is an effect of fire. Dharmakirti added a broad class of relationships all called non-perception, such as non-perception of identity ("There is no smoke here, because it is not seen"), or of effect and of container ("There is no *shimshapa* here, because there is no tree here whatsoever"). Under non-perception he included perception contrary to identity ("There is no cold here, because there is fire"), perception of opposite effect, perception of contrary connection between cause and effect (including multiple causation), perception contrary to the effect, and perception contrary to the container. Finally he distinguished non-perception of the cause, perception contrary to the cause, and perception of an effect contrary to the cause, to complete a list of eleven forms of non-perception.

Inference for the sake of others requires putting the argument in words acceptable to all concerned, for though words themselves are not knowledge, they can educe it when rightly used. All inference is either affirmation or denial, linking terms in ways which produce statements or theses. A thesis is false if it is incompatible with perception, inference, conception or one's previous statements. Fallacies of the middle term occur when any of the requirements it must meet are unproven, uncertain or contradictory. For example, "Sound is eternal, because it is visible" is rejected as unproved, since no one will grant the visibility of sound. "Trees are conscious, because they die if their bark is removed" is unproved if the opponent points to types of trees that survive the removal of bark. The argument "Sound is non-eternal, because it is knowable" is uncertain, for the category of the knowable includes eternal as well as non-eternal members. And the thesis "Sound is eternal, because it is a product" must be rejected because 'product' is not homogeneous with 'eternal', that is, the middle and major terms are contradictory.

In inference for the sake of others, examples already familiar to the listener are offered to illustrate and support the inference drawn. In the argument that there is fire on the hill, the examples were 'like a kitchen' and 'unlike a lake'. The first is homogeneous, being the same as the hill, for both have smoke. The second is heterogeneous, because, unlike a kitchen, it does not have smoke. Homogeneous examples can be fallacious, that is, render the 'syllogism' untenable, when they fail to support the thesis. For instance, in the argument "Sound is eternal, because it is incorporeal, like action", action is not a viable example, since it is not eternal and is therefore excluded from the minor term. In "This man is not omniscient, because he is passionate, like the person in the street", the example fails because it is moot whether the person in the street is passionate and also questionable whether he is or is not omniscient. In Dharmakirti's strict system, refutation (dushana) consists in pointing out any of these fallacies. Refutation does not necessarily prove that a thesis is wrong, but only that it is unsupported or unclear.

Unlike Dignaga, Dharmakirti did not recognize any difference between a contradiction, in which two terms are opposed, and an implied contradiction, in which the terms are opposed if one of them is taken in a certain sense. For Dharmakirti, each term in an argument must be restricted to one meaning. Hence, if a contradiction appears, it will invariably be of the first kind. Since words may carry multiple denotations, the context determines the single relevant meaning. Whilst such an approach cannot exhaust the richness and resonance of scripture, Dharmakirti held that sacred texts are not patently transparent. Their meanings are matters of progressive contemplation which must be tested and clarified through inference for oneself. Ultimately, the meaning of the Teachings will be fully understood through the highest perception. Logic is an aid, but it deals with exposition, both to oneself and to others, and not directly with pure insight. Insight will be clouded, however, if the dialectical basis for knowledge by inference is unsound. These concerns led Dharmakirti to reject Dignaga's non-erroneous contradiction as a fallacy of uncertainty. It arises when opposing conclusions are drawn from syllogisms acceptable to differing schools of thought. For Dharmakirti, the opposition arises from differing, and perhaps hidden, assumptions and has nothing to do with inference. Mere appeal to scripture as authority is useless, for it implies that one's understanding of scripture is perfect and therefore authoritative.

Despite his rigorous focus on logic and dialectic, Dharmakirti saw these as tools to aid oneself and others along the Bodhisattva Path and not as ends in themselves. He expressed disappointment that his work was unappreciated, not because it was challenged – for it was not – but because so few seemed to understand it or recognize its value. Whilst Dharmakirti did not live to see his work widely respected, generations of Buddhists after his death did take it up. Due to the decline of Buddhist tradition in India, however, it was left to Hindu thinkers to advance Indian concerns with logic and dialectic. Dharmakirti would eventually be forgotten in his homeland, though his thought was reflected in subsequent Hindu logical treatises, but he was revered in Tibet, China and southeastern Asia. Although the Buddhist tradition survived in India until the thirteenth century, Dharmakirti knew that he stood at the beginning of the final illustrious chapter in the story. More important for the future, he also stood at the beginning of the magnificent unfolding of the Tibetan tradition, a story entering a dramatic new phase in the late twentieth century.

*Hermes*, December 1985
Elton Hall

# CHANDRAKIRTI

*Shravakas and solitary realizers*
*Spring from the kings of Munis.*
*Buddhas spring from Bodhisattvas.*
*The compassionate mind, non-dual awareness,*
*And the altruistic mind of Enlightenment*
*Give rise to jinaputras, children of Conquerors.*

*Mercy alone is perceived as the seed*
*Of a Conqueror's abundant harvest,*
*As water for growth, and as*
*Fruition in long enjoyment.*
*Thus I hail compassion at the beginning.*

*Homage to compassion for gatis,*
*Powerless migrators, like buckets dropped in a*
*    well,*
*First clinging to some self, an 'I',*
*Then growing attached to things – 'Mine'.*

*Homage to compassion for gatis,*
*Evanescent and empty of inherent existence.*
*Like the moon in the rippling water.*

Chandrakirti
*Madhyamakavatara*

Once Buddhaghosa consolidated non-Mahayana teaching in Sri Lanka and the followers of Nagarjuna elaborated Mahayana doctrines and methodology, the luminous burst of creativity which marked the birth and growth of the Indian Buddhist tradition began to wane. The tradition remained robust, and its focus shifted from discovering hidden dimensions of *Buddhadharma* to transmitting the Teaching to others. During those centuries Nalanda became the undisputed centre of Buddhist education and scholarship, so dominating Indian Buddhist life that when it was destroyed in the Muslim invasion of India, Buddhist thought virtually disappeared from the subcontinent. But if India looked back to its ancient Vedic heritage, the doctrines of Buddha followed the Silk Road and other routes of commerce north and east, dominating Tibet and Mongolia, Southeast Asia, China, Korea and Japan, where it remains to the present day. Several Indian Buddhists exercised far greater influence outside than within India.

Chandrakirti was born in Samanta (or Samana) in southern India sometime in the seventh century. He quickly mastered the knowledge taught in his day and was ordained a monk in the Sangha. After learning the texts revered by various schools, he concentrated on the works of Nagarjuna and attained such pre-eminence as a scholar that he was installed as *Upadhyaya* of Nalanda. Whilst he governed this great monastic university, a lay follower of the Bodhisattva ideal called Chandragomin arrived in the area. When Chandrakirti learnt of his presence, he requested that Chandragomin enter Nalanda with public honours. Since such a reception was technically impossible because Chandragomin was not an ordained monk, Chandrakirti arranged instead for a ceremonial procession in honour of Manjushri, the Bodhisattva who wields the sword of wisdom. It is said that when Chandragomin sang the praises of Manjushri, the statue turned to listen. Later writers mark this moment as the beginning of a seven-year contest of wits between "the two Chandras", but Chandrakirti and Chandragomin treated one another with the greatest respect and enjoyed a deep friendship. Chandrakirti represented the monastic ideal and the fullest control of the mind, "the great Slayer of the Real", whilst Chandragomin represented the generosity of heart which arises from devotion to the Bodhisattva vow, though both men mingled profound intelligence and selfless service.

Even though Chandrakirti assumed the onerous burden of overseeing Nalanda, he acquired remarkable powers associated with deep meditation. Taranatha wrote that he could milk a picture of a cow to give others nourishment, and many saw him put his hand through a stone pillar. Nonetheless, after many years of teaching and tending to the welfare of monks, he retired to a life of intense contemplation. Journeying south to Konkuna, he spread Buddhist teachings through discourse and debate. When he reached a hill known as Manubhanga, he withdrew into a long period of meditation. According to a tradition associated with those proficient in *mantras,* Chandrakirti gained the highest *siddhis* and attained the rainbow body, passing from this world into self-conscious immortality. Philosophically, Chandrakirti returned to the teachings of Nagarjuna and attempted to restate the Madhyamika or Middle Way standpoint.

Sometime in the fifth century Buddhapalita and Bhavaviveka formulated opposing views of the nature of Madhyamika philosophy. Whilst Buddhapalita held that Madhyamika methodology wholly consisted in *prasanga,* reducing the assertions of others to contradictions or absurdities, Bhavaviveka contended that Madhyamika dialecticians should propound and defend positive doctrines. Chandrakirti understood that Nagarjuna's dialectic could lead the intellectually unwary into philosophical nihilism, but he believed that the fundamental insight of Nagarjuna's approach was the recognition that no formulation could be true, and that any affirmation of doctrine is ultimately misleading and a hindrance on the path to Enlightenment. For Chandrakirti, the Yogachara system was unsatisfactory, as its concept of *vijnana,* consciousness without an object, was actually the idea of an *Atman* in disguise. The difference between Yogachara and Prasangika Madhyanilka is found in their responses to *astitva* and *nastitva,* 'is' and 'is not'. Whilst the Yogachara accepts 'is' and 'is not', Prasangika Madhyamika, as formulated by Chandrakirti, rejects both. Chandrakirti shunned every positive formulation of Truth not because he denied its reality, but rather because he doubted the possibility of providing *any* formulation of it.

If formulations of the Truth mislead, however, nihilism is even more in error. The first invites the delusion that belief brings one closer to Enlightenment. The other encourages the delusion that demonstrating the lack of independent existence of phenomena is the same as proving the non-existence of existence, implying that nothing need be done to attain Enlightenment. For Chandrakirti, the denial of the reality of phenomena is not the denial of phenomena, just as the recognition that some collective activity is only a game is not the discovery that there is no activity at all. Rather, discerning things for what they are is part of the process of freeing oneself from their grip on consciousness. Understanding the illusory nature of the world is part of emancipation from illusion, though a number of steps are required to achieve it. Since Buddhas arise from Bodhisattvas, one who would be truly free of the endless round of *Samsara* must ascend the ten grounds *(dashabhumi)* of the Bodhisattva Path. Such an effort depends less on belief, which can at best offer only provisional and temporary support, than on cultivating three practices which radically reorient consciousness and perception: compassion *(karuna)*, non-dual understanding *(gnyis med kyi blo)* and the mind of Enlightenment *(bodhichitta)*.

Of these three, compassion is the cause of the other two. In compassion one comes to identify with others at a level distinctly beyond the opposites of attraction and repulsion (which make others mere mirrors of the likes and dislikes of one's own false ego), and this identification aids in the integration of understanding. Compassion is the basis of the awakening of *bodhichitta,* for in wanting to be of true service to others, one yearns to know the Truth. Thus Chandrakirti began his *Madhyamakavatara (Supplement to the Middle Way)* by paying homage to compassion, the signature of the Bodhisattva and the Archimedean lever which moves one from stage to stage along the Bodhisattva Path. He likened the ignorant individual to a bucket in the well of *Samsara.* The bucket falls easily, clattering against the sides of the well and crashing on the rocks below. Thus it descends, damaging itself, from the realm of the gods at the top of the well to the region of hellish beings at the bottom. The uncontrolled mind gives the windlass free reign to drop the bucket, and the gravity effect of desire, hatred and ignorance pulls it downward. Without compassion, one is indifferent to this state insofar as it describes the condition of others, but one feels it intensely when it results in harm to someone with whom one is intimate. Compassion involves engendering this sense of intimacy with all sentient beings, devoid of mere sentiment which tinctures personal relationships, so that the condition of every living being affects one's own consciousness and impels one to seek to rectify it. Only meditation will stimulate a selfless sense of solidarity with all beings.

If an individual is determined to tread the Bodhisattva Path through each of its ten stages, he will necessarily develop compassion. As *karuna* arises from deep meditation upon the condition of living beings, compassion can assume three aspects corresponding to three levels of *Samsara*. The first type, *sattvalambana karuna,* is compassion in observing nothing but sentient beings. In this phase there is no concern with the transience of every being or with ultimate Reality. Rather, one realizes at this level that all beings share one common characteristic – suffering, *dukha*. Like buckets in a well, beings rise and fall according to the whim of the windlass, the uncontrolled mind. *Dharmalambana karuna,* compassion in observing beings as phenomena, is the realization that beings have no independent nature but are only phenomena, aggregates *(skandhas)* temporarily gathered together into the mind-generated illusion of entities. *Analambanalambana karuna* is compassion in recognizing the inapprehensible, through which one realizes that *shunyata,* voidness or emptiness, is the distinguishing characteristic of all beings.

Two practical means of arousing threefold compassion are preserved in the Tibetan tradition. One, taken from Maitreya, is to contemplate the possibility that, over myriad lives and countless millennia, every person one encounters could have been one's mother. This is to think of having once been nurtured in the womb of every other human being. The second means, inspired by Manjushri and taught by the present Dalai Lama, is to equalize and switch oneself with others. Think honestly of oneself and one's deep longings for happiness, and then think of the fact that others desire the same. In this fundamental respect, all beings are equal. In addition, one contemplates the fact that those who are 'other' to oneself are 'self' to themselves. Each individual is both 'self' and 'other' in senses which are symmetrical from a standpoint outside of humanity but which seem to be asymmetrical from any and every individual's perspective. When these two means are adopted, one's longing for Enlightenment can be transmuted into an aspiration on behalf of all beings. True meditation and study are marked by the conviction they produce, for conviction alone can nurture the mental and moral action essential to treading the Bodhisattva Path.

Though the Path of Renunciation has ten stages or grounds (and eleven if Buddhahood is included), the first five are perhaps the most critical, since without an understanding of them, the remaining stages are beyond comprehension.

> The mind of a *jinaputra*, filled
> With compassion to emancipate *gatis*,
> Consecrated with Samantabhadra's aspirations,
> Abiding in joy, is called the first.

The mind of a child of the Conqueror, a spiritual son or daughter of Buddha, is overwhelmed with compassion for *gatis*, those caught in the cycle of reincarnation. It dedicates itself to Samantabhadra, the Bodhisattva associated with kindness and auspiciousness, and it is the first supramundane mind, consciousness corresponding to the first stage of the Bodhisattva Path. The continuity of consciousness (*samtana*) of this stage is characterized primarily as joy (*pramudita*).

> Born in the Tathagata lineage,
> He utterly renounces the three links.
> The Bodhisattva attains unsurpassed joy
> And can vibrate a hundred world-systems.

As the fledgling Bodhisattva directly recognizes selflessness, he sees through the three links: false views of transience, doubt which pollutes and distorted ethics. They will not affect him again.

> From stage to stage advancing he ascends,
> His paths to lower incarnations are blocked,
> All levels of ordinary beings are closed to him.

Any being who attains the first level of this road to emancipation finds that his growing compassion is naturally translated into *dana*, giving. He may have little to give, but he knows what others have yet to discover:

> Even for beings with little compassion,
> Brutally intent on their own ends,
> Coveted resources arise from giving,
> And cause the end of suffering.

Even if a person thought of nothing but his own happiness, if he were also intent on *dana* he would in time encounter a true Arya, a superior being, who could show him how to cut the continuum of cyclic existence and achieve the emancipation of *Nirvana*. For the Bodhisattva, giving opens the way to hitherto unimagined possibilities for effective service. Therefore, Chandrakirti taught, *dana* is profoundly important alike to those with compassion and those without it. For a *jinaputra*, however, the very thought of giving brings happiness. In time, such a being will recognize the levels of giving.

> Giving void of gift, giver and receiver
> Is called a supramundane perfection *(lokottara*
>     *paramita).*
> But when attachment to these three arises,
> It is called a mundane perfection.

The joyous mind which arises from giving is secured in the second stage, which is called stainless *(vimala)* and is marked by proper ethics *(shila)*. The Bodhisattva who purifies ethics does not think in lesser terms even in dreams. *Shila* involves the renunciation of seven actions: killing, stealing, sexual misconduct, lying, divisive speech, harsh words and senseless chatter. These seven impediments to harmonious conduct, four of which have to do with speech and therefore directly with thought, are eradicated through the motivating influence of desirelessness, harmlessness and freedom from wrong views. Speaking of the Bodhisattva who has attained the *shila* stage, Chandrakirti wrote:

> Like an autumn moon he is ever pure,
> Beautified by *shila,* serene and radiant.

But at the same time, he pointed to the problem of unconscious self-righteousness, the false sense of having completed a task which remains unfinished.

> If he views his *shila* as inherently pure,
> Then its purity will not be complete.

For Chandrakirti, the problem of ethics is not that people have no ethical sense, but rather that they tend to absolutize a faulty, insufficient, or distorted ethical sense. The Bodhisattva realizes that any perception stained with so much as a minute remnant of ignorance or attachment throws a cloud upon ethical clarity, and so he strives to perfect *shila* far beyond the moral demands of the world. Thus his actions assist all beings in ways hardly comprehensible to those who have yet to follow in his footsteps.

> Like the light of an autumn moon,
> The stainlessness from the moon of a *jinaputra,*
> Unworldly, yet the glory of the world,
> Removes the mental distress of *gatis.*

The third stage of the ten-stepped Bodhisattva Path is *prabhakari,* the luminous, whose sigil is *kshanti,* patience. It is called luminous because here the fire of wisdom consumes the objects of knowledge in an orange light, a coppery conflagration that consumes discursive thought like the dawn light dispels darkness. In using this analogy, Chandrakirti also made a veiled allusion to the pervasive orange light that appears to the contemplative when he has attained meditative equipoise. Its seal is patience because the Bodhisattva sees that every form of impatience, all of which are aspects of resentment, are useless to his self-assumed task and an obstacle to its fulfilment.

> If you grow angry with one who harms you,
> Does your resentment eradicate the harm?
> Resentment is utterly useless here,
> And unfavourable for future lives.
>
> How can one justify oneself,
> Who longs to erase effects of previous action,
> To spread broadcast the seeds of suffering,
> Through hating and harming others?
>
> Even a moment of hating by a jinaputra
> Destroys virtues from dana and shila
> Garnered over a hundred aeons.
> There is no sin worse than impatience.

The cultivation of *kshanti* removes the inversions of virtue, gives one a luminous beauty, makes the holy dear, nurtures skill in discerning right from wrong, and leads to exalted future births. The Bodhisattva who secures himself at this stage discovers that the eradication of desire and hatred allows mastery in concentration and the natural development of clairvoyance.

*Archishmati,* the radiant, is the fourth *bhumi,* whose hallmark is *virya,* effort. This effort, "dauntless energy that fights its way to the supernal TRUTH", is the gateway to every conceivable attainment, for it brings the whole being into harmony or resonance with Enlightenment. Tsong-Kha-Pa listed thirty-seven ways in which the Bodhisattva is brought into harmony with Enlightenment through *virya,* including mindfulness in respect to body, feeling, mind and phenomena; renunciation of both vice and virtue; manifestation of aspiration, effort, thought and meditation; emergence of faculties and powers; harmonization of the branches of Enlightenment, including joy, pliancy and equanimity; and perfection in the Noble

Eightfold Path. All this is possible, Chandrakirti wrote, because "what is related to the view of a self is extinguished".

The fifth *bhumi* is called *sudurjaya,* difficult to overcome, because the *dhyana* or concentration which distinguishes this level is so powerful that neither earthly distractions nor the hosts of demons from the astral plane can affect it.

> This great being on the ground *sudurjaya*
> Cannot be vanquished even by all the demons.
> His *dhyana* excels, he gains great skill
> In knowledge of subtle truths of the good-minded.

Since, according to Chandrakirti, *Nirvana* is not different from ultimate Truth and extinction of conditionality and falsehood, including false conceptions of the self, perfection in *dhyana* is the threshold of *Nirvana.* A person who seeks Enlightenment for himself alone has no farther to go. The next step is into the refulgent presence of utterly transcendental *prajna,* the Flame of which cannot be touched because the seeker becomes it. The Bodhisattva refuses to take that final step, however, because he has consecrated himself to enter the Flame only after all sentient beings have been helped to do so. For him, the Path continues through four more stages, whose names can hardly suggest the states to which they point, culminating in the eleventh stage, which is no stage at all but rather is the mystery of the Buddha, He who stands beyond space and time yet can enter into both for the welfare of all beings.

For Chandrakirti, the Path begins and ends in compassion. Compassion is a point drawn out into a line by the effort of the aspirant who eventually realizes that he is the Path himself. Chandrakirti's views, together with the writings of Nagarjuna which he did much to preserve, survived the fall of Nalanda and the dispersion of its schools of thought, and when Tsong-Kha-Pa revitalized the Buddhist tradition in Tibet and founded the Gelukpa or Yellow Hat order, he made the works of Nagarjuna and Chandrakirti the heart of his spiritual philosophy. If Nagarjuna was the progenitor of the Madhyamika, Chandrakirti was the undisputed scion of Prasangika Madhyamika, the Middle Way's most rigorous and sublime expression.

> *He who with equanimity surveys*
> *Lustre of goodness, strife of passion, sloth*
> *Of ignorance, not angry if they are,*
> *Not wishful when they are not: he who sits*
> *A sojourner and stranger in their midst*
> *Unruffled, standing off saying – serene –*
> *When troubles break, "These be the Qualities."*
> *He unto whom – Self-centered – grief and joy*
> *Sound as one word; to whose deep-seeing eyes*
> *The clod, the marble, and the gold are one;*
> *Whose equal heart holds the same gentleness*
> *For lovely and unlovely things, firm set,*
> *Well pleased in praise and dispraise; satisfied*
> *With honour or dishonour; unto friends*
> *And unto foes alike in tolerance,*
> *Detached from undertakings – he is named*
> *Surmounter of the Qualities.*

Shri Krishna

**OM**

*Hermes*, October 1985
Elton Hall

# SHANTIDEVA

*Just as the stem of a banana tree does not exist when it has been divided into parts, the ego likewise becomes unreal when examined reflectively.*

*One might think that because no being can be discovered, there are none on whom to bestow compassion, but what is done even in confusion is because of a purpose.*

*If, however, there is no being, whose is the purpose? The effort is illusory, but because it serves to tranquillize sorrow, this delusion is not forbidden.*

*When, through my effort and by raising a cloud of merit, may I make tranquil those who are troubled in the fire of sorrow?*

*When, by zealous and meritorious deeds for the unveiling of the truth, may I point towards* shunyata *those who see only fantasies?*

Shantideva
*Bodhicaryavatara*

Chandrakirti laid the foundations and initiated the Prasangika Madhyamika school of Buddhist thought, but Shantideva provided it with mystic vision and ecstatic fervour. Born in the eighth century, he was a son of the ruler of Saurashtra, a small kingdom in modern Gujarat. While still a child, he was vouchsafed a vision of Manjushri, the Bodhisattva of wisdom, and the vision was repeated near the time for his accession to the throne. Manjushri declared that he was Shantideva's *alyanamitra*, spiritual friend, and warned him not to take the throne of Saurashtra. At about the same time, Shantideva had a dream in which Tara, the feminine aspect and counterpart of Avalokiteshvara, appeared to him in the guise of his mother and consecrated him. In an act reflecting the renunciation of Buddha, he fled the kingdom and wandered in a forest for twenty-one days. He came upon a woman who offered him sweet water and led him to a *yogin* who initiated him into Buddhist doctrine and meditation. He soon attained *samadhi* and recognized the woman and the *yogin* as Tara and Manjushri. From that moment, the vision of Manjushri remained with him throughout his life.

In time he came to Nalanda, where he received ordination and the name Shantideva from the *upadhyaya* Jayadeva. Since he ate large quantities of rice and seemed to sleep much of the time, many monks suspected that he was a spiritual fraud. To unmask his pretensions, they set up a recitation of the *sutras* from memory, expecting him to fail when his turn came around. When it was his time to recite, he asked if they would like to hear an old *sutra* or something wholly new. They chose the latter, and he at once began to utter the *Bodhicaryavatara (Entering the Path of Enlightenment)*, a poetic and philosophical discourse on the Bodhisattva Path. When he began to utter the verse (IX, 35), "When existence and non-existence cease to be present to the mind. . . ", he rose into the air and became invisible, though his voice could be clearly heard. There was no more gossip in Nalanda regarding Shantideva's routines, and reverence for him was so great that he joined Chandragomin as one of the select few to whom Taranatha gave the sacred title *acharya* in his history of the Buddhist tradition in India.

While at Nalanda, Shantideva also composed the *Shikshasamuccaya*, a compendium of Buddhist doctrines, which drew together citations from a vast number of *sutras* and texts. It emphasizes the moral dimension of the Bodhisattva Path, whilst the *Bodhicaryavatara* focusses on the Path from the standpoint of consciousness. Shantideva also engaged in dialectical debates, advocating a mystical view of the highest doctrines and insisting that logical clarity serve the ends of intuitive insight. According to tradition, he travelled south to a now unknown place to debate a number of *tirthikas* who rejected the teachings of Buddha. He won a great number of them over with his dialectical skills, and though many attested to his magical powers, his memorable "seven wonderful acts" emphasized the conversion of different groups of opponents. Sometime late in the seventh century he disappeared from history, which remains silent on the time, place and manner of his death.

For Shantideva, the key to the Bodhisattva Path is *bodhichitta*, the seed or thought of Enlightenment, and therefore the Bodhisattva is the paradigm of the path to Enlightenment. Because the Bodhisattva pauses at the threshold of becoming a Buddha, who assumes the *Dharmakaya* glory but is cut off from giving aid directly to human beings still mired in the illusion and delusion of *samsara*, he is suspended between the relativity of illusions and the certitude of Reality. He reaches down from the realm of pure thought to help all those willing to attempt to tread the path he has trodden. Whilst the Arhat and the Bodhisattva are the same in their ultimate natures, the Arhat seizes the Enlightenment he has earned and becomes an example for others to follow. The Bodhisattva holds back in some mysterious way, inexplicable to ordinary consciousness, and actually reaches out to help those who would walk the Path. The unfathomable mystery of this aid is bound up with *bodhichitta*, that spark of consciousness which, when activated, turns the aspirant towards *bodhi*, Enlightenment. The difference between Arhat and Bodhisattva is to be found less in states of consciousness than in the linkage between that realm and the world of transient phenomena.

Since *bodhichitta* is not only the idea of *bodhi* or Enlightenment, but also its suffusion through the whole of consciousness as well as the force it exerts in impelling one along the Path, it is *Buddhanubhava*, the gesture of Buddha, which turns consciousness, even if only for a moment, to the good. Like a thunderbolt in the night sky, it permanently transforms one's perception of the world, giving new valence and orientation to everything in *samsara*. Since *dukha*, suffering, is the defining characteristic of temporal existence, *bodhichitta* is the inexplicable infusion of a higher reality into the otherwise seamless fabric of ignorance. *Bodhichitta* is therefore an event which falls outside the causality of ordinary mind and nature, a kind of grace from Buddha or from an enlightened Guru. It is as if *shunyata,* the Void, calls to the Void, and the arising of *bodhichitta* within one is its echo.

> This merit – seed of the world's joy, medicine for the world's sorrow, jewel of *chitta,* the mind – how can it be measured?

*Bodhichitta* contains the potency necessary for the entire pilgrimage to Enlightenment, and it is the womb of *karuna,* compassion. With it goodness can vanquish evil, knowledge can surmount ignorance, and insight can subdue suffering. The arising of *bodhichitta* completes one's birth as a human being, for one becomes a *Buddhaputra,* a Buddha-son, a member of the *Buddhakula,* the Buddha family.

Because *karuna* is born from *bodhichitta,* the ray of *shunyata* activated in human consciousness, it is not a property of the individual or an instrument for the redemption of the individual alone. It is the alchemical source of universal purpose, the ground of *mahartha siddhi,* the great work, and the force within *jagad dhitartha,* the work of the world's well-being. For Shantideva, it is less important that one grasp the ten stages on the Bodhisattva Path than that one understand that the activation of *bodhichitta* compels a twofold practice. *Bodhipranidhichitta,* the thought of the vow of Enlightenment, spontaneously arises with the advent of *bodhichitta,* and it is immediately followed by *bodhiprasthanachitta,* the departure upon the road to realization. When one comes to the fortunate condition in which one can take the great vow, *mahapranidhana,* before a spiritual guide, *kalyanamitra,* one has not only come to an irreversible turning point in this life, but one has affected the entire cycle of *samsara.* The great vow is the Pledge of Kwan-Yin, and the aspiration to achieve Enlightenment cannot be separated from the Enlightenment of all beings. *Bodhichitta* is thus the spark of the Bodhisattva in every being, and once it is truly aroused, it becomes a consuming fire which may have setbacks but which expands without limit and can never be extinguished.

Rejoicing in the seemingly miraculous manifestation of *bodhichitta* within one's deepest consciousness leads naturally to an overwhelming sense of gratitude, which Shantideva expressed in terms of the Tathagatas, the Jewel of the True Dharma and all the Buddha-sons, that is, to the Buddha, the Dharma and the Sangha mystically transfigured in the light of *bodhichitta.* Shantideva calls upon all the great beings represented in these Three Jewels to take possession of him, for he is prepared to enter the strict servitude demanded by the *bhakti,* devotion, which has arisen in him. He recognizes that neither *bodhichitta* nor refuge in the Three Jewels excuses the aspirant from the self-engendered effort which is required on every step of the Path. For Shantideva, the first step after being caught up in spontaneous gratitude is a self-conscious act of purgation through *papadeshana,* the confession of sins. *Papadeshana* is no guilt-ridden indulgence in regret over one's past misdeeds, which at best would amount to an inadequate empirical review dependent on partial memory. Rather, it is a reflection upon the evil in the world and the recognition that, given innumerable previous incarnations, one dare not presume to dissociate oneself from any of it.

> Whatever evil, on the endless wheel of *samsara* or just right here, whatever evil was committed by me or was caused to be committed by me, and whatever was enjoyed foolishly, ending in self-destruction, that evil I confess, stricken with remorseful feeling.

Once one's past deeds and one's connection through karma with every other living being has been honestly faced, one can authentically rejoice in everything that is good, *punyanumodana,* the mirror image of *papadeshana.* With these two comes the capacity to begin fulfilling the Bodhisattva Vow by renouncing whatever meritorious karma one might have or will receive for the uplift of all beings. Together, these form the basis and substance of *bodhichittaparigraha,* seizing the seed of Enlightenment and retaining its efficacious radiance throughout the whole of consciousness, so that at every moment it suffuses thought, permeates intention and manifests in deeds.

Today my birth is completed, my human nature is fulfilled. Today I have been born into the Buddha family and I am henceforth a Buddha-son. It is now for me to behave according to the customs of this family, so that there may be no stain put upon its spotlessness.

Each step on the path to Enlightenment is distinguished by the predominance of a *paramita*, virtue or quality of character, which synthesizes all the virtues from a particular standpoint. Though Shantideva followed the traditional Mahayana list, consisting of *dana*, *shila*, *kshanti*, *virya*, *dhyana* and *prajna*, he depicted them primarily in terms of transformations of consciousness rather than of deeds. Thus *dana*, love identified with giving, becomes *bodhichittapramada*, vigilance in the thought of Enlightenment. Noting the fact that "innumerable Buddhas have passed, seeking all beings", he lamented his self-engendered condition: "Because of my own fault, I have been beyond the reach of their medicine." Because of one's own past actions on the plane of consciousness, one has developed attractions and repulsions which are readily expressed in joys and fears, friends and enemies, pleasures and pains. Desire, hatred and anger are one's real enemies, but since they have no power in themselves, they cannot enslave one without one's own cooperation. "Yet they are dwelling within my own mind and thus smite me at their ease." Ultimately, one can neither claim to be overpowered by them nor pretend that one does not have the resources to banish them. "I am stupid only because I make no effort", Shantideva wrote, In striving for *prajna*, wisdom, one can overcome *maya*, illusion, and this requires vigilance in the thought of Enlightenment.

For Shantideva, *dana* and *shila*, as ethical principles, are on occasion potentially in opposition. From the plane of the mind, however, which is the root of ethical discrimination, they are at one. *Shila*, harmonious conduct, can be undertaken only if one follows *shiksha*, a discipline or rule of life, and this is possible only to the extent that one cultivates *samprajanyarakshana*, complete mental awareness or presence of mind. Since all one's enemies and fears are lodged in consciousness, anger comes easily to one who has not developed considerable mental equipoise. If anger can be eradicated, Shantideva taught, all one's fears and enemies will vanish. Thus awareness is *shila* in consciousness, and all who would walk the Bodhisattva Path must strive for it, though those who have the indescribable good fortune of association with a Guru will find themselves immensely aided. The ability to discern when the dictates of love for all beings requires one to ignore conventional morality, and when dissipative circumstances indicate that one's giving should be checked, is developed through the performance of duty. For the performance of duty to be an effective means of treading the Path, one has to bring one's whole attention to each act undertaken. In addition, one needs to shift attention from self-interested concern with the body to protecting the mind. By strengthening awareness and guarding consciousness from distractions and illusions, one makes oneself an instrument of service in the cause of universal welfare.

*Kshanti*, patience, implies forbearance, forgiveness and tolerance at the broadest possible level. It is patience in respect to oneself and one's imperfections, to karma which is exact, relentless and just, and to others. All levels of patience have hostility as their opposite, and hostility of any kind undermines what one has garnered from the arising of *bodhichitta* and works against the Vow one has taken to help redeem all beings from the bonds of conditioned existence. For Shantideva, the dialectical paradoxes familiar to Madhyamika thought and the theme of the *Prajnaparamita Sutras* are powerful levers for the permanent reorientation of consciousness. Though one wishes to help all beings reach Enlightenment, one also knows that no independent beings actually exist. Rather than appropriating this doctrine to justify inaction, one should recognize that if it is so, there is no one and nothing towards which one need be hostile. If, as Buddha taught, the fundamental condition of *samsara* is *dukha*, then patience is critical to nurturing *bodhichitta* in the world. Through patience, one can come to endure a modicum of suffering without having to flee it or become obsessed with it. That degree of indifference can be extended gradually until neither pleasure nor pain of any intensity can divert one from the self-selected Way. *Kshanti* is therefore the best *tapas*, purgative discipline, and it allows one to take the Bodhisattva Vow at a new level of understanding and dedication.

> Let this, then, be my vow: the honouring of the Tathagata, the complete fulfilment of my own well-being, the destruction of the sorrow of the world.

To the extent that one has secured the foundations of patience, one can begin to manifest *virya*, which for Shantideva is effort, heroism and a kind of pride. Self-mastery, aiming at courage and attainment of strength, identity of self and others, and likewise, exchange of self and others, are all aspects of *virya*.

One's tolerance and patience must not be allowed to lull one into complacency. Rather, they should prepare one for a fierce and unrelenting struggle to achieve the goal. Having learnt to face karma and suffering, one should gain the strength to do something about them. Though Shantideva was well aware of the disease of separative pride, which destroys if not itself destroyed, he saw that even it is only a pitiful reflection of a virtue. True pride, *mana*, is a will to persevere on behalf of all. One should so solidly identify with all beings that one is too proud to labour for the separative and false ego, or to allow distasteful work to be done by others, or even to permit the thought of giving up to cross one's mind. One should think too much of oneself as a being ultimately not different from all the beings in existence to shun ruthless examination of one's faults and fearless correction of one's mistakes.

> As cotton is obedient to the coming and going of the wind, so one should proceed in obedience to one's resolution. Thus *riddhi*, the wonder-working power, is utterly triumphant.

The practice of *virya* as a mental activity manifests as wakefulness, heedfulness and concentration, and it is sometimes called 'unbounded industry'. At the same time, it is a commensurate tranquillity of mind. The energy released by this combination provides the basis for *dhyana*, contemplation, reflection and abstraction, which culminates in *samadhi*, full meditation. *Shamatha*, alert tranquillity, opens the way to *vipashyana*, clear vision. Although vision is possible long before this stage is reached, the recurrence of (or even the potential for) passionate attraction and revulsion discolours it. In *dhyana* one can gain from one's visions the assurance that, though they will be partial revelations of Truth, they will not be distorted or inverted. *Vipashyana* is the recognition of things as they are, and this supreme clarity of mind results in total detachment and renunciation of the fruits of action. Having vowed from the beginning to serve the spiritual welfare of all beings, and making real through detachment the ultimate equality of all beings, the Bodhisattva participates in a great alchemical mystery through *dhyana*, the efflorescence of quiet consciousness.

> Whoever wishes quickly to rescue himself and another, should practise the supreme mystery – the exchanging of himself and the other.

Ethically, this is the recognition of the virtues in others and the faults in oneself, followed by an exchange in which one seeks to emulate those virtues by exalting and not stealing them. On the plane of clear mind, it is the realization that one is not separate from others and that karma is understood fully only at the collective level. Psychologically, it is the willingness to assume the suffering of another and replace it with one's own bliss. But on a deeper, occult plane which does not exclude other levels, it is the alchemical magic of lending one's consciousness and insight to another, giving invisible strength through meditation without removing the responsibility of another for his or her condition. This is the mysterious wonder-working power which Buddha called the highest magic, easily misunderstood as vicarious atonement, but in fact the fundamental force at the root of all the *siddhis* or supernormal powers. Thus the Bodhisattva becomes a pillar of the world, uplifting the whole of humanity, though unseen and unknown to most beneficiaries.

Secure in *dhyana* and beyond the possibility of retreat on the Bodhisattva Path, the traveller finds himself at the threshold of *prajna,* perfect wisdom beyond all conceivable formulation. Relative truths, many of which have been helpful, like a raft crossing a river, are left behind once the raging waters are crossed, and one stands before *paramartha,* "that which is beyond the veiled". Truth, *satya,* is seen to be *shunyata,* a void into which all relativities and partialities are dropped, an emptiness in which there are no attitudes but a universal orientation. In its ineffable radiance one sees that which is beyond form and formlessness, and one rejoices in the realization that there are no beings to be redeemed, though one will labour without cessation to redeem every being. The Bodhisattva now knows, and though that knowledge cannot be communicated to others but only intimated through symbol, metaphor and analogy, he can act on it while not seeing himself as the actor. The fusion of perceiver, perception and perceived is as complete as it is inexplicable. The Bodhisattva now bears that revered designation in its highest meaning, and his signature is selflessness His radical identification with all beings restrains him from disappearing in the release of *Nirvana.* Rather, in *parinamana,* that unspeakable consummation which is attaining the Goal, he now breathes and thinks for humanity, his every word a living balm and every act a benediction.

> As Manjushri walks in ten directions and to the sky's edge for the increase of the prosperity of all beings, let my work be like his. As long as there is space and as long as the world exists, for that long let my existence be devoted to the world's sorrows.

> Wherever is found the sorrow of the world, may it come to fruition in me, and may the world be comforted by the glorious host of Bodhisattvas.

As the only medicine for the world's sorrow, the only cause of happiness and success, may the Teaching – honoured everywhere – endure for long aeons.

I pay homage to Manjughosha by the favour which makes the thought beautiful. I honour the *kalyanamitra*, the good friend, by the favour which he has thus increased.

Shantideva

---

*Regard as true Renouncer him that makes*
*Worship by work, for who renounceth not*
*Works not as Yogin. So is that well said:*
*"By works the votary doth rise to saint,*
*And saintship is the ceasing from all works";*
*Because the perfect Yogin acts – but acts*
*Unmoved by passions and unbound by deeds,*
*Setting result aside.*

Shri Krishna

**OM**

*Hermes*, November 1985
Elton Hall

# SHANTARAKSHITA

*The deputy of the Buddha, the holy Shantarakshita,*
*And the superior master of incantations,*
*  the ascetic Padmasambhava,*
*Kamalashila, the crest jewel of the wise,*
*And Trhisong Detsen. of surpassing thoughts –*
*Through these four, like sunrise in the dark land of Tibet,*
*The light of holy religion spread even to the frontiers.*
*These holy men of unwavering kindness*
*  Tibetans will all forevermore revere.*

Tibetan Song

The history of the Land of Snows is as mysterious as its awesome landscapes, as secret as its fastnesses. It reaches back from chronicle to legend and then to myth, beyond which an impenetrable veil hides the distant past. Ringed by lofty mountains, Tibet was for millennia isolated from the political intrigues of its neighbours to the south, east and west. China's cultural insularity ensured that its historians paid scant attention to Tibet, and the great northern peoples, including the Mongolians, remain almost as enigmatic and remote as the Tibetans themselves. Trans-Himalayan culture was deeply rooted in the oral tradition, and the Tibetan people kept no ordinary written records until the advent of Buddha's teaching.

According to the Tibetans, the first human beings were as radiant and ethereal as the original earth. Gradually the earth condensed and the bodies of men grew dense as well, until both reached their present condition. Sometime during this long evolution Avalokiteshvara in the form of a monkey mated with a terrestrial demoness of the rocks, and their offspring became the ancestors of the Tibetans. Avalokiteshvara gave his children six kinds of grain, and over time this race evolved from a monkey-like appearance into modern human forms. At the same time, society evolved, though disputes over food formed the basis of all the inequities and injustices that sprang up with social progress. Six races emerged, to which a seventh race, directly descended from the primordial egg of heaven, was added. Seven ages of human development culminated in the emergence of the first heavenly king. The first five periods were characterized by the appearance of various classes of lesser deities, and the sixth was marked by the rule of the twelve minor kings. These chieftains were not strong enough, individually or collectively, to rule Tibet and to protect it from the great powers at the four cardinal points – China, India, Iran and Gesar – but they were wise enough to discern the need for a mighty ruler.

Having come together and worshipped the holy mountain, the twelve kings sent messengers up the mountain to heaven to petition for a single monarch. According to ancient scrolls found in the Tun-huang caves, "The divine king of Great Tibet, of magical power, came from the gods as ruler of man", and the seventh age began. This line of seven divine kings ruled the earth by day but returned to their natural abodes at night by ascending the *dmu,* a rope whose name means 'sky'. When the first king's son reached the age of thirteen, the king's body dissolved into the *dmu* and the rope returned to heaven. Each successor followed the same practice, and so there are no tombs for the divine kings save for the *dmu* tombs, the celestial vault. Trigum, the last king in the line, was an exception, however. Though still of celestial origin, he had an arrogant personality and he once challenged all comers to a duel in magic. Only one man dared to accept the challenge, and in their ferocious contest first near Mount Kailas and, later, renewed southwest of Lhasa, the king accidentally severed his *dmu.* The rope rose to heaven and Trigum became the first king to leave a corpse. Though one of his sons, Rula-kye, later overthrew the challenger and ascended the throne, the line of divine kings had come to an end.

Rula-kye built mountain fortresses, baled hay, introduced charcoal and the smelting of metals, and taught the people to make ploughs and yokes. For the first time, Tibetans had ploughed fields and built bridges over otherwise impassable waterways and a system of channels for irrigation. According to tradition, the Bon religion in its pure form entered Tibet at this time from Iran, or from Gilgit or Gurnawatra (northwest India). The art of religious story-telling and that of singing genealogies and riddles also appeared during this period. Rapid social and agricultural progress initiated by Rula-kye continued under the six human kings of the Lek dynasty, but the eight kings of the succeeding De dynasty focussed their attention upon the development of law and the political order. With the death of the last De king, the queens of Tibetan monarchs ceased to be incarnate goddesses, and the subsequent kings of the Tsen dynasty married among their subjects, at once diluting and sharing the divine inheritance. When the fifth and last Tsan king ascended the throne, a casket descended from heaven containing two Buddhist *sutras* and a golden *stupa*. Though no one could read the sacred texts, they were preserved and revered as the "Mysterious Helper", and the king was vouchsafed a prophecy that during the fifth reign after his, the meaning of the heavenly casket would be known.

The fifth king of the prophecy was the great Songtsen Gampo, who gave Tibet a firm and unified political structure and accepted the *Buddhadharma*. Born about A.D. 569, he ascended the throne at age thirteen. Establishing legal codes throughout Tibet, he subjugated the petty chieftains and formed a single army of a hundred thousand men. He brought water mills, silkworms and mulberry trees, paper and ink, from China and adapted the Chinese calendar, but he turned to India for a system of writing. Marrying a Nepalese princess, he accepted her Buddhist faith and built temples in Lhasa for the images she brought to Tibet of Akshobhya, Maitreya and Tara, and the image of Akshobhya survives into the present. Songtsen Gampo also married a Chinese princess who was a Buddhist, and she brought an image of Gautama Buddha, originally made in Magadha, and a temple was built for it. He built the first structures of the Potala in Lhasa and founded a number of monasteries which were not successful. His stunning invasion of India and China made Tibet an Asian power that could not be ignored. Diplomats and soldiers came to Lhasa, trade flourished, China and Nepal paid annual tribute to the king, and some sacred texts were translated into Tibetan. Within two or three decades Tibet became a literate nation, a military power and nominally a Buddhist country. When Songtsen Gampo died in 650, Tibetans had already come to believe that he was an incarnation of Avalokiteshvara. His Nepalese wife was recognized as the green Tara, whilst the Chinese princess was seen to be the white Tara (Kwan-Yin).

Though Buddhist thought and practice waned and fell into degradation after the death of Songtsen Gampo, traditions hint at a much older stream of *Bodhi Dharma*, the secret Wisdom Religion, that had abided in the Himalayas and the Gobi Desert from the beginning of man's spiritual awakening. Perhaps this is why the most arcane teachings of Gautama Buddha rooted themselves in Tibet when the Good Law came there. For the time being, however, a succession of rulers had to fight just to preserve the integrity of Tibet against Chinese incursions, North Indian revolts and internecine disputes. In 742 a Chinese wife of the reigning king gave birth to Trhisong Detsen, who ascended the throne in 755. Tibet's dwindling fortunes were now reversed. The Pala kings of Bengal became tributaries of Tibet, and Trhisong Detsen extended his borders to the Ganges, where he set up an iron column to mark his frontier. He invaded China and even enthroned a new emperor who ruled briefly, and he generally secured Tibet against the outside world. Then he turned his attention to Buddha's teachings and decided to adopt the religion and make it the religion of his country. His lifelong labours for Buddha's teaching led to his being recognized as an incarnation of Manjushri, Bodhisattva of wisdom.

Trhisong Detsen knew that Bon priests opposed most aspects of the Buddhist tradition, and so he did not attempt to force acceptance upon the people. Quietly, he sent emissaries to Nalanda to seek help. Tibetan tradition holds that at that time Shantarakshita was *Upadhyaya* of the great university and monastic community, though he was met by the Tibetans in Nepal. Shantarakshita may have been born in Bengal, the son of a king of Zahor, and though nothing is known of his early life, he was an ordained monk who combined a remarkably logical mind with a deep understanding of tantric magical practices. He had written the *Tattvasamgraha*, a sweeping analysis from the Yogachara standpoint of every known Buddhist and non-Buddhist philosophical tenet. The Tibetan emissaries who interviewed him were deeply impressed by his intelligence, erudition, energy and will. Lengthy discussions followed in which Shantarakshita came to a full understanding of the possibilities and limitations of working in Tibet. Despite his immense learning and renowned skill in dialectical disputations, he was determined to explain the fundamentals of Buddha's teachings to Tibetans. Trhisong Detsen's ministers, however, were sharply divided over the importation of Buddhist doctrines. Some strongly supported the king, whilst others backed the Bon resistance to any change in Tibetan culture. Shantarakshita patiently waited in Nepal until the balance of opinion shifted to the king's party, and only then he made the arduous journey to Lhasa in response to a royal invitation.

Shantarakshita, who is called in Tibet Shiba-'tsho, Shantijiva and, simply, Bodhisattva, was warmly received in Lhasa. The king, however, wished to be assured that his choice had been wise before supporting the monk's proposed programmes. He knew that the monks surviving from Songtsen Gampo's time were lax in respect to practices and austerities and often shockingly dissolute. He did not want to infect Tibet with another of that breed. The deputies sent to interview Shantarakshita did not understand his language and considerable consternation resulted. Eventually, Ananta of Kashmir offered his services as interpreter, and soon the deputies could report that Shantarakshita "was virtuous and had no obscene thoughts". He was invited to the palace and received by the king. According to one Tibetan historian, when Shantarakshita was asked about his doctrine, he replied:

> My doctrine is to follow whatever proves correct
> under examination by reason, and to shun all that does
> not agree with reason.

The king was convinced of the soundness of his decision by Shantarakshita's keen mind and impeccable moral conduct. He gave him freedom to preach and to teach in Tibet and offered to support any undertaking the monk might advise.

Perhaps more than the remarkable work Shantarakshita was about to undertake, the stupendous testament to his character might be the change in approach he initiated in his own consciousness. The most brilliant dialectician of his day, he realized that the recondite disputations of which he was the unchallenged master were utterly meaningless to a people who had hardly heard of the Enlightened One and who had discovered the written word barely a century before. He laid aside all his sophisticated learning and undertook basic education in *Buddhadharma*. With the help of the interpreter Ananta, he spent four months teaching Trhisong Detsen and his court. Beginning with the Four Noble Truths – suffering, its cause, its cessation and the Noble Eightfold Path – he proceeded to explain the six and ten virtues, from *dana* to the highest attainment of the Bodhisattva. He taught the king about the eighteen states of corporeal existence and expounded the eight fundamental prohibitions.

Then Shantarakshita turned to the twelve *nidanas* which form the links in the circular chain of conditioned existence. Sentience leads to consciousness *(vijnana)*, and consciousness gives rise to name and form *(namarupa)*. *Namarupa* in turn produces contact *(sparsa)*, and this in turn leads to emotion *(vedana)*. Feelings arouse thirst or desire *(trishna)*, which produces attachment and revulsion *(upadana)*. The ceaselessly changing tension between attraction and repulsion initiates the condition of existence *(bhava)*, and this makes necessary birth *(jati)*. Birth is the ultimate cause of death, since whatever comes into being must necessarily perish. From old age and death, the inevitable end of all embodied existence, come grief, lamentation, pain, depression and misery. Thus, Shantarakshita taught, the endless chain can be broken only through Buddha's way of Enlightenment. This was the justification of Buddhist practices from meditation and morality to the austere life of the monk.

For the first time, the basic message of Gautama Buddha was taught in Tibet, and the Bon priests felt directly threatened by Buddha's doctrine. In particular, the code of conduct expounded by Shantarakshita came into uncompromising conflict with some Bon practices. Besides bringing considerable political pressure to bear on the king, the Bon priests employed their formidable magical powers. In the words of Bu-ston, they "brought the malignant deities of Tibet into a fury. Phan-than was carried away by a flood, lightning struck Mar-po-ri, and diseases fell upon men and cattle." Soon the people, cunningly guided by the Bon priests, cried out against Shantarakshita, and the king's ministers urged Trhisong Detsen to expel him. When the king discussed the deteriorating situation with Shantarakshita, he expressed concern for the monk's safety. Though he was loath to give up his effort to make Tibet a Buddhist country, he thought it wise to send Shantarakshita away. Shantarakshita saw no value in imposing the *Buddhadharma* on Tibetans through force, but he devised a plan to preserve and expand the gains already made. He left Tibet for Nepal, and upon his suggestion Trhisong Detsen invited the great tantrist Padmasambhava to Tibet.

Padmasambhava accepted the invitation, understood the situation in Tibet, and engaged in magical combat with the aroused demons. His victories over Bon machinations were softened by his skill in absorbing some Bon traditions into the framework of Buddhist thought and practice. The custom of giving a place to the Bon chief priest in the Dalai Lama's governing council may ultimately date back to Padmasambhava's work. Before long Shantarakshita was able to return in safety to Tibet. Together he and Padmasambhava established the great Samye monastery some thirty miles southeast of Lhasa. Taking the then modern monastery of Odantapuri as a model, they constructed a number of buildings before any monks were chosen. Bu-ston wrote that Shantarakshita "made a plan containing the forms of Mount Sumeru, the twelve continents, both the sun and the moon, and these surrounded by a circumference of iron".

Samye was built about 787; its upper portions were constructed in Chinese style, its middle in Indian style and its foundations in the Tibetan manner. Named "the academy for obtaining the heap of unchanging meditation", Samye became the repository of many Indian texts brought by Shantarakshita, and a number of them survive today. Though Padmasambhava left shortly after Samye was built, Shantarakshita remained for thirteen years and made it into the first full-fledged monastery in Tibet, complete with provisions for resident monks and for teaching and training. Samye naturally became the first important centre for Buddhist learning in Tibet, and it served as a platform from which to promulgate the Good Law across the land.

In the few years left to him, Shantarakshita initiated two lines of work which profoundly affected the subsequent history of Tibet. On the one hand, he trained a group of scholar-monks who could translate Buddhist *sutras* into Tibetan. At the same time, he persuaded a number of Indian Buddhists to come to Tibet and join in their labour. Difficult as it is to imagine under the adverse circumstances of the time, within a few years Shantarakshita had overseen the translation of most of the over forty-five hundred texts which came to constitute the Tibetan canon, the Kangyur and the Tengyur, the scriptures and the commentaries. On the other hand, Shantarakshita took twelve novices and tested them thoroughly, choosing from them seven for ordination. These revered "seven selected ones" became the core and foundation of Tibetan monasticism. Though there had been ascetics among the adherents of the Bon tradition and even Buddhist monks of a kind, Shantarakshita saw to it that his disciples followed the proper *vinaya* rules.

Shortly before he died Shantarakshita foresaw a gradually developing conflict within the ranks of the Tibetan monks. Knowing that their disagreements would eventually centre on the nature of the path to Enlightenment and therefore upon the validity of the disciplines he had established, Shantarakshita prophesied that his own Indian disciple, Kamalashila, would come from across the Himalayas and settle the dispute before the king himself. Though he was still healthy, his immense self-sacrifice in the cause of the *Buddhadharma* in Tibet was finished. He had renounced an ascetic but comfortable existence at Nalanda, where many disciples could appreciate his exceptional intellectual gifts, and like Buddha among the masses, had come to an alien land to raise the edifice of the doctrine and discipline from the beginning. Despite adversity and danger to himself, he had accomplished his chosen mission in a few years, and suddenly one day he was accidentally kicked by a horse and died.

Kamalashila came to Tibet on the invitation of the king and in fulfilment of his teacher's prediction. Even though Chinese Buddhists had supported Trhisong Detsen's attempts to bring Shantarakshita to Tibet, they inclined to a lackadaisical view of monastic discipline and angrily resented the monks who followed Shantarakshita. When Kamalashila challenged them to debate, the king himself chose to preside over it. The Chinese monks argued that all action produces karma and that it is better to do nothing rather than perform good deeds. By abstaining from all deliberate action, Enlightenment is at once assured. Kamalashila replied that discursive wisdom is essential to meditation, the source of *prajnaparamita* or transcendent wisdom. Studied inaction is a denial of discriminative wisdom, and without it, meditation is little more than a swoon. Without real meditation and the ethical disciplines that support it, Enlightenment is impossible. Having stated his view, the king and chief ministers ruled decisively in favour of Kamalashila's standpoint, and Shantarakshita's teaching became the official doctrine of the Buddhist tradition in Tibet.

There is a *stupa* in Nepal associated with the central figures in Shantarakshita's life. It is called *Bya-rung-kha-shor,* which means, "It's all right to do it, he said." Legend says that once Avalokiteshvara wept at the sight of the uncounted multitudes floundering in the ocean of *Samsara*. He dedicated his tears to the service of humanity. Two of them became daughters of Indra, but one fell out of heaven and was reborn as the daughter of a chicken-keeper in Nepal. Eventually she had four sons, all of whom became moderately prosperous, and late in life she determined to build a shrine. Since she was a humble keeper of chickens, she sought the king's approval and he readily gave it, saying, "It's all right to do it." She and her sons began to build the *stupa* but she died before it was complete. Following her wish, the four sons finished her *stupa* and placed the relics of the former Buddha Kasyapa in it. Owing to their fidelity to their vows, they were reborn together. One became Trhisong Detsen, another was born as Shantarakshita, the third as Padmasambhava and the fourth as Trhi-sh'er of Ba, who took charge of Shantarakshita's translation program. Thus was mankind, and Tibetans in particular, served by a tear shed from the divine eye of Avalokiteshvara.

*Hermes*, January 1986
Elton Hall

# PADMASAMBHAVA

*Some people believe that I revealed myself upon the pollen heart of a lotus in the Dhanakosha Lake in Uddiyana, and some believe that I was born a prince there. Others believe that I came in the flash of a thunderbolt to the Namchak hilltop. Many are the beliefs of different people, for I have appeared in many forms. Twenty-four years after the Parinirvana of Buddha Shakyamuni, Amitabha, the Adi-Buddha of Boundless Light, conceived of bodhichitta, the thought of Enlightenment, in the form of Mahakaruna, and from the heart of Mahakaruna, I, Padmasambhava, the Lotus-Born Guru, was emanated as the syllable Hri. I came like falling rain throughout the world in innumerable forms to those who were ready to receive me. The actions of the Enlightened Ones are incomprehensible. Who is to define or measure them?*

*Terma* of Yeshe Tsogyal
*Life of Padmasambhava*

When Shantarakshita went to Tibet, he soon realized that resistance to the Teachings of Buddha was strong. The metaphysical and psychological content of *Buddhadharma* was of little concern to the indigenous religion, but the prospect of an association of self-disciplined individuals bound by vows and their allegiance to a spiritual preceptor promised to initiate a powerful new social and political force in Tibet. The Bon priests and ministers made common cause in two directions against Shantarakshita's plan to construct Samye Monastery. The ministers argued against the alteration of tradition and the introduction of a new political entity in Tibet, and the priests employed their skill in magic to create diverse ominous omens which they claimed showed the unhappiness of local gods and spirits with Shantarakshita's presence. Trhisong Detsen was not an absolute monarch, and when he felt compelled to forestall his plans to establish the Buddhist tradition in Tibet, Shantarakshita proposed that he himself withdraw and that Padmasambhava be invited to Lhasa.

The myriad classes of elementals and Nature spirits were well known to the Tibetan people. Bon priests had learnt the modes of magic used to manipulate them, whilst keeping secret the means for doing so, and many of the people had become superstitious about the potencies of the gods and demons and of the priests who could propitiate and pacify them. Shantarakshita decided that an individual who was accomplished in magic as well as in Buddhist doctrine and ascetic discipline would have to confront Bon resistance on its own ground, and Padmasambhava excelled in all three.

Padmasambhava's life is immersed in a medley of elaborate legends, and little is known of the historical individual outside them. He was not a composer of doctrinal texts or commentaries, and his remarkable feats in subduing the deities of Tibet were celebrated in tales which grew richer with repetition. The repression of *Buddhadharma* and the monasteries under King Lang Darma and also the disintegration of a unified Tibet into numerous chiefdoms together destroyed most historical records. The lives and activities of early Buddhist teachers survive in *terma*, documents said to have been hidden away and discovered centuries later by *tertons* or treasure finders, often monks who came upon hidden manuscripts, compiled old records, or wrote what they learnt from deep meditation upon and union with a *mandala* devoted to a teacher. *Termas* expounding the life of Padmasambhava – or Guru Pema, as he was sometimes called – abound, for the 'old school' reveres him as the second Buddha. These revealed accounts are *namtars*, life stories told in ways which aid disciples on the path to emancipation, and they do not claim to be literal.

According to several stories, Padmasambhava, the Lotus-Born, was the son of King Indrabhuti of Uddiyana and husband of Mandarava, Shantarakshita's sister. It is said that Amitabha, Lord of Boundless Light, sent a manifestation of himself in the form of a red ray of light flashing like lightning into the sacred lake of Uddiyana.

There King Indrabhuti discovered a great white lotus open to the morning sun, and on its petals sat a handsome boy eight years old, luminous like a god and holding a sceptre. Hence he was called Lotus-Born. He evinced wondrous powers as he grew up, but he renounced the throne of Uddiyana for a life of meditation. When he accepted the invitation to travel to Lhasa, only Mandarava of his many wives chose to journey with him. Other stories say that he was born in Zahor, where Shantarakshita was the son of the king. Whilst the location of these kingdoms is a matter of scholarly disagreement, many place them in Bengal, seat of early tantric practices. Uddiyana was renowned for its magicians and Zahor was a centre of Buddhist tantra, and all sources agree that Padmasambhava excelled in both magic and tantra.

In Tibet the tension between Hinayana and Mahayana forms of Buddha's Teachings was resolved by invoking a hierarchical understanding of their relationship. Hinayana doctrine and practice is suitable for all aspirants and leads the individual who follows it faithfully to individual Enlightenment. In this sense it is the path of the Pratyeka Buddha, who achieves emancipation for himself. The Mahayana is the path of the Bodhisattva, who wants Enlightenment only for the sake of helping all beings and who renounces the fruit of emancipation in order to work in the world for the redemption of humanity. To these is added Vajrayana (the diamond vehicle) or Mantrayana (the *mantra* vehicle), which is the secret way to highest Truth and ever remains secret to one whose mind has not become that Truth itself. The *Shriguhyagarbhamahatantraraja* teaches: "The *dharma* which is the utmost secret is the intrinsic secret behind manifold manifestation, utterly secret through self-existence, than which there is nothing more secret." Since absolute Truth is *sui generis,* consciousness must necessarily transcend all habitual, discriminative and differentiated modes of activity to behold it. Wisdom, *jnana,* is incognizable and yet is hidden within the stream of consciousness. It is the source of every good quality, but just as light radiating from the sun veils the orb which is its source, so too the qualities pouring forth from the fount of *jnana* hide their point of origin.

Put in another way, Hinayana constitutes the public teachings of Buddha, Mahayana consists of his instructions to pledged disciples, and Vajrayana is the discipline he taught as *guru* to those who had fully prepared themselves for the undertaking. Precisely because Vajrayana is potent and involves the totality of an individual's life and being, it is dangerous. Like a ship crossing a stormy sea, where the slightest divergence from its plotted course will cause it to perish on the rocks rather than enter the calm harbour, Vajrayana requires total self-mastery and precision in thought, feeling and act. The possibilities for abuse through misunderstanding and desire for personal glorification and the chances of terrible spiritual and psychological damage are so great that Tsong-Kha-Pa in the fourteenth century based his sweeping Buddhist reform on the principle that one had to master Mahayana before entering into Vajrayana. His reformed order, the Gelukpa or Yellow Hat school, is the tradition of the Dalai Lamas, and though the 'old orders', and especially the Nyingma, did not accept the reform, they nonetheless quietly assimilated many of its elements. Even in modern times, H.P. Blavatsky found it necessary to warn against attempting tantric practices, for anyone who cannot "slay the lunar form at will" would be subject to misunderstanding from the start, and if persistent, would end in perversion and even soul destruction. Since the incognizable Truth can only be alluded to, one has to be wholly detached in regard to the colourful and creative, violent and erotic, imagery used in Vajrayana to point to the depths of the mystery of being and becoming. Vajrayana is never taught in books, save in code language; its meaning is imparted by *guru* to *chela*, tailored to the nature and needs of the consciousness of the disciple.

Vajrayana deals with the fusion of *prajna* and *upaya*, insight and means, doctrine and discipline. According to the Kangyur this confluence of meditation and action occurs on four levels. The first deals with disciples still attached to and involved with outer action, including ritual and magnetic purification. This is Kriya Tantra and is represented by laughing deities. Carya Tantra is for those who enjoy outer and inner action in equal measure, and it is represented by gazing deities. Intertwined deities represent Yoga Tantra, used by those accomplished in meditation to overcome their attachment to the life of the mind. Anuttara Tantra is for those wholly absorbed in inner yoga and who delight in it, and it is depicted by deities in complete embrace. Tsong-Kha-Pa found it necessary to remind monks that the imagery corresponds to transcendent psychological and inexpressible metaphysical states and not to entities, just as the occult physiology of the human form does not refer to physical anatomy and physiology. In the subtle vestures are to be found three *nadis* or channels, *rasana, avadhuti* and *lalana,* corresponding to the Hindu *pingala, sushumna* and *ida,* to the right, middle and left of the spinal column. Along the central channel are *chakras,* or centres of force and energy, which correspond to states of consciousness. According to Tsong-Kha-Pa, the waking consciousness finds mind in the navel, the *nirmana* centre which the Hindus know as *manipura.* In dreams consciousness rises to the neck, the *sambhoga* centre, called by the Hindus *vishuddha.* In dreamless deep sleep the mind abides in the heart, or *dharma* centre, known in the *Upanishads* as the *anahata.* When all the polarities are united in consciousness, it rises to the *mahasukha (ajna)* centre in the head. Total control of consciousness within the subtle vestures prepares the disciple for the transfer of the *guru's* wisdom-light in initiation.

No one knows the levels of *prajna* or kinds of *upaya* Padmasambhava found it appropriate to teach, but all the stories of his life extol his unequalled attainments as a *yogin* and a *siddha* who had mastered the supranormal faculties. He was informed by Shantarakshita of the resistance to the *Buddhadharma* in Tibet, and he entered the country with a plan to face the Bon priests as their superior by their own criteria and yet to win their allegiance by making them protectors of the Teaching. When Padmasambhava entered Tibet, he did not go straight to Lhasa, but rather roamed the plateaus and valleys in search of local spirits and deities. In a *terma* ascribed to Yeshe Tsogyal, Padmasambhava recounted the story of his life and listed the demons he faced:

> On the banks of the Nyimakhud Lake in Tibet, I subdued the cruel mountain gods and barbaric cannibal spirits: all these were

bound under oath to the Dharma. On the Khala Pass I subdued the twelve guardian protectresses of the White Mountain. . . . I subdued all the lords of the earth of the northern regions. In Tsang I subdued the pestilential spirits of Oyug: all these were bound under oath to the Dharma.

The elaborate *Padma Ka'i Thang (Life and Liberation of Padmasambhava)*, a *terma* also ascribed to Yeshe Tsogyal, explained how Padmasambhava managed to win over his invisible and visible antagonists by making them responsible for the safety of the Teaching:

> In the autumn, Padma came to the castle of Mang Yul. A demoness of the region of Zhang Zhung, Jamun the eminent enemy, thought she could crush the *guru* between two stone mountains. But he rose up in the sky, and the humiliated demoness offered the heart of her life. As her secret name was Debt of Turquoises and Diamonds, the *guru* gave her a great treasure to watch over.

In regard to all the entities Padmasambhava encountered, including priests, magicians, sorcerers and shamans, he first subdued them by evading their traps and snares and then by offering them something precious to protect. Each treasure was symbolically illustrative of an aspect of the *Buddhadharma*. He also altered the meaning of signs and omens:

> On Mount Kailas, I bound the Stellar Forces of the Lunar Mansions, and on Targo I brought the dark Planetary Forces under the control of Dharma.

When Padmasambhava eventually met King Trhisong Detsen, he did not mince words:

> I am the Buddha who is Lotus-Born, possessing the precepts of highest insight. Skilled in the fundamental Teachings of Sutra and Tantra, I elucidate the Buddhist Ways without confusion.

I am the Dharma which is Lotus-Born, possessing the precepts of progressive practice. Outwardly I don the saffron robes of a monk; inwardly I am the highest of Vajrayana yogins.

I am the Order which is Lotus-Born, possessing the precepts which unite insight and practice. My knowledge is higher than the heavens.

Soon Padmasambhava exorcised the site of Samye Monastery, and Shantarakshita was recalled from his voluntary retreat in Nepal to oversee its construction and consecration. Once novices were trained and monks ordained, Shantarakshita's stupendous translation programme began. Bon ministers of the king still resisted the work of Shantarakshita and Padmasambhava, but the priests gradually adopted a different mode. They built their own monastery, and the sagely among them adapted various Buddhist tenets and practices to the Bon religion. Thus Reformed Bon emerged and eventually became deeply involved with Nyingma or 'old school' traditions. Tsepong Ze, one of the king's wives, attempted to undermine Buddhist efforts by destroying the translation programme. Though she could not easily attack the Indian and Chinese translators, she managed to force some of the Tibetans into exile. Accusing Vairotsana of rape, a charge the king did not believe, she forced him into banishment, though he remains to this day one of the most revered of the first monks of Samye. She exiled Namkhai Nyingpo, but he went to Bhutan and became famous for spreading the *Buddhadharma* there. Tsepong Ze's worst fury, however, was reserved for Padmasambhava and his disciples. Padmasambhava was exiled to Turkhara in Turkestan for seven years, and when he returned, his opponents waited for some pretext on which to force him to leave Tibet again.

Even though some ministers sought the downfall of Padmasambhava, King Trhisong Detsen was drawn into his circle of intimate disciples. When he asked to be initiated into Vajrayana,

Padmasambhava placed him on a year's probation, and the king took the time to devise the gift he would give his *guru.* Yeshe Tsogyal was born a princess of Kharchen, and while still young she married Trhisong Detsen. She had been drawn to the *Buddhadharma* and to the teachings of Padmasambhava, and when the time came for the king's initiation, she willingly allowed herself to be given to her teacher. Offering a princess and wife of a king as a disciple and companion to a wandering ascetic violated the social traditions of the time. Tsepong Ze and the Bon ministers were incensed, and many others were scandalized and remained silent when there was a clamour for Padmasambhava's exile. Fearing that both his *guru* and Yeshe Tsogyal might be murdered, the king acceded to the demand for banishment, but instead of sending them to the distant regions decreed as their places of separate exile, he saw to it that they secretly retired to Tidro to meditate.

*Guru* and disciple remained together in Tidro for a number of years. According to the *termas,* including *The Secret life and Songs of the Tibetan Lady Yeshe Tsogyal,* the princess excelled in meditation and successfully passed through a number of initiations. She became one in consciousness with Padmasambhava and was eventually sent by him to Nepal, where she visited the ancient E Vihara. Though long gone, this monastic community is believed to have existed on the site of the Kashthamandapa temple in Katmandu. Shaivite *yogins* resided there from the twelfth century until recently, but a small group of *tantrikas* still perform ancient Buddhist rites there. Nearby is the cave where Padmasambhava is said to have attained Enlightenment before his sojourn in Tibet, and the area is as sacred as Bodh Gaya to Nyingma monks. When Yeshe Tsogyal returned to Tidro, she brought disciples with her.

Events after this retreat are confused. The king recalled Padmasambhava and his disciples to Lhasa. For a time religious and social peace was restored to the kingdom, and Trhisong Detsen felt confident enough to disperse trained monks throughout Tibet. The wise Drenpa Namkha Wongchuk was invited to Samye, and he provided a bridge between Buddhist and Bon standpoints, since he knew and practised both. When Kamalashila, Shantarakshita's disciple, led the great Samye debate between Chinese and Indian perspectives, the Indian modes were secured for Tibet. Trhisong Detsen, however, was careful to see that the retiring Chinese monks were treated with reverence and honour. It is said that Yeshe Tsogyal played an important role in resolving the debate. When Trhisong Detsen died, court intrigue threatened to destroy the unity of Tibet. Tsepong Ze poisoned her own son, Mune Tsenpo, shortly after he ascended the throne, in part because his Buddhist beliefs led him to propose a programme of land redistribution. His brother was crowned as Mutik Tsenpo and ruled for a decade. Though Yeshe Tsogyal stopped the internecine war and persuaded the ministers to renounce schism, Tsepong Ze exiled her. Padmasambhava decided his work was completed in Tibet and announced his intention to travel south, where he disappeared from history and remains a mystery in long-standing tradition. Shantarakshita died and Kamalashila became the second abbot of Samye. When King Repachan ascended the throne, Yeshe Tsogyal returned to pay homage to Shantarakshita's *chorten* at Samye and died shortly afterwards. Repachan revered her memory and declared her *parinirvana* in about AD. 817.

The *termas* tell of Padmasambhava's departure. The king and many disciples followed him to the top of a great pass. There he took his leave and rose into the sky, speeding southward and leaving a rainbow trail in the sky. Then they sat in meditation and "they saw him like a ray of the sun, passing beyond India without touching upon Uddiyana; they saw him reach the top of Mount Jambuza and alight. . . . Near the Fire City, he sat in the cool shade of a celestial magnolia tree." Yeshe Tsogyal spoke for all of the disciples when she lamented.

> *Alas! The Precious One of Uddiyana,*
> *The luminous circle of the sun which gave us light has gone.*
> *The crystal moon which relieved suffering has disappeared.*
> *The stem of the poison-curing plant has gone dry.*
> *The father has withdrawn his impartial mercy.*
>
> *The friend who saved us from the ocean of Samsara has taken leave.*
>
> *The flame of the torch dispelling the night of ignorance is*
>     *extinguished. . . .*
>
> *Broken is the calyx of power of the one who cultivated those ready to*
>     *become pure vessels.*
>
> *Departed is the Lotus-Born, adept in all methods.*
>
> *The Lama who revealed his soul in pure essence has gone.*
> *The Lama adorned with the three vows has departed. . . .*

---

> *Since the virtues of the guru are ineffable,*
> *May future beings revere the image of Padmasambhava.*

*Hermes*, February 1986
Elton Hall

# ATISHA

*One who neglects the branches of tranquillity*
*    (shamatha),*
*Even though he struggles mightily to meditate*
*For millennium upon millennium,*
*Never will attain concentration (samadhi).*

*When the tranquillity of yogins is attained,*
*So too are the transcendental faculties (abhijna).*
*Nonetheless obscuration is not destroyed*
*Without the perfection of insight (prajnaparamita).*

*Sacred texts teach that bondage arises when*
*Insight (prajna) is severed from means (upaya),*
*And means is cut off from insight as well.*
*Therefore, never neglect this union.*

Atisha
*Bodhipathapradipa*

   Repachan, the grandson of Trhisong Detsen, was the last
Buddhist king of Tibet. His devotion to Buddha, the Dharma and
the Sangha is alluded to under his informal name, which refers to
the matted locks *(re-pa)* of ascetics. Like Ashoka a thousand years
before him, Repachan developed a foreign policy centered upon
peace. Having defeated the Chinese in a lengthy battle, he drew up
a permanent peace treaty which invoked as protectors the Three
Jewels, the host of *arhats,* the sun, moon, planets and stars. Earlier,
peace had been made with the great caliphate to the west, and both
treaties held firm until the fall of the monarchy. At the same time,
Repachan inaugurated a revision of the Tibetan translations of
Sanskrit texts. Since the original translators had devised a technical
Tibetan vocabulary to accommodate the subtleties of Sanskrit, even
literate Tibetans could read the *sutras* only with great difficulty.

Repachan commissioned translations which were both accurate and in ordinary language, and it is said that he was responsible for half the texts in the Kangyur and Tengyur, the vast Buddhist canon in Tibet.

Though *Buddhadharma* spread across Tibet during the reign of Repachan, and though he was sufficiently popular and powerful to keep opposition out of his councils, the aristocracy saw its independence threatened. Those who were not followers of Buddha by conviction joined forces with the Bon priesthood, and eventually they found in the king's younger brother someone whom they could use for their own ends. Sometime around A.D. 840 Repachan, already considered by many to be the incarnation of Vajrapani, was assassinated. His queen, whose honour was mercilessly slandered, committed suicide, and his son, already a monk, was banished. Then the throne was taken by Lang Darma, who was sympathetic to Bon.

Though allied with an aristocracy which saw in the rise of monks and monasteries the diminution of its own wealth and power, Lang Darma seems to have been a passive supporter of the anti-Buddhist movement during the first years of his rule. Buddhist nobles and monks could not exonerate him from the persecution they experienced, and after a few years they managed to depose him. Returning to the throne a year later, Lang Darma launched a violent retaliatory offensive. Monks were dispersed, translators killed or banished, shrines attacked and the Buddhist aristocracy routed. Though he ruled for only a year after the persecution began, he managed to destroy the structure of the Tibetan Sangha. Ironically, the disruptions caused by this forceful reassertion of Bon produced exactly those results which the Bon priests had prophesied if *Buddhadharma* were allowed in Tibet. When Lang Darma died, the monarchy collapsed along with Tibetan unity. Descendants of the royal line and petty chieftains seized territories for themselves, imperial territories revolted, and China looked again to the possibility of conquering Tibet. Only those rulers who migrated to Western Tibet near Mount Kailas remained faithful to the Teachings of Buddha. But until King Khorre of Ngari abdicated in favour of his brother and took the monk's robe as Lha Lama Yeshe , the Buddhist tradition in Tibet would not experience its first great renaissance. When Yeshe sought to purify and renew the Good Law in Tibet, he discovered that Atisha alone possessed the training, dedication and energy to undertake the enormous task of reform and dissemination.

Atisha was born in 982 to King Kalyanashri and Queen Shriprabha of Zahor in Bengal. Tibetan authorities hold that he was born in Vikramapura to the royal lineage which had produced Shantarakshita two centuries earlier. The middle of three sons, he was called Chandragarbha and enjoyed the duties and privileges of royalty. He received an education suitable to a prince, married five wives while still young and fathered nine children. One day he went hunting in a local forest and happened upon the ascetic Jetari. When he showed him homage, the ascetic surprised him by rebuking him for his pride. Rather than take offence, Atisha declared that he wished to renounce the world and become a disciple of Jetari. The ascetic recognized Atisha's potential but, instead of accepting him as a disciple, instructed him to go to Nalanda. By the tenth century the tantric tradition had so infused Indian Buddhist institutions that the preceptor who welcomed Atisha to Nalanda soon sent him to the Black Mountain for tantric initiation under Rahulagupta. Although the early portion of his life as a Buddhist is not well chronicled, it is evident that he rapidly became an enthusiastic initiate whose knowledge served him well in his later work. His skill in *tantra* did not weaken his mental agility, and after a few years he sought the metaphysical and spiritual knowledge without which such practices and rituals tended towards meaningless excesses and psychic delusion.

According to Tibetan historians, Atisha was associated with the four great monastic centres of his day. Having mastered the *tantras* at Uddiyana and finding them lacking, he became a novice at Nalanda and was eventually ordained under the name Dipamkara at Odantapuri or Vajrasana (Bodh Gaya). Though he learnt both

Pali and Sanskrit Buddhist texts, mastered the *Tripitaka* and the *sutras* and studied under the best teachers of his time, he was dissatisfied with what he found. Some scriptures had already been lost, the tradition of study was waning and few individuals cared for anything but tantric practice. Indian Buddhist tradition had strayed so far from the pure Mahayana teachings that the few disciples who wanted them had to go elsewhere for instruction. Like them Atisha turned to the Far East. At that time, the greatest Buddhist scholar was Dharmakirti, the namesake of the illustrious Indian logician, who resided in Suvarnadvipa (Sumatra). Many of the eminent Buddhist teachers of Atisha's time had studied under him, and Chinese monks travelling to India were advised to stay with him for two years, since they would learn Sanskrit more thoroughly there than they could hope to do in Buddhist India.

Atisha set out on the difficult journey to Suvarnadvipa, and it took him almost a year to arrive there. He was delighted to find that Dharmakirti was a brilliant exponent of the Mahayana, firmly rooted in the tradition of Nagarjuna, Maitreya and Chandrakirti. During the twelve years he remained with Dharmakirti, Atisha mastered the abstruse and arcane doctrines of the Mahayana and cultivated a mature insight into the pure forms of practice and the Bodhisattva Path. Though he never rejected *tantra,* he discerned numerous ways in which its expressions had obscured *Buddhadharma,* and he longed for a radical reform that looked improbable in India. He knew that Muslim incursions into his homeland, the decline of the monastic communities and the growing disinclination to meditate upon the *sutras* meant that the path of Buddha was disappearing in India. Nonetheless, despite the natural enticement to remain in the golden glow of Sumatra, he took leave of his beloved *guru* and returned to work in the monasteries as Dipamkara Shrijnana, renowned teacher and scholar.

Atisha was over forty years of age when he returned to India. Though he was entitled to retire with a few of his best disciples to a quiet life of teaching, he launched a programme of monastic renewal. King Nayapala of Magadha invited Atisha to become high priest of Vikramashila and he spent most of his time there. He wrote a philosophical treatise at Nalanda and assisted in administrative functions at Odantapuri and Somapuri. During the fifteen years he devoted to these activities, he became known as the greatest Indian monk and scholar of his time. The remarkable combination of dialectical and administrative skills with a synthesis of *sutra* and *tantra* gave him an authority far beyond that of the offices he held. He collected texts threatened with destruction, wrote commentaries, trained monks, established criteria for tantric practices and even expelled dubious monks and unregenerate tantrists. These activities brought Atisha to the attention of the devout King Yeshe .

Although Yeshe had abdicated in favour of his brother and had entered the Sangha, he remained the real ruler of Western Tibet. Convinced that the pot-pourri of Buddhist practices around him were impure and debased, he sent twenty-one carefully selected young men to India to learn the pure doctrines. Yeshe did not know that Vajrayana had almost totally eclipsed Mahayana, and he was surprised when the two sole survivors of the mission returned with new tantric practices. Nonetheless, seeing that the new *tantra* was superior to the old forms, he supported the tremendous reorganization launched by Rinchen Sangpo, one of the two survivors. After a number of years, however, Yeshe decided to seek out an Indian teacher who could promulgate the purest doctrines. When he decided to invite Atisha to Tibet, the great scholar was around sixty years old, and Yeshe sought to amass a great quantity of gold with which to persuade Atisha to undertake the arduous journey into the Land of Snows. During one of Yeshe's sojourns near Lake Manasasarova, he was captured by some dynastic enemies and held for ransom. When his nephew offered to make the gold already collected available for this purpose, Yeshe refused and begged him to take the gold to Atisha instead. Atisha eventually heard of Yeshe's self-sacrifice, and he was so deeply moved that he renounced his natural reluctance to undertake a dangerous mission to Tibet. He agreed to go there for three years.

Atisha delayed his journey long enough to secure peace in the conflict between his friend King Nayapala and the Hindu King Karma. Both were permanently reconciled and became friends of Atisha. He dispersed the gold he was given among the monasteries and made arrangements for their good management. Then, after a visit to Bodh Gaya, he set off for Tibet sometime around 1040. He spent about a year in Nepal and gradually made his way northwest from Katmandu, past Annapurna and Dhaulagiri to Jumla. From there he made his way to the Karnali River and along it to Khocharnath and Taklakhar; then he turned north to Manasasarova and followed the Sutlej River to Toling ('high flying') Monastery. Despite the enormous hardships of the journey, Atisha remained cheerful and even optimistic, as if he felt himself entering upon his real work in life. It is said that Atisha so enjoyed his first cup of Tibetan tea that he declared, "So excellent a beverage must have originated from the moral merits of the monks of Tibet." Tibetans still possess a poem he is alleged to have written in praise of tea.

Atisha was received with a joy and warmth that surprised him. Though he found the rituals and practices of the western Tibetans degenerate, he discovered an unusual willingness to learn and an openness to reform which had been sadly absent in his homeland. Only Rinchen Sangpo, who had brought the new *tantra* to Tibet and was now eighty-five years old, was a little annoyed at Atisha's devaluation of *tantra*. Atisha visited him at his own residence at Toling and spontaneously composed an exquisite verse for each of the deities represented in the shrine, and he taught Rinchen Sangpo the magic mirror of Vajrayana, in which all the *tantras* can be mystically synthesized in a single meditative practice. Rinchen Sangpo recognized that Atisha's proposed reforms were not based on any prejudice against *tantra,* but rather represented a diamond-like penetration of its true essence in the light of the best teachings. At once he became Atisha's devoted disciple and, despite his great age and seniority, threw himself into Atisha's projects of translation and instruction in the *Mahayana.*

Amidst the hectic activity inaugurated at Toling and around Mount Kailas, Atisha found time to compose his seminal *Bodhipathapradipa (Lamp for the Path of Enlightenment)*, consisting of a quintessential presentation of the path to Enlightenment in sixty-eight eloquent verses and a detailed auto-commentary filled with statements from Mahayana *sutras* and great Teachers. By weaving monastic practice and the Bodhisattva ideal into a seamless garment dyed with the pure colours of the exalted mystical Vajrayana, Atisha created the model for Tibetan spiritual literature. These *lam-rim* instructions or aids in the gradual steps on the Bodhisattva Path became the foundations of the Kadampa Order, which was organized by Atisha's chief Tibetan disciple and of which Atisha was the founder. When Tsong-Kha-Pa initiated his great reform, he based the 'new Kadampa' or Gelukpa Order on his own vast *lam-rim* teaching which repeatedly invoked Atisha's message. *Kadampa* means 'instructed by the word' rather than by ritual and stresses the need for understanding and mental and moral purity in the unfoldment of spiritual potentials and powers in human beings.

Atisha began the *Lamp* with obeisance to the Buddhas, the Dharma and the Sangha. In the dedicatory verse of his commentary, he paid homage to Tara (Kwan-Yin) and Manjushri, Chakrasamvara (a tantric deity) and Lokeshvara (who is Avalokiteshvara and Shiva), and to the *gurus* Maitreya, Asanga and Dharmakirti of Suvarnadvipa, as well as Manjughosha, Shantideva and Bodhibhadra. "The instruction I give here", Atisha wrote, "came like drops of honey and nectar to me from the holy *gurus* Dharmakirti and Bodhibhadra . . . I am going to gather up those drops of individual guidance I received and follow what my *gurus* gave me and what the *sutras* and texts teach." Atisha divided all human beings into three distinct types. The inferior individual "seeks but the pleasure of *Samsara*" and is therefore wholly egotistical. The mediocre individual renounces wrongdoing and is indifferent to pleasure, but is concerned with his own peace of mind. The superior individual "seeks a complete end to the entire suffering of others because their suffering belongs to his own *samtana*, stream of consciousness". Since only the latter type possesses the purity of consciousness required to sustain an authentic aspiration for highest Enlightenment, Atisha addressed his instructions to superior individuals.

One makes aspiration practical through worship, which begins with images to which offerings can be made but soon passes into meditation. The first phase of meditative adoration is sevenfold, including homage, offering pleasing objects, admission of faults and wrongdoing, rejoicing in the virtues, desiring the Doctrine, seeking the blessing of Buddha, and offering whatever merit one has attained to others. The second phase of meditation "is contemplation with *prajnaparamita*, perfection of insight: there is no object of worship, no worshipper, no substances for worship". Atisha repeated Buddha's words in the *Prajnaparamita Sutra*:

Whoever sees me as form or knows me as a voice, that person sees me falsely. He does not see me. The Buddhas are the *Dharmakaya*, the vesture of Truth, and those who are guided have studied that Truth. Yet its true nature is not to be seen, and no one can be conscious of it as an object.

When one nurtures a mind that does not turn back, the heart of Enlightenment is reached, for that heart is the essence of Truth. According to the *Gaganaganja Sutra*, "The Heart of Enlightenment is Space; Enlightenment has the characteristic of Space." If one has taken refuge in the Buddha, the Dharma and the Sangha, one is prepared to engender the thought of love.

> Because the thought of love
> For all creatures is essential,
> One looks upon the whole world,
> Suffering in death, in transmigration,
> And in rebirth in the triple evil destiny.
>
> Beholding that suffering, one suffers,
> And whosoever, to liberate the world
> From the very cause of its sufferings,

> Must beget the thought of Enlightemnent
> That is pledged never to turn back.

This pledge can be realized only if one follows the inner disciplines of the monk, which include self-restraint, self-forgetfulness and service. But such discipline is possible only if one is willing to take vows which embody the possibility of progress towards perfection. When that is done, one is prepared for the Bodhisattva Vow.

> One takes the Vow from a good guru
> Who has the requisite characteristics.

> One who knows the rites of the Vow,
> And lives the Vow he has taken,
> And in compassionate forbearance
> Will impart it – he is the good guru.

If one is truly ready to take the Bodhisattva Vow, even if one cannot find a proper *guru,* one can take the vow in one's heart, where the inner *guru* is always available to hear and to instruct the disciple. When one meditates upon the Bodhisattva Vow and the vast array of correlates it entails, one will nurture and perfect *sambhara,* virtue and knowledge, the equipment needed to attain Enlightenment.

When one is strong in self-mastery, one-pointedness of consciousness and unconditional love, one can safely use the six *abhijnas* or transcendent faculties to speed one's way towards Enlightenment. Divine sight, divine hearing, awareness of others' thoughts, remembrance of one's previous lives, supernormal powers, and overcoming all obscurations are valuable to the *yogin* who is faithful to the Bodhisattva Vow, but they are a menace to all others. *Shamatha,* calmness, must be cultivated, and it will allow one to develop all transcendent faculties save the last: to overcome obscurations, one must nurture *prajnaparamita,* the perfection of insight. Thus *prajnaparamita* must be fused with *upaya,* skilful means, which include *dana, shila, kshanti, viraga, virya* and *dhyana.*

*Prajna,* insight, is distinct because it recognizes *shunyata,* the voidness of all things.

> Not to perceive some intrinsic nature
> In any phenomena whatever
> Is to contemplate its *anatman.*
> The same is contemplation with *prajna.*

> The world of change springs
> From conceptual thought, its very nature;
> The uttermost removal of such
> Thought is the supreme *nirvana.*

Only when one's feet are firmly set on the Path and one is well advanced in the union of virtue and knowledge, means and insight, can one practise the Mantrayana and Vajrayana. For that, however, one must be initiated by a *guru* who knows the initiations, and he will bestow his blessing and guidance only on one whose mental and moral nature is purified to the degree of "falling snow".

Towards the end of his third year in Tibet, Atisha made plans to return to India. But a brief war on the Nepalese frontier prevented him from crossing over the border, and Atisha read the karmic indication that he should accept invitations he had received to visit other areas of Tibet. He journeyed to Lhasa and was pleased to find some followers of Buddha there. When he visited Samye Monastery, founded by Shantarakshita and Padmasambhava, he was delighted to find a few monks in residence, but he was amazed to discover Sanskrit *sutras* and Tibetan translations of texts which had been lost in India. Atisha realized that Tibet would continue to revere what it had received from Mother India long after the subcontinent had let these treasures perish. Altogether he spent eighteen years in Tibet, carrying his reforms across the entire land. He died near Lhasa when he was well into his seventies, and the place of his death remains to this day a centre of pilgrimage. Atisha, whom the Tibetans also called Joborje, the Noble Lord, renowned in India, became the most illustrious of Indian teachers in Tibet. He is praised even as he taught others to invoke Buddha:

*O Omniscient One, epitome of wisdom,*
*Purifier of the Wheel of Life,*
*I have no refuge in any Lord,*
*Except at your lotus feet.*
*O Hero of creatures! May the Mahaguru*
*Bestow his kindness upon me.*
*May that Holy One grant to me*
*The supreme thought of Enlightenment.*

*Hermes*, March 1986
Elton Hall

# MARPA

*Fixated neither on Samsara nor Nirvana,*
*Free of both acceptance and rejection,*
*Not hoping for fruition from others,*
*With mind free of preoccupation and complexity,*
*Avoiding all of the four extremes,*
*Non-meditation and non-wandering,*
*Free from thought and speech,*
*Beyond any analogy whatsoever –*
*Through the kindness of the Guru, I realized these.*

*Since these realizations have dawned,*
*Mind and mentation have ceased,*
*And space and insight are inseparably one.*
*Faults and virtues neither increase nor decrease;*
*Bliss, shunyata and luminosity are unceasing.*
*Therefore Light arises beyond coming and going.*

Marpa
*Kagyü Gurtso*

*Viharas* or monastic centres preserved the inextinguishable presence of Buddha and the vitality of the Dharma in India for fifteen centuries. They were also the bases from which Buddha's teaching spread along royal highways to the northwest, across silk routes north and then east, and over sea lanes to Southeast Asia, China and Japan. The Sangha or Order was the community of committed disciples who had taken vows to practise and propagate the Four Noble Truths and the Noble Eightfold Path through realization and service. Over the centuries the Order gradually formalized its monastic functions and emerged as the preserver and interpreter of the sacred texts. Lay disciples always had a place in the Buddhist tradition, however, as was shown by the enthusiastic welcome extended to Chandragomin at Nalanda by the great monk and teacher, Chandrakirti. Nonetheless, the greatest monastic centres were not free of the vulnerabilities of religious and educational institutions, and they suffered from ossification of venerable practices and from scholastic aridity.

The rise of tantric systems first threatened the traditional relationship of monastic and lay communities by drawing lay disciples away from the broad umbrella of monastic influence. But in time the monastic community absorbed *tantra* and helped fashion it into Vajrayana, the diamond vehicle, for which it provided texts, techniques and commentaries. Though Vajrayana infused the *viharas* with new vigour, many individuals still found that the heavy hand of scholasticism impeded their efforts to realize Buddha's message in the core of their own being. By the tenth century the tradition of tantric adepts who mastered their practices independently of the formal Sangha had grown to include monks who were trained in the *viharas* and who had left them to deepen their own insights under the guidance of a teacher who set his own rules and based his instructions on the lineage of teachers to which he belonged. On the positive side, the monastic community provided continuity for *Buddhadharma,* whilst the tradition of independent lineages of teachers broadened and redefined the idea of the Sangha. Both cast shadows: the monastic community sometimes violated the spirit of Buddha's teachings by engaging in such technical disputations over their dead letter that monks sacrificed spiritual striving to cerebration, and lineages not subject to the consensus or guidance of the community could drift into psychic delusion or even black magic. Nevertheless, the Vajrayana tradition gave potent meaning to the *guru-chela* relationship and invoked one critical aspect of Buddha's own activity. Both traditions entered Tibet with Shantarakshita and Padmasambhava and have remained there until the present day.

Marpa was born into a wealthy landowning family in Lhotrak in A.D. 1012. Lhotrak lies almost due south of Lhasa near the border with Bhutan, and its Buddhist contacts were not lost during the persecution of Lang Darma and the subsequent disintegration of the Tibetan empire. Marpa was hearty and dynamic to a degree which led his parents to decide to educate him as a Buddhist. He began his education at the age of twelve and soon mastered reading, writing and the teachings available in the region, receiving the name Chökyi Lodrö (Dharma Mind). His thirst for the teachings was countered by an inability to control his temper – one of the most difficult tasks, according to Buddha in the *Dhammapada* – and his parents agreed to send him to Western Tibet for advanced training.

In 1054, when he was already middle-aged, Marpa came to the Nyugu Valley, where Drogmi had established a monastic community the year after Atisha entered Tibet. Drogmi had studied in India and had brought valuable texts to Tibet, where he translated them. They found their way into the Tibetan canon, and Drogmi became the philosophical parent of the Sakya tradition in Tibet. Marpa remained with Drogmi for three years, learning Sanskrit along with Buddhist teachings, and prepared himself so well for his own work as a *lotsawa* or translator that he is sometimes known to history as Marpa the Translator. Although he made great strides in self-discipline, his thirst for *Buddhadharma* was unassuaged, and he decided to follow the familiar but treacherous route to India. After winning the approval of his reluctant parents, he converted his possessions to gold and set out on the journey which was to mark the real beginning of his spiritual odyssey.

Marpa made the hard journey far to the west into the Kungthang region above Nepal, and then he descended along the Trisuli River Valley into the cis-Himalayan kingdom. Since Tibetan wayfarers had always found the descent into the plains of the subcontinent hazardous to their health, Marpa chose to remain in Katmandu for three years in order to adjust to the climate. There he met Chitherpa and Paindapa, disciples of Naropa, his future *guru*. Never for a moment did he think that the encounter was by chance; for him, it was the re-establishment of an ancient connection. He studied under the Nepalese disciples and prepared himself to meet their teacher, and then he made his way across dangerous territory to

Phullahari near Nalanda, where Naropa lived. Naropa immediately received him, declaring that he would hold the lineage in Tibet, for his own teacher, Tilopa, had prophesied the appearance of Marpa and his worthiness as a disciple.

Tilopa has been enshrined in human memory as one of the eighty-four *mahasiddhas,* fully enlightened adepts of Vajrayana. After practising meditation as an ordained monk at Somapuri for twelve years, he left the *vihara* and worked at secular occupations for another twelve years whilst perfecting his meditation and fusing it with his daily round. Thereafter he became a wandering teacher whose renown spread throughout Bengal. Tradition holds that Tilopa received his quintessential spiritual knowledge from no embodied *guru* but from *Vajradhara*, the pure essence of Buddha's mind, which is Enlightenment itself. It is also said that he had received the transmitted teachings of a number of important lineages, which included in their lines Vajrapani, Saraha, Nagarjuna and Indrabhuti. Tilopa accepted Naropa, who is also one of the *mahasiddhas,* as the disciple to whom he passed the entire lineage. Naropa began as a monk and eventually occupied the distinguished and responsible position of academic gate keeper at both Nalanda and Vikramashila. Despite his remarkable attainments, Naropa realized that without Enlightenment all else was valueless, and he left the monastic community in search of a teacher who could speak from experience. When he met such a teacher in Tilopa, he was subjected to twelve trials of his worthiness, and these tests have been given such epic proportions by tradition that it is said his teacher had to restore him to physical health after each one. Naropa was in the end successful, and in combining learning with *yoga,* he became a teacher worthy of his *guru's* full confidence. He left Tilopa and moved to Phullahari to teach and await the arrival of Marpa.

Even though Naropa assured Marpa of his eventual success, he insisted that Marpa must earn his wisdom. It is impossible to specify the exact nature of the teachings passed on to Marpa, for the tantric texts do not constitute spiritual transmission. They may be given to a disciple, but it is the oral instruction of the *guru* which brings them to life and which illumines the disciple's understanding. In addition, the *guru* gives his *chela* suitable *abhishekas* or initiations which empower the disciple to practise the teachings transmitted. In doing so, the disciple is linked with various deities – peaceful, mildly wrathful and wrathful – including the *yidam* or personal deity of the disciple. These deities are simultaneously aspects of the Buddhas and therefore pure representations of the Buddha-mind; the active fusion of insight and compassion, *prajna* and *karuna;* the awakened nature of the disciple himself; and the path to realization of which the *guru* is the link, threshold, portal and guide. For the disciple, the *guru* is the awakened mind of the disciple, and only he who totally fuses his mind with that of the *guru* is worthy to receive the whole of the *guru's* mind or teaching. The lineage which the disciple enters, in being given one or more *abhishekas,* is a direct translation of Buddha's relationship with his Arhats. The unswerving faith in the first of the Three Jewels thus becomes unshakeable faith in the *guru,* receptivity to the Dharma becomes total acceptance of the *guru's* instruction, and the mutual support of the Sangha becomes the discipline imposed by the initiation. Marpa's *yidam* was Hevajra, a mildly wrathful deity of energy, skilful means and bliss. His initiation introduced him to the Vajrayana doctrine that the world itself is sacred, bound him to the path of realization of the sacredness in every thought, word and deed, and set him upon his way through devotion to the *guru.*

Though Naropa could teach Marpa everything, he followed the tradition of sending his disciple to other teachers who were adepts in particular Vajrayana practices. Among others, he went to Maitripa, who had once taught Atisha to learn the skill of singing *dohas,* spontaneous songs which express the essence of one's insight and experience. Marpa's *dohas* inaugurated the *doha* tradition in Tibet in the form which has persisted to the present day. Although the inner teachings of the lineage cannot be recorded in writing, Marpa's *dohas* show the significance, value and effect of what he assimilated. Maitripa also gave Marpa the great *mahamudra* teaching. *Mahamudra* literally means 'great gesture' or 'great seal', but according to the mysterious *Chakrasamvaratantra, mu* represents the wisdom of *shunyata*, Voidness; *dra* refers to emancipation from *Samsara*, the ocean of illusion and cyclic existence; and *maha* signifies their ultimate indivisibility. When one sees with a pellucid mind that reality is free from illusion, it becomes the self-validating symbol of Enlightenment. The ground of existence is *dharmata*, unchanging, indestructible, unceasing reality, best represented by empty space. Realization of this ground is perfect insight, self-luminous and therefore capable of manifesting anything and everything. *Mahamudra*, the union of *dharmata* and *prajna* beyond even the intimation of duality, is thus the seal of that spiritual alchemy in which the fusion of *Nirvana* and *Samsara* is both understood and lived out. Upon assimilating this teaching, Marpa sang:

> This unceasing *dharmata*
> Is self-luminous insight without obstruction.
> Within innate insight, unity,
> Spontaneous wisdom is the view. . . .
>
> The essence of realization is nowness,
> Occurring all at once, with no plus or minus.
> Self-emancipation, innate great bliss,
> Is the fruition free from hope or fear.

Marpa returned to Naropa, who confirmed the instructions he had received from other teachers, and after twelve years he began the journey back to Tibet. After numerous adventures, many of which tested his hard-won knowledge, he settled down in his native Lhotrak, took a wife, and began to teach disciples even while he raised a family. In one sense, Marpa's life in Lhotrak was unexceptional for a farmer and family man with all the duties of a landowner and a householder. In another sense, his behaviour, especially with his disciples and in the performance of magic, was quite unusual. In time Marpa made a second trip to India, which took six years and followed the pattern of his first sojourn. When he took leave of his *guru* for the second time, however, Naropa sang an enigmatic song in code language and promised special instruction on his return. Back in Lhotrak, Marpa farmed and waited for the disciple Naropa had told him about – Milarepa. Since Milarepa had been impetuous in the use of psychic powers, Marpa compelled him to undergo a number of trials which seemed designed to inflame his ego and ignite his impetuosity, yet aimed to purify his whole nature. During this time, Marpa ordered Milarepa to build stone towers for no very clear purpose. Remnants of these constructions survive to support the story of Milarepa's labours. When Milarepa was ready to receive Marpa's teaching and to go into retreat to master them, Marpa suddenly understood Naropa's cryptic song and hastened to return to India.

When he reached the vicinity of Phullahari, he made a horrifying discovery. Naropa had taken up an extremely advanced stage of Vajrayana practice called *spyodpa la gshegspa* – entering the action – in which one abandons any fixed abode and encounters the world directly. Like a Taoist Immortal, Naropa was glimpsed everywhere but found nowhere. The geography of Marpa's journeys had become unconscious reference points in the mind, presumed certitudes which have no place in enlightened consciousness. All such reference points, mental, psychological, moral and physical, were torn from Marpa during his desperate search of eight months for his *guru*. When he finally met Naropa, he joyously thrust the gold he had brought as a gift into Naropa's hand, but his teacher cast the gold into the forest, as if the traditional offering were meaningless. Then he touched the earth, and where his fingers felt the ground, the earth became gold. He said, "All the world is gold for me", and at once the innermost meaning of the *mahamudra,* the actuality of the great seal, arose in Marpa's mind. He no longer thought of the world as sacred, because he now *saw* that it was so. And so he was ready for the highest teaching, arcane truths which could be put in no ordinary tongue nor traced with pen on paper. Rather, they were written with the diamond stylus of insight on Marpa's spiritual heart.

Yet one final test was given to Marpa. Naropa magically formed the *mandala* of Marpa's *yidam* in the sky. When Marpa beheld Hevajra in the vault of the heavens, he prostrated before it rather than before his *guru*, forgetting that it was only through the *guru* that such a marvel could come to be. He corrected himself but became terribly ill. When his sickness eventually passed, Naropa explained that it was the immediate purgation of the karma which produced and was generated by that fateful, if momentary, error. Restored to wholeness by this final realization, Marpa returned to Tibet for the last time, sad in heart at leaving his *guru* but aware that his *guru* was one with him for all the days of his life. In addition, Naropa told Marpa that Milarepa would be his successor in receiving the entire lineage and that he in turn would give rise to four related noble lineages which would preserve the teaching. Marpa had hoped to pass his teaching to his own son, Tarma Dode, but the youth died in an accident. His death deeply affected Marpa, his wife and his circle of disciples and became the focus of their understanding that nothing in manifest existence is permanent and worthy of being considered real.

The sublime and arcane teaching which Marpa passed on to his disciple can no more be put into ordinary words than can the instructions given to Marpa by Naropa, Maitripa and eleven other adepts. When the disciples gathered as a group, however, Marpa often answered general questions by singing a *doha*. Many of these were preserved in the *Kagyü Gurtso,* a collection of such songs from the whole Kagyü tradition, and in a biography of Marpa. Their expression of the fruits of insight and understanding are meant to provide inspiration for disciples and to serve for meditation and reflection. On one occasion Marpa sang:

> The three worlds are primordially pure.
> Ultimately, there is naught more to understand.
> Absence of negation, unceasing continuity,
> Unchanging – such is the view.
>
> Innate essence is by nature luminous.

Unconditioned, meditation is unceasing.
Free of negation, beyond loss and gain,
Without desire or attachment – such is meditation.

Arising from natural coincidence,
The play of illusion is unhindered.
Free of negation, all things
Are unpredictable and sudden – such is action.

Mind shines as *bodhichitta,*
The three *kayas* of Buddha are not attained.
Free of negation, beyond hope and fear,
Groundless and without root – such is fruition.

Besides providing guidance, orientation and focus for disciples, Marpa sometimes provided commentaries on difficult and confusing doctrines in his songs. For example, in addition to the mysterious conception of the three *kayas* of Buddha – *Dharmakaya, Sambhogakaya* and *Nirmanakaya* – Marpa spoke of the *Svabhavikakaya,* the essential unity of the three *kayas,* and of the *Mahasukhakaya,* the indivisibility of the other four *kayas.* When asked about the teachings of Maitripa at a sacred feast in honour of the *gurus,* Marpa declared, "There is no harm in revealing some aspects of Maitripa's intention in a song." Then he expounded the doctrine of the *kayas:*

The *Dharmakaya,* like the sky,
Is Buddha, the great Vajradhara.
The thick rain clouds of wisdom
Are the two Bodhisattvas. . . .

Self-luminous unchanging insight
Is characterized as unborn *Dharmakaya.*
Unceasing self-born wisdom
Is described as the manifold of
    *Nirmanakaya.*

> These two fused in coemergence
> Are described as *Sambhogakaya*.
> And these three, free from origination,
> Are called the *Svabhavikakaya*.

> All these, transcending conditions,
> Are the *Mahasukhakaya*.
> These are the five ultimate *kayas*.
> O friends of the heart! Are your minds
>     gladdened?

Marpa repeatedly reminded his disciples of the centrality of devotion to the *guru*, for the union of the receptive mind of the disciple with the omniscience of the *guru's* mind alone permits the full transmission of the Dharma. Paradoxically, the spiritual submission of the *chela* awakens his real consciousness, so that he begins to grow into his innate nature, increasing understanding and attracting those spiritual forces – the Sangha – which support striving towards realization.

> The merit of praising the *guru*
> Is equal to offering to the Buddhas.
> Through praising the masters,
> May all beings serve spiritual friends.

When Milarepa returned from his secluded meditations, Marpa gathered his disciples together and gave them the full transmission of the teachings he had received from his *gurus*. True to Naropa's prophecy, which was also a command, Milarepa received the most advanced doctrines. Then Marpa sent them on to their own work while he himself retired to his farming duties. Save for his effortless display of magical powers, he lived out an ordinary life in the world, for his real life was on planes of consciousness inconceivable to unawakened minds. Though the Kagyü lineage traces its origin to Vajradhara and Tilopa, Marpa was its founder in Tibet and his disciples organized the Kagyü Order, which survived the tumults of Tibetan history and has recently spread to India, Europe and America. Its strange and easily misunderstood rituals and practices cannot be penetrated without the perspective provided by Marpa in his spontaneous *dohas,* sung to his disciples.

> If I explain all of my realization,
> Some of you would not be able to hold it in your mind.
> If I were to explain just an aspect, it would be this:

> Confidence in luminosity
> Is perception free from bias or partiality.
> Meditation is continuous, like the flow of a vast river.
> By refusing to limit meditation to the four periods,
> And by renouncing even the vestige of hypocrisy,
> There is no distinction between meditation and what
>     comes after it.

> By gaining the power of *prana* and mind,
> The fear of *Samsara* disappeared long ago.
> This is my realization.

*Hermes*, April 1986
Elton Hall

# MILAREPA

*The Buddha, the Dharma and the Sangha*
*Are the three outer Refuges.*
*In taking them as my shelter,*
*By putting my whole trust in them.*
*I gain joy and fulfilment.*
*Fortune will come, if you take refuge here.*

*The Guru, the Patron Buddha and the Dakinis*
*Are the three inner Refuges.*
*In taking them as my shelter,*
*By putting my whole trust in them,*
*I gain joy and fulfilment.*
*Fortune will come, if you take refuge here.*

*The Nadis, Prana and Bindu*
*Are the three secret Refuges.*
*In taking them as my shelter,*
*By putting my whole trust in them,*
*I gain joy and fulfilment.*
*Fortune will come, if you take refuge here.*

*Form, Voidness and Non-distinction*
*Are the three real Refuges.*
*By putting my whole trust in them,*
*I gain joy and fulfilment.*
*Fortune will come, if you take refuge here.*

*If you do not look to the Refuges,*
*Who will shield you from eternal suffering?*

Milarepa
*Mila Grubum*

Vajrayana, the 'third stream' of Buddhist thought closely allied
with Mahayana, is mysterious and often alien to outside observers.
Arising independently of the Buddhist monastic tradition, its rituals
and practices can seem bizarre, especially to those who have not

learnt to discern the fine line between fact, symbol and that unseen reality to which symbols point. Perhaps the most mysterious of Vajrayana lineages is that which began with Tilopa and passed to Naropa and his disciple Marpa, who took it to Tibet. And Marpa's chief disciple, Milarepa, is the most enigmatic figure in the line. His life is a summation of the heights to which the human spirit can rise and the depths to which it can plunge. It draws together vivid contrasts that the mind prefers to see kept separate, and it shows how intermingled good and evil, insight and perversity, white and black magic, can become. If Milarepa's life is a study of degradation made larger than life, it is equally a story of unsurpassed spiritual triumph.

According to the *namtar* or life story composed to help individuals towards Enlightenment, Milarepa was born in A.D. 1052, a descendant of the Khyungpo clan and the Josey family. His ancestors included the son of a Nyingmapa lama who was esteemed in Upper Tsang for his capacity to subdue demons, and his father was a trader who had become affluent in Kya Ngatsa far to the west of Lhasa in Gungthang, above the Tsangpo River (which becomes the sacred Brahmaputra when it flows into India). His father named him Good News because he had heard of his birth whilst engaged in trading business at Tiger Point. Milarepa grew up in a warm and loving family, replete with the relatively luxurious life of country gentry. Although his upbringing and education were ordinary, his childhood and early youth were marked by precocious psychic sensitivity, a keen mind and a deep devotion to his parents. He also possessed a marked spiritual inclination which remained largely latent but was never wholly obscured. Even as a child he was aware that, though his family was respected, their prosperity was envied by those who were jealous of the success of people who had moved to Kya Ngatsa from elsewhere. When Milarepa's father discovered that he was dying of a wasting disease, he established a trust for his wife and son, making his brother and his wife trustees.

Milarepa's father died and soon the bereft family discovered the enormity of the hatred in those who were less affluent. His aunt and uncle provided little support in the name of preserving the trust, and former servants began to mock them. Greed conquered whatever worthy impulses the trustees may have had, and eventually they claimed that all Milarepa's inheritance had always been theirs, given on loan to Milarepa's father while he lived. Rather than stoop to throwing herself on the mercy of her husband's relatives, Milarepa's mother determined to take up the life of a beggar, but her own relatives managed to provide enough for her to maintain a small homestead by spinning and weaving. But she resolved not only to survive and to provide for her children, but also to avenge the wrongs she had suffered. Whilst Milarepa's sister, Peta, spun and wove and begged when circumstances compelled it, he was sent to a renowned monk to learn reading.

Milarepa's first teacher was a magician of the Nyingmapa or Ancient Order, which traces its origins to Padmasambhava. He possessed the serpent powers of the Eight Nagas, which include the capacity to change one's form at will, to communicate exactly what one wishes, to maintain full awareness and to expand the mind to include many worlds, and to serve all living beings. Milarepa thus gathered some sense of the mystery and depth of meditative practices while he learnt to read. When he returned to his mother, she sold half her little homestead and bought turquoise and a white horse for Milarepa, and then she commanded him to seek out a teacher of magic. After some travel and enquiry Milarepa went to the region of Ü, sold his turquoise and horse for gold and sought out Yungton Trogyel, who lived in the region of Yarlung. Offering everything to Yungton Trogyel, Milarepa became his disciple. In time, the lama learnt his story and was moved by his determination to serve his mother. Although concerned about Milarepa's strong will and his mother's immense hatred, he sent Milarepa to Yonten Gyatso, who lived in Nub Khulung, where he learnt the magical art of destruction.

Milarepa undertook a two-week retreat for spells and incantations. Just as his greedy aunt and uncle had filled their house with guests for the wedding of their son, the house was torn apart by elemental forces and collapsed, killing thirty-five people and sparing only the heartless couple. Terrified villagers recognized the power of malevolent magic and suspected its source, and they prevented the pair from seeking revenge, instead giving Milarepa's mother additional land to pacify her. She was not to be placated, however, and so she sold the land for gold and sent it to Milarepa with the demand that he do more damage. He went back to Yungton Trogyel, gave him the gold and learnt to control the weather. Then he made his way back to his village, and from a cave in which he secreted himself he brought down a fierce hailstorm upon the fields just before the beginning of harvest. Escaping with some difficulty, he made his way back to his teacher.

Nothing could be the same for Milarepa thereafter. He had fulfilled his mother's wishes and thereby discharged what he had perceived as his duty, but despite his moral blindness and warped sense of justice, he understood the inexorable working of the Law of Karma. He saw that evil begets evil and that his own actions, however he might rationalize them, were unspeakably terrible and would rebound on him.

> I was filled with remorse for the evil I had done by magic and by hailstorms. My longing for the Dharma so obsessed me that I forgot to eat. If I went out, I wanted to stay in. If I stayed in, I wanted to go out. At night sleep escaped me. I dared not confess my sadness or my longing for emancipation to the lama. While I remained in his service, I ardently asked myself again and again how I might practise the true teaching.

During this period his teacher's wealthiest patron died and his teacher fell into a deep reflection upon Karma and the Dharma. When he told Milarepa that he had decided to retire and begin working to reverse his own black karma, Milarepa asked for help. Yungton Trogyel told him to seek out Rongton Lhaga for instruction.

When Milarepa met Rongton Lhaga, he confessed his whole life and threw himself upon the lama's compassion. Rongton Lhaga told him that the deepest meditation involved direct insight and release from all hindrances, provided one's karma permitted its perfect practice. So exhilarating was Milarepa's sense of having escaped a fatal burden that he ignored the caveat and went to sleep believing that he was already a Bodhisattva. The next morning, however, Rongton Lhaga summoned him and explained that he knew his would-be disciple's mind and, because of such thoughts, he could not teach him. He told Milarepa to journey to Lhotrak and find Marpa the Translator. The two were connected by ancient bonds of karma, he said, and only Marpa could instruct him in the Dharma. Milarepa set out, and Marpa divined in a vision that his greatest disciple and most difficult challenge were approaching. When Milarepa found Marpa, he threw himself in desperation at Marpa's feet, but his teacher seemed cold and hard, offering him either food and shelter or the Teaching, but not both. Milarepa chose the Teaching, but then Marpa demanded that he exercise his magic to qualify: he was to send hail on the fields of those who persecuted Marpa's disciples and sow discord amongst the mountaineers who robbed them. Milarepa quickly did both and then asked Marpa to teach the Dharma. Marpa replied:

> Ha! Is it to reward your many crimes that I went to India at the risk of my life? . . . Restore the harvest and heal the mountaineers. After that I will teach you. But never come back if you cannot do this.

> Thus Milarepa discovered that instruction in the Dharma is not easy.

Rather than comforting Milarepa or assuring him that his fresh intentions would overcome his wilfulness, emotional intensity and perversity, Marpa brought them to the surface, where they had to be confronted. He had Milarepa build a round tower from stones he gathered, but then ordered the half-constructed edifice torn down – and the stones replaced where they had been found – on the grounds that he had not sufficiently considered the matter. Next he had his disciple construct a semicircular tower in another place, only to be demolished because Marpa had supposedly been intoxicated when he gave the order. Then he gave instructions for the building of a triangular tower, only to rescind them when the tower was half built, this time denying that he had any memory of giving them. Finally, he had a nine-storey tower built, which after numerous false starts was almost completed. Before it was finished, Marpa's actions, reminiscent of extreme forms of Zen instruction, convinced Milarepa that he would never receive the Teachings. Not once did he blame Marpa, but rather thought that his frustration was entirely due to his own past deeds. With a heavy heart Milarepa left to find instruction under one of Marpa's disciples. Marpa finished the tower and then summoned his disciples and Milarepa to its consecration. There he forbade anyone to teach Milarepa, and this broke the reformed sorcerer's heart. Only when he was on the verge of killing himself did Marpa appear to relent. With Milarepa prostrate before his feet, Marpa explained that his seemingly arbitrary actions and simulated anger were devices used to initiate Milarepa's initial purification. The magician had proved himself worthy to be a disciple.

Marpa had the *Chakrasamvara mandala* set up, the *yidam* or tutelary deity of which represents transcendental wisdom in the form of *shunyata*, or the voidness of luminous clarity. He then initiated Milarepa through this *mandala* and at a critical moment pointed to the vault of the sky, where the deity appeared in the living *Akasha*, space. Milarepa was given the initiation name Pal Zhepe Dorje – Resplendent Laughing *Vajra* – by the *yidam* Chakrasamvara. And in him was awakened the fire of *tummo*, which is hidden in the *tsa-u-ma (sushumna)* in the psycho-spiritual nerve channels. Milarepa went into secluded meditation for eleven months, after which he confessed to his teacher:

> I understand that in this body lies the vital choice between profit and loss, relating to eternal happiness or misery on the border between good and evil. Relying upon your power of

compassion as the venerable guide of sentient beings, I am hopefully endeavouring to achieve emancipation from the ocean of existential bondage, from which escape is very difficult. . . .

From this point, progressively ascending the Path, it is necessary to observe one's vows as carefully as one guards one's eyes. Even in failure, remedies must be employed. By not seeking one's own liberation on the path of Hinayana, one develops *bodhichitta*, which seeks to work towards the liberation of all sentient beings.

Even though the *namtar* which gives the life of Milarepa explains his efforts in meditative absorption at considerable length, little of the inner realm of experience is intimated. Milarepa had entered that subtle path which leads far beyond the reach of descriptive language and the range of discursive consciousness.

Eventually, Marpa held a great ritual feast at which he gave each of his chief disciples a particular charge and teaching. Milarepa was given the teaching of the fire of *tummo*, whose danger is as great as its promise, and both match the extreme energies Milarepa had already summoned in the wrong direction. Milarepa's will, originally cultivated to a remarkable degree of intensity, had to be channelled along a path equal to it despite the risks involved. Marpa sent his disciples across the high Tibetan plains and mountain fastnesses, but Milarepa remained near him in secluded meditation for some months. Then, as Marpa prepared to visit his teacher, Naropa, in India, Milarepa felt the need to return to his village. His journey was not a happy one, for when he arrived he found that his mother had died in wretched poverty and that his sister, Peta, was disinherited and impoverished. His greedy uncle and aunt tried to kill him, the villagers hated him and he had to threaten – though he resolved not to use – sorcery to make them withdraw. After meditating to the point of starvation near his mother's abandoned house, which was now his, he was visited by his sister. Enjoining her to follow the way of Dharma, he gave his small inheritance to his aunt and then decided to leave. Though befriended by his original tutor and nourished by his admiring sister, his homecoming served only to teach him the utter delusion of *Samsara* and of all attachments. Whilst meditating upon this insight, he found various supernormal powers released in him, and so he flew to the Cave of the Eagle's Shadow for total privacy. Having discerned the range and limit of his inestimable powers, he flew back to Horse Tooth White Rock near his village and decided to enter the world for the sake of sentient beings.

Suddenly his *yidam* spoke to him:

> Devote yourself wholly to meditation in this life, in accordance with Marpa's instructions. There is nothing greater than serving the teachings of Buddha and thereby saving sentient beings through meditation.

Milarepa realized that he could never touch the feet of his teacher in dwelling without distraction in the external world. Yet through meditation he could serve all beings in a way that would honour Marpa. Thus, it is said that Milarepa knew he could never be as great as his teacher, though he is also revered for his greatness in a different direction. Milarepa remained near his village and was periodically tended by his sister, who, though admiring him, was inconsolable regarding her lot and had little sympathy for Dharma. In the end Milarepa won her over and she became detached from the world and, more importantly, from her own bitter memories. When Milarepa's uncle died, his aunt was filled with remorse for the life she had lived. She sought out Milarepa and begged his forgiveness, and eventually he instructed her in Dharma and she became a *yogini* renowned for her meditation.

Having completely righted the relationships which had been so twisted in his youth, Milarepa now freely renounced all concern with the world and entered a series of retreats for meditation. His luminous powers of absorption became so strong that numerous disciples were attracted to him, and he instructed each according to his capacities and his karma. Knowing from experience that the interplay of the forces of knowledge and light with the demonic forces of ignorance and evil was precarious and intense, he focussed attention on the boundary between them. Where ordinary consciousness would recognize nothing at all, Milarepa realized that in the interstices between light and darkness was to be seen the reflection of the highest truth. He instructed his famous disciple Gampopa by assimilating this insight to the language of the *bardo*, the intermediate state between death and rebirth.

> Sentient beings in *Samsara*
> And all Buddhas in *Nirvana*
> Are equal in nature, the same in essence:
> Son, this is the *bardo* of view.
>
> The manifesting red and white (positive and
>     negative) forces
> And the indescribable essence of mind
> Are the true non-differentiated state:
> Son, this is the *bardo* of practice.
>
> The myriad forms of illusion
> And the non-arising mind itself
> Are one, not two, in the Self-existent:
> Son, this is the *bardo* of action. . . .
>
> The five tainted *skandhas*
> And the pure Buddhas in the five directions
> Are one in the *yoga* of perfection,
> The state of non-discrimination.
> Son, this is the *bardo* of the Path.
>
> Self-benefit is reflected in changeless
>     *Dharmakaya,*
> Altruism in *Sambhogakaya* and *Nirmanakaya,*
> Yet in their primordial state they are one:
> Son, this is the *bardo* of *Trikaya.*

> The impure body which comes from the womb
> And the pure form of Buddha's body
> Are one in the great light of *bardo:*
> Son, this is the *bardo* of attainment.

The highest reality, briefly experienced in the post-mortem state, is everywhere present but unnoticed so long as one is even minimally caught in the pairs of opposites.

After instructing a number of disciples over the years, Milarepa felt that his mission was finished. A monk, Geshe Tsakpuhwa, took pride in his learning and mocked the humble ascetic when they met at a feast. Milarepa responded with a song, which ran in part:

> Having meditated on my lama,
> I forgot those who are influential and powerful.
> Having meditated on my *yidam,*
> I forgot the coarse world of the senses.
> Having meditated on the teaching of the secret
>     tradition,
> I forgot the books of dialectic.
> Having maintained pure awareness,
> I forgot the illusions of ignorance. . . .
> Having made a monastery within my body,
> I forgot the monastery outside.
> Having embraced the spirit rather than the letter,
> I forgot how to play with words.

The monk was furious and planned to kill Milarepa. He prepared a draught of poison and paid a woman to give it to the ascetic. Milarepa's clairvoyance revealed all to him, but he initially refused the drink, forcing Geshe Tsakpuhwa to pay her a handsome sum to try again. Only then did Milarepa accept the drink, but he told the woman that he knew of the plot. When in remorse she begged to be allowed to drink the poison herself, he refused, saying that the time for leaving the world had come, and drained the cup while swearing her to silence until he had died. He also told her to keep the monk's bribe and to seek out the Dharma. Then Milarepa called his disciples together and gave them instruction:

> Strive unceasingly for purification,
> Banish ignorance and gather merit.
> Doing so, you will not only see
> The Dharma-loving gods come to listen,
> You will even perceive within yourselves
> The *Dharmakaya*, holiest and highest of all gods.
> Seeing that, you will then behold
> The whole truth of *Samsara* and *Nirvana*
> And you will free yourselves from karma.

The wicked monk came to see that Milarepa was indeed enlightened and, prostrating before him, confessed his evil deed. Milarepa instructed him in the Dharma and sent him away to work to reverse the karma that no hand can still.

When Milarepa announced his impending death, he added, "There is no reality in my sickness; there is no reality in my death", and explained that he simply manifested both. He sent his most energetic monks ahead to Chuwar, but both those who accompanied him and those who went ahead found that he had preceded them, though they were with him at all times. Thus he showed the illusory nature of all form. When all his followers had gathered in amazement at Chuwar, he delivered his final instructions:

> The practice of the secret path is the shortest way.
> Realization of emptiness engenders compassion.
> Compassion abolishes difference of self and other.
> If there is no duality between oneself and others,
> One fulfils the aim of sentient beings.
> He who recognizes the need of others will discover me.
> He who finds me will achieve Enlightenment.
> To me, to Buddha and to the disciples,
> You should pray as one, thinking of them as one.

Entering a state of profound meditative absorption, he passed into *Nirvana* at the age of eighty-four.

Though many signs and wonders followed his passing, and certain classes of gods and goddesses appeared, there was no marvel as great as the life he had lived and offered to others as an example of what one should not do and of what should be done. He embodied the spirit of his teaching to his closest disciples:

> *Samsara and Nirvana are a single reality*
> *In the state of ultimate awareness.*
> *To perceive ultimate reality,*
> *I mark everything with mahamudra, the great*
> *seal of emptiness.*
> *This is the quintessence of non-duality.*

*Hermes*, May 1986
Elton Hall

# TSONG-KHA-PA

*Dhyana is the kingly faculty of the mind. One-pointed, it remains immovable like a mighty Mount Meru. Projected, it permeates any virtuous object at will. It leads to the exhilarating bliss of applying body and mind to any task. Knowing this, the yogins of mental control have devoted themselves continuously to one-pointed concentration which overcomes the enemies of mental wandering.*

*I, the yogin, have practised just that. If you would also seek emancipation, cultivate the same.*

*Prajna is the eye with which to behold profound shunyata and the path by which to uproot ignorance, the source of cyclic existence. It is the treasure of genius exalted in all the scriptures and is renowned as the supreme lamp that eliminates the darkness of the closed mind. Knowing this, the wise who have wished for emancipation have advanced along this path with every effort.*

*I, the yogin, have practised just that. If you would also seek emancipation, cultivate the same.*

Tsong-Kha-Pa
*Lam-rim Bsdus-don, 19-20*

Just as the creative ferment in ancient Greek thought had prepared the way for Plato, and the Buddhist reformation in India had provided the context for Shankaracharya, so too the Buddhist renaissance and proliferation of schools in Tibet laid the groundwork for the remarkable Tibetan teacher, the great synthesizer Tsong-Kha-Pa. Despite the influx of diverse streams of Buddhist teaching at various times and from different parts of India, Khotan and China, there persisted a singular unanimity regarding *Buddhavachana,* the Word of Buddha. But whilst the Sangha stagnated in India through loss of contact with lay people and owing to its emphasis upon intellectual rigour to the neglect of ethics, it was retarded in Tibet by its laxity in discipline. This was in part due to divergences of practice in the various lineages and in part due to a growing gap between theory and practice under the harsh conditions of Tibetan life. The political entanglements of the monasteries, undertaken in the prolonged search for patrons and aggravated by the increasing concern for wealth, power and prestige, contributed to a pervasive corruption in self-discipline. Continuity of the Buddhist tradition in Tibet had been ensured despite formidable cultural and religious obstacles, radical differences in language, significant alterations in Tibetan political modes and ambivalent magical practices. The price paid had been considerable laxity, distortion and inversion in the monastic orders, whilst the threat of irreparable damage from within rose in direct proportion to the diminution of external influence.

Tsong-Kha-Pa's parents were blest by a variety of unusual dreams before his birth. His mother dreamt that a statue of Avalokiteshvara as huge as a mountain appeared before her and gradually diminished in size until it entered her through the *brahmanda* or crown opening. Tsong-Kha-Pa's father dreamt of Vajrapani, who sent a *vajra* or lightning-bolt sceptre from his celestial realm into his wife. These and other symbolic dreams indicated that Tsong-Kha-Pa was the emanation of both Avalokiteshvara and Manjushri. In time, he would be recognized as the boy who Buddha had told Ananda would be reborn in Tibet as Sumati Kirti – 'glory of wisdom' – Losang Drakpa in Tibetan. When he was born in the onion country of Amdo in eastern Tibet, an auspicious star appeared in the heavenly vault. Choje Dondrup Rinchen, Tsong-Kha-Pa's first teacher, was returning to Amdo from Lhasa when Tsong-Kha-Pa was born. Divining the descent of an emanation of Manjushri, he hurried back and presented sacred gifts to Tsong-Kha-Pa's father. At the age of three Tsong-Kha-Pa took layman's vows from Rolpay Dorje, the Fourth Karmapa, and then entered into such profound communion with Vajrayana deities – Heruka, Hevajra and Yamantaka – that he was ready to receive the vows of a novice at the age of seven. Choje Dondrup Rinchen then took charge of Tsong-Kha-Pa and watched over him until his sixteenth year, when he travelled to the great cathedral in Lhasa to take the Bodhisattva vow before the image of Buddha.

Knowing that he would never again return to Amdo, Tsong-Kha-Pa accepted his first teacher's parting advice to meditate on Yamantaka for continuity of practice, Vajrapani for freedom from distraction, Manjushri for wisdom and discrimination, and Amitayus for long life, amongst others. Then he set out to master the teachings of all the lineages. His travels would require a book merely to catalogue, though the pattern they followed was simple: in every case, he went to the best teachers of a particular school or doctrine, or to those who alone knew a particular text or treatise. As a little boy he went to Drikung Monastery, whose head *lama* of the Kargyu Order imparted to him the teachings of *bodhichitta* – the altruistic seed of Enlightenment – *mahamudra* – the great seal of perfection – and medicine. By the age of seventeen Tsong-Kha-Pa had become a proficient doctor of medicine. Moving on to Chodra Chenpo Dewachen Monastery, he rapidly learnt the *Prajnaparamita Sutras* and the works of Maitreya, and by his nineteenth year he was renowned as a scholar. He debated at Samye Monastery, received the Heruka initiation at Zhalu and took his examinations in the *Prajnaparamita* at Sakya. Then he met Rendawa Zhonnu Lodro, who was to become a lifelong spiritual companion, and received from him the essence of the Madhyamika or Middle Way philosophy. Here he inaugurated a method which was to provide the foundation of his reform. He became a disciple to Rendawa in some respects and his teacher in others. His application of dialectics to the *guru-chela* relationship eventually led to his recognition as the undisputed master of all the lineages and teachings.

Taking up the works of Chandrakirti – the Mahayana version of the philosophical *Abhidharma* – of Vasubandhu and Dharmakirti, he began to teach Buddhist philosophy. His reputation spread rapidly, and soon he was invited to various monasteries to instruct senior monks in the highest subtleties of the *Buddhavachana*. Whilst at Choday in northern Tibet he was initiated into a number of tantric practices. Upon his return to Lhasa he found an entire delegation from Amdo waiting to plead with him to come home. He felt that such a journey would interrupt his studies dedicated to the welfare of all beings, and so he renounced the offer, but he sent his mother a portrait of himself which spoke to her when she opened it. Later, he refused an invitation to become imperial tutor for the emperor of China. Journeying to Narthang, he consulted the complete texts of the Kangyur and the Tengyur and studied the treatises of Nagarjuna. Then he returned with Rendawa to Sakya, where he finished his examinations. Tsong-Kha-Pa had become a powerful dialectician, in large measure because of his utter calm and fair-mindedness in the midst of heated and intense debates. People were both fascinated and awed by him, but in his presence they were soon put at ease. His respectful and patient treatment of every sincere question infused teaching and learning with a sanctified joy that regenerated listeners and motivated them to uphold their vows and persevere on the Path.

Although his matchless intelligence and depth of mystical insight amazed those who came into contact with him, his utter selflessness and transparent morality demonstrated a seemingly effortless translation of sublime ethics into the visible arena of daily activities. This led many monks and laymen to recognize in Tsong-Kha-Pa one of those great beings who choose their incarnations for the sake of universal Enlightenment. When he began to write at the age of thirty-two, many who had known him only by reputation could benefit from his teachings. Tagtsang, a monk and translator who had previously been critical of Tsong-Kha-Pa's eclectic doctrines, was stunned by his *Golden Garland of Eloquent Teaching*. Writing to Tsong-Kha-Pa, he confessed, "As your sun of wisdom rises, my flower of arrogance disappears." During this period Tsong-Kha-Pa was ordained, received the teachings which had been preserved by the lineage founded by Marpa, and undertook an extensive study of the *kalachakra tantra* cycle, the heart of which is Shamballa conceived as a spiritual, mental and physical centre of reality. Though his outward movements can be traced for the remainder of his life, his arcane practices and secret activities cannot. He cultivated the super normal *siddhis*, including the meditation wherein the body can be made to generate and radiate remarkable amounts of heat. He travelled north and south from Lhasa to give initiations, and also, with Rendawa, performed initiations on Potala hill, where the palace of the Dalai Lamas would later be built.

Tsong-Kha-Pa now made a systematic study of the four levels of the Vajrayana, involving deep understanding of the mysteries of Sarasvati, the Black Manjushri, Manjushri Dharmachakra and the *Guhyasamaja*, 'king of *tantras*' He then entered upon an intensive retreat during which he determined the course of the remainder of his life. It may have been during this period that he took the decision to inaugurate a seven-century plan in which Bodhisattvas would take incarnation in the Western world to relight the Mystery fires there and to help receptive human beings free themselves from deadly dogmatism and growing materialism. It is said that when he emerged from this retreat, he was thereafter able to question Manjushri at will, consulting him and receiving guidance from him in all important matters. From this time onward Tsong-Kha-Pa alternated extended retreats with his disciples, during which many mystic visions occurred, with very specific meetings and religious activities. He assimilated, for example, the Kadampa tradition founded by Atisha and made it the basis of his own reform. When he met the Nyngma *lama* Khenchen Namkha Gyaltsen, there was an instantaneous mutual recognition. Khenchen saw Tsong-Kha-Pa as Manjushri, and Tsong-Kha-Pa recognized him as Vajrapani. When Tsong-Kha-Pa thought of going to India, Vajrapani advised against it, not only because of the difficulties involved in such a journey, but also because Tsong-Kha-Pa, with his mystic powers, would be of greater service by remaining in Tibet. He did so and used the time he would otherwise have spent in travels to write his great *lam-rim* treatise, the *Great Exposition on the Stages of the Path*.

Tsong-Kha-Pa took the spirit of Nagarjuna's dialectic and applied it to Atisha's teaching (which he felt expressed the methodology of Buddha) to create the *lam-rim* teachings. A vision in which Maitreya appeared confirmed his intuition. Beginning with *Guru Yoga* as the basis for all spiritual growth and advancement, he explained the path to Enlightenment in terms of gradual stages and progressive awakenings. Such a conception, which subordinates the radical methods of insight of the Vajrayana, requires a balanced development of the whole individual and places meditation on the foundation of morality. Integral to this approach – a fusion of doctrine and method, theory and practice – is a strict understanding of the disciplinary rules for monks. Where self-mastery through self-restraint is ignored, attempts to deepen insight are rapidly inverted or distorted into psychic excesses. The growth of the whole being towards the Bodhisattva goal requires a dedication to self-control in thought, feeling, word and deed. When he completed this *Exposition*, Sarasvati approved it and Manjushri told him that he need not seek advice on the nature of reality, since his own powers of insight – *prajna* – were sufficient for any task. Shortly thereafter, Tsong-Kha-Pa entered into a full understanding of *shunyata*.

By the time he was forty Tsong-Kha-Pa was ready to devote all his time to teaching. He visited the monastic centres of various orders and taught every form of Buddhist practice. Having mastered all doctrines and practices, he was able to insert his reform into each of the orders without giving offence or generating resistance. Everyone wanted to claim him as their own because he was the unexcelled master of every discipline and he backed his words by his own conduct – the quintessence of the method of *upaya*, skilful means. In 1409 he realized one expression of his religious reform by inaugurating the Great Prayer Festival at Lhasa in which eight thousand monks participated. The twenty-one-day event, which draws all the orders together, continues even at present in Dharamsala under the auspices of the Dalai Lama. When the festival ended, Tsong-Kha-Pa decided to remain in one place and chose Dongri (Nomad Mountain) as the site for the monastery. Called Ganden, the Tibetan word for Tushita, the celestial abode of Maitreya, its construction was placed in the hands of Gendun Drub, who would posthumously become the First Dalai Lama.

During his last years Tsong-Kha-Pa composed many valuable commentaries on various texts while continuing his teaching. In

1419 he was invited to Drepung Monastery, where he taught the most advanced disciples. One day he halted his discourse halfway through a text, saying that he would continue another time. Everyone present knew the significance of this act: to stop midway through a cycle of teachings indicated the intention of resuming the discourse with those who were worthy in a future incarnation. He returned to Ganden and left it again only to consecrate the ground for Sera Monastery. At the age of sixty-two he gathered his chief disciples together, gave his last instructions, assumed the lotus posture, passed into high meditative states and ceased to breathe. After his funeral he appeared to various disciples a number of times. Even his closest disciples found it hard to believe that such a Great Teacher had lived in their midst. He seemed to have spent his whole life writing, so numerous were his treatises. But it also seemed that he devoted himself exclusively to meditation, so constant was his practice. Yet he spent his life in almost ceaseless discourse to monks and disciples. He had done the work of three exceptional men at one time, even if his most arcane activities are left out of account.

Unlike many other teachers, Tsong-Kha-Pa did not offer his own life as an example to be emulated, for no one could hope to do so. Nonetheless, he spoke of his life in terms of the various stages of study, practice and attainment he had experienced, thus showing others what can be done and enjoining them to take what they can use. Advising his disciples to "seek transcendence first of all", he wrote in *The Three Principles of the Path:*

> By constant meditation, your mind will let go
> Of desires even for life's successes,
> And your aim, day and night, will be
>     emancipation.
> Transcendence without *Bodhichitta*
> Cannot yield the supreme bliss
> Of unexcelled Enlightenment.
> Therefore the Bodhisattva conceives supreme
>     *bodhichitta.*

Warning that efforts at transcendence can easily get off track because residues of ignorance, selfishness and preconception plague the aspirant at every stage, Tsong-Kha-Pa set forth the inner spirit of the Middle Way:

> Appearance as inevitably relative
> And *shunyata* as free of assertions –
> When these are understood as separate,
> Buddha's intent remains unknown.
> When they are simultaneous and not altered,
> The mere sight of relativity
> Becomes sure knowledge free of objective habits. . . .
> While appearance eradicates absolutism,
> *Shunyata* eliminates nihilism,
> And you know *shunyata* manifest as causality,
> And are freed from extremes in views.

Tsong-Kha-Pa held that an individual was supremely privileged to have gained a human form, from which alone the path to Enlightenment can be entered. But that form has to be made ideally receptive to spiritual growth, and this requires the cultivation of a fundamental ethical sensitivity which is accurately translated into moral practice. In addition, one has to take a positive line of action regarding one's karmic inheritance through self-purification and the restoration of vows broken in this and in previous lives. One needs to meditate upon suffering as the universal human condition – but not in terms of one's own dissatisfactions and delusions – so that one can come to understand whatever happens to oneself in light of the whole of humanity.

All these disciplines, which are taken up together and deepened by stages, have as their pivot *bodhichitta*, the seed of Enlightenment manifest as altruism.

> Ever enhancing your enlightened motive of *bodhichitta* is the mainstay of the path of the supreme *yana*. It is the basis and foundation for the great tide of altruistic conduct. Like an elixir which produces gold, it turns everything into the two treasures of

merit and insight, forming a storehouse of merit gleaned from infinitely collected virtues. Knowing this, the Bodhisattvas have held this supremely precious *bodhichitta* as their innermost mental bond.

Cultivation of the *paramitas* and meditation conjoined with one-pointedness, when connected by a rigorous dialectical logic, can cut the grip of *Samsara*. The unpractised, however, will marvel at the possibility of a total fusion of complete mental tranquillity and unlimited spiritual insight, but nothing less will be successful.

Having reached this union, meditate on the *shunyata* of empty space while absorbed in one-pointed meditation, and meditate on the *shunyata* of illusion when in the world. By doing this, your union of method and insight will be perfecting the conduct of the Bodhisattvas. They have made it their custom never to be content with partial paths.

Tsong-Kha-Pa was aware of the myriad ways in which one may drift away from balanced practice. In his *Letter of Practical Advice on Sutra and Tantra,* he warned a disciple and friend:

> Suppose we were to take as our foundation the self-deception of having only a partial and intellectual understanding of the stages of the path and then heard, thought and meditated on this basis. . . Despite our noble claims, I think the way our mind will probably have been working will have been nothing other than aiming for benefits in this life, or for certain pleasurable results of cyclic existence to which we have given the name 'Emancipation', or for some partial end for ourselves which is not Enlightenment at all.

Tsong-Kha-Pa dared to see why the path to Enlightenment is trodden by so few, and he knew that even after the kaleidoscopic distractions and self-rationalizing temptations of the world have been firmly set aside, the difficulties of the path only begin to manifest themselves. He knew in exact detail every possible pitfall along the way, and yet he was not for an instant discouraged, either for himself or in respect to humanity. He was firm in his faith that any and every human being could attain Enlightenment if only motive, persistence and renunciation of expectation were combined. This indescribably noble and profound conviction was as natural to him as breathing, and it is why he is considered to be Tibet's greatest Bodhisattva.

When Tsong-Kha-Pa and Rendawa first met, they became at once intimate spiritual friends. Rendawa's pure response to Tsong-Kha-Pa has become the *mantram* by which his blessing is sought by the sincere aspirant and devotee:

> *Avalokiteshvara, mighty treasure of immaculate love,*
> *Manjushri, lord of stainless knowledge,*
> *Vajrapani, destroyer of the demonic host,*
> *O Je Tsong-Kha-Pa, Losang Drakpa,*
> *Crown jewel of the sages of the Land of Snow,*
> *Humbly I request your blessing.*

*Hermes*, July 1986
Elton Hall

# THE FIRST PANCHEN LAMA

*I bow down to Prince Shakyamuni, all-knowing,*
*God of gods, who drew the great ones to follow him,*
*Who subdued the inner and outer demons four*
*And gathered to the utmost merit and wisdom. . . .*

*I bow down to him who, conquering darkness*
*By unfathomable wonderful marvels,*
*Led innumerable beings to the heights of Man or God,*
*To emancipation and the path of perfect Buddhahood.*

*I dedicate all merit accumulated by expressing*
*The merest atom of these wondrous deeds*
*From the jewel mountain of the Teacher's knowledge,*
*That I might gain omniscience for the benefit of all.*

*The Tathagata's form,*
*His attendants, life and sphere,*
*And his extraordinary marks —*
*These attributes may I and others attain.*

*Since the Teacher visited this world,*
*His Teachings illumine like the solar rays.*
*By brotherly accord between disciples of the Teaching,*
*May there be good fortune that the Teaching remain long.*

The First Panchen Lama

Tsong-Kha-Pa's immense visible and invisible reforms cannot readily be classified as social, political or religious. Whilst he vowed to rejuvenate Buddha's Teaching in Tibet, he initiated a mission for the spiritual regeneration of all humanity. Its mysterious force has reverberated through seven centuries, culminating in the present. The dynamics of his universal vision and the efforts made by lineages of adeptic Teachers to translate it into practice cannot be encompassed by what is ordinarily called history. For Tibetans and many others who sense the living presence of wise beings in the affairs of humanity, the chain of Teachers and Guides passes beyond the world of the five senses into invisible realms accessible only to spiritual vision. Tsong-Kha-Pa himself is held by many to be an incarnation of Sangyas, Shakyamuni Buddha, a manifesting aspect of Amitabha, supreme spiritual intelligence.

From the beginning of Tsong-Kha-Pa's work his reforms had spiritual, ethical, social and political ramifications. By founding the great monasteries – Ganden, Sera and Drepung – in the vicinity of Lhasa, he made it the focus of a unified Tibet. When his disciple Gedun Truppa founded Tashilhunpo near Shigatse, the whole of central Tibet came under Gelukpa influence. Yet just as the religious reforms of Tsong-Kha-Pa slowly suffused all Tibetan orders over time, so their social and political analogues gradually spread throughout Tibetan culture. Although Sonam Gyatso, the Third Dalai Lama and the first recognized by that title, consolidated the political structure of Gelukpa reform, it was only Ngawang Lobsang Gyatso, the 'Great Fifth', who secured it firmly. His brilliant statesmanship and remarkable intellect reveal him as a ruler of almost superhuman capacities, but he was equally a monk of luminous spirituality who took upon himself the responsibility of transmitting tantalizing intimations of the work inaugurated by Tsong-Kha-Pa. It was the Great Fifth who initiated the line of Panchen Lamas.

Gedun Truppa, who would later be called the First Dalai Lama, looked after Gelukpa affairs from Tashilhunpo, which was founded in AD. 1447. Gedun Gyatso, the Second Dalai Lama, served in succession as abbot of Drepung, Tashilhunpo and Sera monasteries. Sonam Gyatso, the Third Dalai Lama, travelled as far as Mongolia to spread Gelukpa reforms. Yonten Gyatso, the -Fourth Dalai Lama, was the Mongolian great-grandson of Altan Khan and ruled from Drepung. By the time the Fifth Dalai Lama ascended the sacred throne, Tibetans recognized him as the fourth reincarnation of the original Dalai Lama. But they must have realized much more, for when he ventured to acknowledge that he and his predecessors were incarnations of Chenrezi (Padmapani or Avalokiteshvara), he was accepted as such with enthusiasm. Perhaps because of the faithful and joyous response he received, he felt free to release a *terma*, a hidden text, which showed that his teacher, Lobsang Choekyi Gyaltsen, the abbot of Tashilhunpo, was the latest in a succession of incarnations going back to Khetrup, a great disciple of Tsong-Kha-Pa. These incarnations, the *terma* showed, were aspects of Amitabha, the Buddha of Infinite Light. From this standpoint, Amitabha blesses and renovates the world through three great lines – that of Buddha and Tsong-Kha-Pa, that of Avalokiteshvara through the Dalai Lamas, and that represented by the Panchen Lamas who reside at Tashilhunpo.

Traditional accounts of lives of the Panchen Lamas are complex, arcane and relatively inaccessible, especially in English. Scholars have attempted to explain the relationship between the Dalai Lamas and the Panchen Lamas without meditating upon the idea of spiritual hierarchies, concepts of individuality which have no reference to empirical dimensions of personality, or upon the nature of compassion and universal causation. All of these are inextricably involved in the idea of voluntary reincarnation and commitment to a particular kind of selfless sacrifice over lifetimes. Opinions as to which of the two Lamas is the higher incarnation, the more spiritual, the more senior, or any other such comparisons, cannot be more than ignorant and, at best, irreverent speculation.

Lobsang Choekyi Gyaltsen was born in the region of Tsang in the Iron Horse year, 1570, half a century before the birth of the Fifth Dalai Lama. When he was a young monk, the Third Dalai Lama died and his reincarnation, the Fourth, was discovered in Mongolia. Whilst the Fourth Dalai Lama strengthened Tibetan-Mongolian relations and laboured to secure Gelukpa authority throughout the land, Lobsang Choekyi Gyaltsen studied and sought to exemplify the spiritual orientation indicated by Tsong-Kha-Pa, combining meditation and ethics in a synthesis of the *sutras* and *tantras*. After the Fourth Dalai Lama died in 1616, it took only a year to find his reincarnation, the Great Fifth, and Lobsang Choekyi Gyaltsen, now senior in the Gelukpa Order, became his teacher. The profound mutual respect which arose between them is shown in the effects the teacher's instruction had on his disciple and the high honours the student bestowed on his former teacher. When the Fifth Dalai Lama built the Potala in Lhasa and settled there, the First Panchen Lama remained in Tashilhunpo, which was refurbished for his work. Between them, Tibet received a powerful spiritual and temporal guidance that kept the lineages strong for three centuries. When Lobsang Choekyi Gyaltsen died in 1662, the Water Tiger year, the Fifth Dalai Lama saw that he was interred with great ceremony, and he personally supervised the search for his reincarnation. The Second Panchen Lama, born a year later, was educated by the Dalai Lama. Since that time the elder of the two Lamas has been the teacher of the younger.

Despite the onerous burdens of looking after the welfare of the Gelukpa Order, encouraging reforms in the other orders, managing the extensive holdings of Tashilhunpo and seeing to the welfare of its lay citizens, as well as serving the Great Fifth as teacher and acting as a ruler in his own right, the First Panchen Lama sought to provide Gelukpa monks with the quintessence of *Buddhadharma* as formulated in the *sutras* and in the writings of Tsong-Kha-Pa. His writings reveal a profound experiential understanding of meditation and an equally deep insight into its pervasive connection with every arena of waking life. He wrote poems, each of which encapsulates some aspect of Buddha's Teaching in vivid, memorable form whilst intimating arcane meanings to the sensitive and receptive disciple. He also wrote synoptic texts which allowed monks to grasp the architectonics of the *sutras* and *tantras* even while threading their way through essential details of theory and practice. In his writings the First Panchen Lama emerges as a consummate teacher and guide in the spiritual quest.

There is a story, found in the *Damamurkhanama Sutra* in the Tibetan Kangyur, which tells of Buddha's confrontation with six Indian pandits. So vast was their learning that when they taught what they knew, their discourses took the form of seemingly miraculous phenomena. Buddha, in response, raised dialectic to alchemy and replied with magic. In his poem on Buddha's fifteen-day response, the First Panchen Lama showed the nature of this magic rising to the highest spiritual degree, passing beyond phenomena as ordinarily conceived. On the first day Buddha placed a tiny stick into the ground which grew into a wish-fulfilling tree, satiating the desires of men and gods. On the second day he caused jewel mountains to rise up around the place where he was sitting, and they burgeoned with succulent foods for humans and cattle. The third day witnessed a change in Buddha's reply: rather than satisfy desires rooted in the senses, he formed a lake "on which bloomed lotuses of laughing, radiant light". And the next day he manifested a pool from which eight streams flowed in a circular path, creating sounds which emitted the doctrine of the three vehicles – Shravakayana, Pratyekabuddhayana and Bodhisattvayana.

Having gained the enraptured attention of every mind present, Buddha again changed the level at which he manifested marvels. On the fifth day Buddha allowed his smiling countenance to radiate a golden light which suffused the three thousand worlds, purifying those far from Enlightenment and giving them a foretaste of *samadhi*. On the sixth he granted them the power of faith by enabling them to read one another's minds and to see clearly their own dark and pure thoughts, making it possible on the seventh day for each individual present to experience existence as would a universal sovereign in possession of the seven magical jewels. And on the eighth day he completed this dimension of his Teaching by sending forth Vajrapani and five demons, who subdued the six pandits and freed their followers. Beginning with the ninth day he disclosed something of his own nature – that realization towards which all beings strive – by expanding his form to the limits marked by the heaven of Brahmā and manifesting all the virtues of *Nirvana* and *Samsara* within it. And on the tenth day the luminosity of his form encompassed *Samsara*, forming a cloud from which a rain of happiness showered on all beings.

Buddha remained unmanifest on the eleventh day, but he expounded the Dharma with the voice of Sarasvati. Then, meditating on love throughout the twelfth day, he caused all beings to love one another as parents love their children. On the thirteenth day two rays of light emanated from his navel, and at the end of each was a Buddha from whose navel came forth more rays of light. This pattern repeated until the whole universe was filled with Buddhas of light. He took flowers offered by Udrayana on the fourteenth day and transformed them into bejewelled chariots which graced the three worlds. Then, on the fifteenth day, he shared the ambrosia of the gods with all beings and radiated from his fingertips streams of golden light which brought joy to beings in even the lowest hells. In his poem the First Panchen Lama characterized each day of marvels in such a way that the intuitive disciple can see each as a mystical stage on the path to Enlightenment and the Bodhisattva quest. Such Teaching, he warned, remains accessible only so long as it is followed in a spirit of universal brotherhood.

Two monks known for their persistent spiritual striving petitioned the First Panchen Lama to write an introductory text to *mahamudra* practice. *Mahamudra,* sometimes called the Great Seal of Voidness, constitutes the fulcrum of Tsong-Kha-Pa's teaching and is essential to an understanding of Mahayana and Vajrayana thought. The First Panchen Lama provided an overview of its nature and complexity in a short treatise, where, having made obeisance to *mahamudra* itself and to his *guru,* he defined *mahamudra* as "the all-pervasive nature of all things, the indistinguishable single nature of both objects of the Void and of the Void itself". Rather than restate the available written accounts of *mahamudra,* he combined the essentials of the *sutra* and *tantra* doctrines of *mahamudra* with the oral transmissions of Gelukpa and Kagyupa teachings.

> In order to enter the gateway and framework of Buddha's Teachings in general, and specifically those of the Mahayana, it is essential for you to take refuge and develop an enlightened attitude of *bodhichitta* sincerely from your heart, not merely from your mouth.

Since realization of *shunyata,* the Void, depends both upon merit and the removal of obstacles, one may prepare oneself through prostrations and mantramic invocations. (Both Marpa and Tsong-Kha-Pa followed this practice before the thirty-five Buddhas.)

> Then you must make repeated heartfelt requests to your root *guru*, whom you recognize as inseparable from the Buddhas of the past, present and future, to be able to realize *shunyata*.

Although one may approach the *mahamudra* teaching in many ways, these can all be placed under two heads – *sutras* and *tantras*. To follow the *tantra* system, one must successfully complete the difficult task of concentrating attention on the *nadis* or psycho-spiritual energy channels in one's *vajra* or diamond body, focussing on the central *nadi*. This can only be done under the direct guidance of a qualified teacher, and, when successful, it leads to the attainment of the clear light of *shunyata*, approached only through *anuttara yoga*, the controlled exercise of the highest purified consciousness. Such a method requires degrees of knowledge, access to a teacher and levels of self-control beyond the resources of most individuals. The First Panchen Lama therefore turned to the *sutra* method, which is within the reach of everyone. According to him, Nagarjuna held that outside these two approaches, there is no way that leads to Enlightenment.

The *sutra* method involves meditating upon *shunyata* in ways prescribed in the *Prajnaparamita Sutras* and expounded by an unbroken line of *gurus*. Their teachings involve methods of meditation which have received a variety of names, among them 'simultaneous production and union', 'the four letters' and 'the great encompassment'. In 'the joined amulet box', meditation involves combining bliss, *ananda*, and the Void, *shunyata*, like the two halves of a closed amulet box. The 'six equal tastes' method involves transforming six generally adverse conditions into modalities of wisdom. The six adverse conditions are distorted conceptions, moral defilements and mental delusions, sickness, harm from gods and spirits, suffering, and death. Transformation of distorted conceptions, for instance, involves altering whatever one hears into a *mantra*, whatever one sees into a deity worthy of meditation and so on. The 'profound Madhyamika theory' is the method devised by

Tsong-Kha-Pa and based on the teachings of Nagarjuna. Whilst these oral instructions bear different names, a *yogin* experienced in meditation will readily see that they are complementary and aim at a full understanding of *shunyata*.

Whichever approach one might adopt, there are two general ways to practise *mahamudra*. The first begins with a preliminary understanding of the conception of *shunyata* and then seeks one-pointed concentration upon that understanding. The second reverses the order, beginning with tranquil one-pointedness of concentration and using it to strive for an understanding of *shunyata*. In this, one should select a suitable place reserved for meditation and settle in a comfortable but erect posture, the lotus position being preferred. The grossest irrelevant thoughts can be dispelled with a few breathing exercises. When dull states of mind have been put aside and clarity remains, one takes refuge in the thought of *bodhichitta* with a pure motive. Then one should meditate upon the *guru*, and with intense devotion imagine the *guru* dissolving into oneself. Now one is ready to concentrate on a wholly unstructured and undetermined state of mind.

> This is a state of mind devoid of any preconceptions, doubts, wishes or aspirations for either temporary or ultimate purposes concerning past or future. This does not mean, however, that you should cease all conscious attention as if you were asleep or in a swoon. Rather, you should fix your unwavering memory firmly on the task of watching your mind from a distance and keep yourself constantly prepared with mental alertness to sense any mental wandering.

When equilibrium has been achieved, one can turn one's attention to the nature of mind itself as an impermanent phenomenon which is capable of clear and valid knowledge. Now attention should be 'tightened', and one should try to see the bare nature of the mind with stark clarity. If extraneous thoughts arise, one should either recognize them for what they are or cut them off as soon as they appear. With the mind focussed and clear, one should maintain meditation in a relaxed manner without letting memory slacken.

> Another method of settling the mind is not to block whatever extraneous thoughts arise, but to concentrate on the nature of the train of thought that has arisen and try to comprehend it. What happens is like the example of a caged pigeon released from a ship in mid-ocean. As the scripture says, 'A bird that has flown from a ship in mid-ocean, after flying here and there, must inevitably land back on the ship from which it left.'

This practice of meditation, undertaken with patience and persistence, brings the mind to a state of clarity without obstruction or predisposition.

> Although this state of mind lacks any form or structure, and in this way is as bare as space, yet it is precisely on this mind, as on a mirror, that whatever arises to consciousness appears vividly. Although you can behold this nature of the mind most obviously, you can never hold onto or point to any particular thing as 'my mind'.

The First Panchen Lama notes that most meditators claim that, having attained this stage, one can now realize whatever one's mind turns to, and that this is henceforth an easy path to Enlightenment. He suggests, however, that at this stage one has merely settled the mind, and he then goes on to expound the oral teachings of his own root *guru*.

From the stance of one-pointed, clear consciousness, one should, "like a small fish swimming through clear undisturbed water", explore the identity of the meditator. Who is this meditator? One will find that it is not the gross or subtle matter of the body, not the space it occupies and not consciousness. Given this, one will realize that the person who is ordinarily said to exist is only a label in the realm of the senses. Seeing that one has no ultimate or independent existence, one should proceed to meditate on that discovery. "In this way you cultivate the placement of one-pointed concentration on *shunyata* which is like space." Now one should concentrate on the stream of continuous clarity which is the mind until one realizes that this continuity is not a thing or particular existence but a modality beyond the ordinary categories of existence. This is the beginning of the dawning of *shunyata*. If one can concentrate one-pointedly on that, one will have achieved a wondrous feat.

When the period of meditation is over, one should return to the world of the senses systematically. First of all, one should dedicate the virtue gained from meditation to attaining Enlightenment for the sake of all beings. Secondly, one should closely examine the objects of sense which come to hand so that one will see their bare mode of existence. Thus one will see that they are not what they appear to be and should not be grasped. By nurturing understanding in this way, one can begin to realize that all things in *Samsara* and *Nirvana* share a single ultimate nature – *shunyata.*

> Thus in your formal meditation session, when you concentrate one-pointedly on *shunyata* according to proper methods, you will become convinced that all things in *Samsara* and *Nirvana*, whether validly existent or not, are void of independent existence, which is only a mental fabrication. Moreover, when you rise from your meditation session and make further analysis of things, you will then be able to witness the unmistakable operation of independent origination based merely on the way the mind labels things. In this way things will naturally appear to you as similar to dreams and hallucinations, like mirages and the reflection of the moon in water.

The First Panchen Lama wrote such works to bring sincere disciples in line with *Buddhadharma* and the Bodhisattva Path. By respecting tradition while subtly pointing to the distinctions between belief and knowledge, ritual and effort, venerable tradition and direct experience, he sought to purify the ascendant Gelukpa Order and alchemize every aspect of transmission of eternal wisdom. The tone he set has reverberated throughout Tibet until the present day.

*Hermes*, September 1986
Elton Hall

# TARANATHA

*Long ago, in an age before which there was nothing else, the Jina, the Tathagata Dundubhishvara [some say Amoghasiddhi] came into existence and was known as the Light of the Various Worlds. The princess Jnanachandra, 'Moon of Wisdom', had the highest reverence for his Teaching, and for ten million and one hundred thousand years she made offerings to this Enlightened One, to his shravakas and to the countless host of the Sangha of Bodhisattvas. . . Finally, after all this, she awoke to the initial steps of bodhichitta. At that time some monks said to her, "It is as a result of these, your roots of virtuous actions, that you have come into being in this female form. If you pray that your deeds accord with the Teaching, then surely you will change your form to that of a man, as is befitting."*

*After much discourse, she replied, "In this life there is no such distinction as 'male' and 'female', neither of 'self-identity', 'person' nor any perception of such, and so attachment to 'male' and 'female' is quite worthless. . . . Therefore may I, in a female form, work for the welfare of beings right until Samsara has emptied.". . . Then the Tathagata Dundubhishvara prophesied, "As long as you can possibly continue to manifest such supreme bodhi, you will be exclusively known as Goddess Tara."*

Taranatha
*The Origin of the Tara Tantra*

The Teachings of Buddha entered Mongolia long before they influenced Tibet. Travelling along the silk and trade routes through Kashmir and Afghanistan, crossing the great northern deserts and following the sea lanes of Southeast Asia into China and then westward, a rich variety of Buddhist views vitalized Mongolian culture. During the period of Tibetan unity under Buddhist kings, however, the foundations of Tibetan Buddhist orders were firmly established, and the resurgence of *Buddhadharma* inspired by the succession of remarkable teachers from Shantarakshita to Tsong-Kha-Pa gradually gave the orders temporal responsibility to match their spiritual authority. From the thirteenth century the Mongol political rule in Tibet grew, whilst the Tibetan Buddhist orders undertook the spiritual guidance of Mongolia. The great Mongol emperor Kublai Khan, who founded the Yüan Dynasty as China's first Mongol emperor, gave the rulership of Tibet to the Sakyapa Order.

Tsong-Kha-Pa, the founder of the Gelukpa or 'School of the Virtuous' Order in Tibet, reformed Buddhist practice and purified the Teachings from centuries of superstitious dross and diverse accretions. Having established Ganden Monastery near Lhasa in A.D. 1408, over the next fifty years his disciples founded Drepung and Sera monasteries, also in the Lhasa region, and mysterious Tashilhumpo in Tsang. Tashilhumpo's first spiritual head would come to be known as the First Dalai Lama. After the death of Bu-ston in 1364, Sakyapa influence was eroded by internal difficulties, and even as the Mongolians withdrew their favour, Gelukpa monks extended their teaching missions into Mongolia and secured the confidence of its rulers. Altan Khan, King of Thumed Mongolia, met the Third Dalai Lama and immediately became convinced that the spiritual head of the Gelukpas was a reincarnation of Phagpa, the remarkable Sakya head who had instructed Kublai Khan two centuries earlier. Since Altan Khan saw himself as Kublai reborn, he readily declared the Gelukpa abbot as Talé (Dalai) – one whose wisdom is as vast as the ocean – and placed the government of Tibet in his hands.

Although the Gelukpas enjoyed the patronage and protection of the most important Mongolian ruler, different orders sought protection from various clans that constituted a ceaselessly changing Mongol confederacy. Early in the fourteenth century, a Tibetan with the Sanskrit name of Digvijayi broke with Sakyapa tradition and founded a new order in Jonan, about a hundred miles northwest of Tashilhumpo. These Jonanpas, close to the Sakyapas in doctrine but equally close to the Gelukpas in spiritual practice, eventually allied themselves with the Chogthu Mongols of Kokonor, established a great monastery known as the Perfect and Eternally Firm Island and built a printing press. They produced a number of excellent scholars, the greatest of whom was Taranatha. Shortly after Taranatha's death, however, the Chogthu patron was assassinated by Gushri Khan, a Qoshot Mongol, in 1642. The Fifth Dalai Lama, known to history as the 'Great Fifth', was profoundly aware of the necessity of uniting Tibet politically and spiritually if its integrity was to prove a bastion for the Buddhist tradition. He was distressed by the divisiveness inherent in Chogthu patronage of the Jonanpas, and though he did not act so long as Taranatha lived, he subsequently took the occasion of Chogthu reversals to absorb the Jonan monasteries into the Gelukpa Order. Thus the Jonanpas disappeared as a distinct order, but the historical writings of Taranatha were preserved and venerated under Gelukpa auspices.

Almost nothing is known about the life of Taranatha. Although he wrote a spiritual autobiography which has survived, it is so rich in metaphorical and symbolic language that no scholar has yet felt competent to render it in a foreign tongue. For Taranatha, the so-called empirical facts of everyday life are nothing more than a veil cast across noumenal realities and arcane causality. Though they might provide sufficient hints and intimations for one with some spiritual insight to read them aright, they mislead the ignorant and unwary. Life as ordinarily lived and understood is a diversion and delusion, for the workings of karma and the significance of events can be understood only on the plane of the purified mind illumined by *bodhichitta*, the seed of Enlightenment. Born in 1575, Taranatha entered the Jonanpa monastic community at Jonan, where he emerged as a lama of exceptional insight and brilliance whose interests covered every aspect of Buddhist tradition. His unconditional love of Buddha effortlessly overflowed as unqualified reverence for the Dharma and deep respect for the Sangha. For Taranatha, the Three Jewels constituted a noumenal unity, every aspect of which deserved the fullest attention. Though he became the most famous scholar of his day and the beacon light of the Jonanpa Order, he was also Tibet's greatest historian and one of its chief exponents of esoteric wisdom.

Taranatha became the student of Buddhagupta, an Indian teacher who travelled extensively in the subcontinent before coming to Tibet. Taranatha seized every opportunity to assimilate Buddhagupta's knowledge of the history of the Buddhist tradition in India and to learn many stories of particular teachers and monastic centres. Taranatha studied the Buddhist scriptures and all the major commentaries on them and then wrote commentaries of his own which demonstrated a thorough grasp of diverse points of view, including the distinctive Jonan standpoint. He was drawn to the mysterious *Kalachakra* philosophy, upon which Tsong-Kha-Pa had based much of his own teaching, because it intimates the secret causality and continuity behind the play of events and succession of states of consciousness. The exceptional care Taranatha took in distinguishing and tracing the various lineages associated with the *siddhas* – men of knowledge, insight and power who transmitted the spiritual heart of *Buddhadharma* in the form of tantra – revealed a remarkable sensitivity to the delicate refinement and unbreached secrecy required to assure an unsullied continuity of oral teaching. His histories sought to demonstrate the spiritual vitality and essential unity of Buddhist tradition within various currents distinguished by philosophical perspectives, ritual modes and organizational structures.

Even without knowing the details of Taranatha's life, it is clear that he was much more than a scholar. The quality of his insights into philosophical and historical issues shows that he practised the system he described. At the same time, he was active in the affairs of his order, personally seeing to the renovation of at least two temples in his district. Late in life he journeyed to Mongolia, where he taught and worked. He remained in Urga, the region of ancient Mongolia known for its mysterious manuscripts and centres, where tradition holds that he died sometime before the middle of the seventeenth century. His remains were eventually interred in a silver *chorten* in a temple at Dzingji, east of Lhasa, where they remained at least until 1949. Taranatha so deeply influenced the Mongolian Buddhist community that he is believed to reincarnate in Jetsun Dampa, the reincarnating lama of Urga.

The Jonan Order to which Taranatha belonged was similar to the Kagyupas and the Gelukpas but was known for its distinctive view of *shunyata,* the Void. All the orders agreed that *shunyata* refers to the voidness of all phenomena, the fact that no phenomenon has any independent reality or existence. This standpoint is the natural complement of Buddha's doctrine of dependent origination, in which each individual, thing, quality and event is seen as dependent upon something else for its existence. In the fourteenth century the venerable founder of the Jonanpa tradition, Digvijayi, enunciated a doctrine of a second *shunyata,* He argued that in addition to what might be called ordinary *shunyata,* which is merely the absence of qualities and inherent nature, there is an absolute voidness, utterly unqualified and indescribable, which is reality in itself. This view, akin to that suggested in *The Voice of the Silence* in the phrase "the fullness of the seeming void", could be traced through antecedents to Nagarjuna and beyond. But it was generally shunned in Tibet because it seemed close to Tirthika perspectives, especially as found amongst some philosophical Hindus. Nonetheless, Tibetan schools recognized that the Jonan teaching, though unorthodox, was defensible and could not be declared outright heretical. Tsong-Kha-Pa, who had studied under a renowned Jonan teacher, understood the Jonan standpoint completely. Intriguingly, despite his myriad refutations of biased, partial and inadequate views, he never once raised his voice against the Jonan view of *shunyata.* Rather, he remained completely silent regarding it. The speculation of some later scholars that the Fifth Dalai Lama absorbed the Jonan Order into the Gelukpa school in order to abolish its supposedly heretical doctrines seems unlikely. Political turmoil and the need to unify Tibet under a strong spiritual and temporal authority more likely dictated the decision. Taranatha, the last distinguished Jonanpa, was honoured by the Gelukpa Order and his works were carefully saved for posterity after the close of the Jonan press. Thus, his name was entered in the roll of illustrious Tibetans who sought to uphold *Buddhadharma* in trans-Himalayan Asia.

Taranatha did not compose histories out of curiosity about the past. He thought that historiography was a mode of meditation upon the inner meanings of events and the Teachings of Buddha. Just as an individual, if he intends to understand his own life, must examine himself dispassionately from the standpoint of the soul, so too the history of the Dharma and the Sangha could illumine the essential core of Buddha's Enlightenment, the path to it and the pitfalls along the way, revealing the secret of its vitality in all circumstances. Thus, he recorded Buddhist history straightforwardly without presuming to sort out actual events from hagiographical embellishments. Where the account of some event seemed impossible under the circumstances, he noted the difficulty, and where different accounts conflicted, he pointed out the problems involved and occasionally suggested solutions. In general, however, he let tradition speak for itself, since even legendary happenings can reveal profound meanings to those who are able to meditate wisely upon them.

He wrote *The Origin of the Tara Tantra* in 1604 almost as a prelude to his monumental *History of Buddhism in India*. Tara is the active compassionate aspect of Avalokiteshvara. Tradition teaches that when Avalokiteshvara shed a tear over the plight of humanity, it fell to earth and formed a crystalline lake. A lotus rose from its shimmering surface and opened to reveal Tara in its heart. The Chinese and Nepali wives of the first king of Tibet are believed to have been incarnations of Tara. The Chinese princess embodied Sitatara, the White Tara, who holds the opened lotus of purity eternal. When she is depicted with the Third Eye on her forehead and with eyes on her palms and feet, she is the Tara of the Seven Eyes. The Nepali princess was an incarnation of Syamatara, the Green Tara, the consort of Avalokiteshvara and holder of the closed blue lotus. Together they represent ceaseless divine compassion working by day and night to mitigate suffering and eventually to bring it to an end.

According to Taranatha, the Tathagata Dundubhishvara conferred the name Tara on the princess Jnanachandra before the world appeared in its present recognizable form. In the subsequent aeon, named after the Tathagata Vibuddha, she subdued all of Kamadeva's demons and received from the Tathagata Amoghasiddhi the names Saviouress, Mainstay, Swift One and Heroine. When in the era called All-Pervading a monk named Radiant Pure Light became Avalokiteshvara, Tara was born from his heart. They descended together to earth in the form of a monkey and a demoness and created the ancestors of the Tibetan people. In the aeon called Vastly Good, Tara was reborn from the sky, and in the Asanka era the Buddhas collectively transformed themselves into Tara as supreme Mother. All of this happened before time began.

In the aeon which includes the present, Avalokiteshvara stationed himself at the centre of the world on Potala Mountain, a secret mountain in South India, after which the palace of the Dalai Lamas in Lhasa is named. There Avalokiteshvara intoned the Tara tantra and *mantra* in a form appropriate for each of the four *yugas* or ages. In Kali Yuga that intonation takes the form of a thousand Tara verses. Thus Tara fills all space with light from "the space between her eyebrows" whilst abiding in the heart of *bodhi*. When she saw Buddha and the Tathagata Akshobhya become one, she taught her tantra to transcendental beings. Then, retiring to Potala Mountain, she gave this wisdom to the Bodhisattva Vajrapani, the guardian of Secret Teachings, who became King Indrabhuti of Oddiyana and created a Dharma Treasury of arcane wisdom. Tara tantra arose in the world, however, about three centuries after Buddha's *Parinirvana.* Out of South India there appeared to various celestial beings the volumes of the great *Avatamsaka Sutra.* In confirmation of its spontaneous appearance and divine source, eight Mahatmas and five hundred Yogachara adepts beheld Avalokiteshvara, Manjushri – the Bodhisattva of Wisdom – and Maitreya, the Buddha to be.

From this celestial source all the divisions of the secret tantras arose.

Having given a tantalizingly enigmatic account of the transmission of wisdom, Taranatha then tells a series of stories which illustrate the multiple guises under which Tara protects humanity.

A twelve-year-old girl was gathering flowers in the forest, when Kuni, a fierce elephant, confronted her. He seized her in his trunk and threatened to crush her. Remembering Tara's name, the girl called upon her for help, and Tara at once restrained the elephant. The elephant placed the girl on a stone outcropping and saluted her with his trunk. He took her to the local town's marketplace, council chambers and temple, and then circumambulated the palace. The king heard of this girl and her stock of merit and he took her as his queen.

Once at Vajrasana, an elderly lady constructed a Tara temple in which the Tara image faced outwards. When the temple was complete, the lady grieved because the image faced away from the Mahabodhi shrine, thinking it inauspicious to do so. Suddenly the image spoke: "If you are not happy about this, then I will look on the Mahabodhi shrine." At once the image looked around, and from then on was known as 'Tara of the Turned Face'.

Taranatha reminded his readers that Tara had encouraged Nagarjuna to attain perfection, had protected Chandragomin on two occasions, and that she had told numerous others edifying tales and given assistance to many *siddhas,* including Tilopa and the disciples of Naropa. He refrained, however, from setting down the detailed teachings of the Tara tantra, for that belongs to the oral instruction passed from *guru* to *chela.* He nonetheless showed why a dedicated disciple should seek its eternal wisdom.

In 1608 Taranatha composed his *History of Buddhism in India.* He originally called it *That Which Fulfils All Desires* to indicate that it was no mere history but rather an auspicious undertaking. Taranatha attempted to speak about every notable figure in the history of Buddhist tradition, but rather than writing a chronicle exclusively in terms of divergent and sometimes conflicting schools, he chose to treat the whole history in phases delineated by the reigns of famous kings, such as Ajatashatru, Ashoka, Kashyapa and Shila. When representative kings could not be found, he marked the passage of the centuries by the greatest teachers of the times – Nagariuna, Aryadeva, Asanga, Dharmakirti, among others. Whilst recognizing differing movements, he preferred to delineate the flavour of a period to suggest distinctive phases of development. He warned, however, that "even the learned chroniclers and historians, when they came to discuss India, exhibited with their best efforts merely their poverty, like petty traders exhibiting their meagre stock". Within this framework he deftly mingled putative fact with events which seemed miraculous. For Taranatha, the visible world of everyday life and the marvellous happenings associated with Arhats, Bodhisattvas, kings and abbots are mixed at every point. Since it is impossible to give out the true, secret history of spiritual events, the most useful alternative is to provide an account which can lead the contemplative aspirant towards real knowledge of the operation of eternal Truth in the ocean of *Samsara*.

Wherever Taranatha's sources can be examined or his work can be compared with other accounts, he has proven to be accurate. He seems to have had a carefully considered view of history which succumbed neither to a blind belief that *Buddhadharma* would prevail under some principle of historical inevitability, nor to a depressing conviction that the Good Law was doomed to be lost in the world of men, He knew that the deeds of men and women – at the levels of thought and meditation, will, feeling, word and act – released Buddha's Teaching in the world or obscured it. Yet he also recognized that there is an inner power to the *Buddhavachana* – the Word of Buddha – that no being in mortal form can stay. History is the vast field where the aspirant must struggle and come to terms with both forces, the one promising freedom and bliss beyond comprehension, the other degrading and destructive. For Taranatha, the history of humanity is not simply an account of events, nor even a resume of changing economic and social conditions overlaid with political motivation: true history is the story of inner heroism, the manifestation of that in humanity which is changeless, unfettered and ever striving to be spiritually free. Jonan Taranatha, the last great representative of one of the sparkling streams of wisdom from which Tsong-Kha-Pa drank, saw the voidness of the seeming full because he saw the fullness of the seeming void. For him, history is a magnificent tapestry woven of threads which shimmer with the noumenal light of *bodhi,* and embroidered with the lives of those who made heroic efforts to blazon forth that light for the world to behold.

*Hermes,* August 1986
Elton Hall

# THE FIFTH DALAI LAMA

*By the clear compassion of Maitreya,*
*May we reap the rich harvest of victory*
*And cool the sufferings of karma and*
   *delusions.*

*O Maitreya, Incomparable Lord,*
*This fortunate aeon's fifth Buddha,*
*Inspire me and every sentient being*
*With the touch of your arm of compassion.*

*In the presence of the Master,*
*Whose eyes blaze with light,*
*I kneel down, hands joined, and pray*
*That the promise of the Throne,*
*Like a carving in adamant,*
*May never perish,*
*And the fruit of reciting your mantra*
*May be experienced.*

*O Protector, you emancipate*
*From the world's boundless sufferings.*
*I constantly seek refuge in you,*
*My able captain.*

The Fifth Dalai Lama

Ngawang Lobsang Gyatso, the Fifth Dalai Lama, was the first to be known as the 'Great'. Whilst tremendous reverence was shown to all the Dalai Lamas throughout Tibetan history, he alone held that appellation until the Great Thirteenth, the immediate predecessor of the present Dalai Lama. And in circumstances that seem to echo the times of the Great Fifth, some Tibetans have begun to speak of the Great Fourteenth. The Fifth Dalai Lama's historical eminence is due to the exceptional insight, skill and discipline he brought to his reign, despite the peculiar and complex conditions in which he exercised his authority. He secured the smooth spiritual transmission of Tsong-Kha-Pa's reforms and established a stable political foundation for Tibet which survived three centuries of invasion, duplicity and betrayal. He inspired in the Tibetan people a trust and confidence that has never wavered, a feat unmatched by priests, popes, kings or presidents elsewhere in the world.

When the 'religious kings' ruled Tibet and the Teachings of Buddha poured into the Land of Snows from India and, to a lesser extent, from China, there existed no monastic tradition. Beginning with Shantarakshita and Padmasambhava, monasteries were built but distinct orders did not emerge until much later. During this period there was a clear though not rigid distinction between political and spiritual authority. In retrospect, the persecution of *Buddhadharma* and its fledgling Tibetan institutions during the rule of King Lang Darma was disastrous. Whether Lang Darma really despised the Buddhist tradition, as many Tibetan histories aver, or whether he merely accommodated the Bonpa leanings of the aristocracy to secure his throne, as some sources suggest, the consequences were tragic. Central kingship vanished in the ceaseless strife of kinglets and warlords, while monks were isolated in little (and sometimes clandestine) groups to continue as best they could. When the 'second foundation' was established by Atisha and others, Tibet stood in great need of spiritual reform at a time when the Indian sources of renewal were exhausted and prone to corruption. The initial emergence of the Tibetan monastic orders provided continuity for the religious community, and Tsong-Kha-Pa's reforms consolidated the spiritual life of the country. The Fifth Dalai Lama seized the opportunities afforded by his time to unify Tibet politically.

By the time the Third Dalai Lama had received the title 'Dalai' from Altan Khan, Mongolian intervention in Tibet had become customary, since Tibet was a strategic piece in a complex game played out between Mongolia and China. The Buddhist orders had sought the patronage of local rulers and over time had been drawn into political intrigues. Once the Mongolian presence was firmly established, the orders sought to ally themselves with strong tribes amongst them. First the Sakyas dominated, and then the Karmapas gathered strength even as the Third Dalai Lama won the support of Altan Khan. His reincarnation, the Fourth Dalai Lama, was Altan Khan's great grandson. Mongolian influence, however, centred in Kokonor and only sporadically extended west and south to Lhasa and beyond. With the help of the kings of Tsang, the Karmapas persecuted the Gelukpas, as did the Bonpas and other older orders on good terms with them. Lobsang Choekyi Gyaltsen, who would become the First Panchen Lama, was enthroned as the abbot of Tashilhumpo in 1600. As the most prominent lama after the Dalai Lama, he looked after the daily affairs of the Gelukpa community in the south, whereas the Fourth Dalai Lama, who ruled from Drepung, gave much of his attention to northeastern Tibet and Mongolia.

After the Fourth Dalai Lama died in 1616, Lobsang Choekyi Gyaltsen supervised and confirmed the discovery of the Fifth Dalai Lama in 1617. Even during the reign of the Fourth Dalai Lama, the rulers of Tsang had attempted to exploit divisions amongst the Mongolian tribes and rivalries within the Tibetan Buddhist orders. Now that the Dalai Lama was a child, they redoubled their efforts. An attempt was made to assassinate him, and though he escaped, his mother was murdered. Lobsang Choekyi Gyaltsen protected his young lord and inaugurated an intense programme of education. He instructed the Dalai Lama in every aspect of the *sutras* and *tantras* and nurtured his inherent propensities for devotion and meditation. At the same time, he trained the Dalai Lama for rulership, showing by word and example that soaring spirituality and scrupulous ethical conduct are compatible with wise and effective leadership. By the time Ngawang Lobsang Gyatso assumed the full powers of the office of Dalai Lama, he fully understood the potentials and precariousness of his position. Knowing that every action would have enormous consequences for good or ill, he reflected carefully and then moved boldly. Beginning with total trust and faith in his Teacher, he gave him supreme authority over the region around Tashilhumpo and turned his own attention to resolving conflicts in Tibet as a whole.

Tsang rulers attacked Sera and Drepung, slaughtering hundreds of monks, and handed over smaller monasteries to the Karmapas. Knowing that he could not prevent such activities on his own, the Fifth Dalai Lama looked to the fragmented Mongols for assistance. Part of his genius as a leader was revealed in his capacity to recognize the karma of leadership in others. He began quiet negotiations with Gushri Khan of the Qoshot Mongols, a man of uncommon political ability and genuine sympathy for Buddhist teaching and Gelukpa practice. Gushri Khan launched an effort to conquer the whole of Tibet, defeated the king of Tsang, killed the head of the Karmapa Order, subdued eastern Tibet and marched west to the Ladakh border. By 1642, when the Great Fifth was twenty-five years old, Gushri Khan had brought the whole of Tibet under one ruler. To the surprise of many, but not of the Fifth Dalai Lama, Gushri handed over all spiritual and much temporal authority to him. Retaining the title of Po-Gyalpo, King of Tibet, he appointed a regent to work with the Dalai Lama, but he refrained from involving himself in the internal affairs of the reunified country save to assure its military protection.

The Fifth Dalai Lama embarked on a variety of activities to strengthen Tibet and the Buddhist tradition. He prompted the orders to enter the Gelukpa fold and induced the great orders to initiate those reforms which would acknowledge his spiritual authority, withdraw them from independent political alliances with external powers and restore their inner integrity. In doing so, he diffused the spirit of Tsong-Kha-Pa's reforms throughout the orders, whilst honouring the traditions of each and protecting their spiritual independence. In 1645 he began the construction of the Potala, the great palace in Lhasa which is the seat of the Dalai Lamas. Choosing the site of the ancient palace of the great 'religious king' Songtsen Gampo, he created an edifice which became one of the architectural marvels of the world and the symbol of Tibetan unity. Naming it after the secret mountain abode of Chenrezi (Padmapani or Avalokiteshvara) in South India, he prepared the way for startling revelations. Meanwhile, he managed so delicately to balance his increase in authority with excellent relations with Gushri Khan and his regent that within a century even the title 'King of Tibet' had disappeared. Simultaneously, he cultivated warm relations with the new Manchu dynasty in China, thereby lessening threats from the east. When Gushri Khan died in 1655, the Fifth Dalai Lama deftly secured the right to appoint the Tibetan regents of the Mongol king of Tibet. He selected as regent his nephew Sangye Gyatso, a man of remarkable talents, and instructed him to complete a census of all monasteries and to revise the system of taxes and revenues. Sangye Gyatso also supervised the continuing construction of the Potala, a task which took a total of forty-four years.

Although Tsong-Kha-Pa had abolished the traditional principle of monastic continuity through hereditary succession of abbots when he enforced celibacy upon Gelukpa monks, the alternative principle of governance by reincarnated abbots had its own problems. Despite the overall secrecy which had veiled the doctrine of rule by reincarnation, the idea had become partly exoteric when Altan Khan saw in the Third Dalai Lama the reincarnation of the great Sakya Pandita. The Great Fifth chose to reveal much more: whilst confirming that the same being had reincarnated in each Dalai Lama from the First, he added that each had been and would continue to be a personification of Chenrezi, the Bodhisattva who protected Tibet. Thus the reigns of the Dalai Lamas were not only wise but also hallowed. Further, he declared that his Teacher, the abbot of Tashilhumpo, was not merely a reincarnation of a close associate of Tsong-Kha-Pa, but indeed the embodied presence of the celestial Buddha Amitabha. The moral and spiritual effect of these revelations has been joyous and profound, for they have meant that the continuity assured by the reincarnations of the Dalai Lama has been preserved in the complementary reincarnations of the Panchen Lamas, who have transmitted the arcane tenets of

Tibetan Buddhism. When his Teacher died, the Fifth Dalai Lama oversaw the discovery of his reincarnation as the Second Panchen Lama, and since then the older of the two lamas has supervised the studies of the younger.

According to some accounts, the Fifth Dalai Lama ruled actively for only two years before entering a prolonged retreat for meditation. Whether or not this claim is strictly accurate, all sources agree that he did retire in his later life, appearing only for certain ceremonial occasions and in order to take fundamental decisions. During the Fifth Dalai Lama's long withdrawal from public view, Sangye Gyatso administered the affairs of Tibet. By the time the Great Fifth died in 1682, Tibet was a land unified politically and spiritually. Sangye Gyatso was well aware, however, of the fragility of Tibet's accomplishments. The Mongols had once again taken a political interest in Tibet and the Chinese were looking for ways to extend their influence in Tibet as a way to check Mongol expansion. In the face of these dangers, Sangye Gyatso proved to be as bold as his lord. Whilst taking only the most senior abbots and palace officials into his confidence, he initiated a successful secret search for the Sixth Dalai Lama. He found an old monk who resembled the Great Fifth and hid him in the Potala. For thirteen years no announcement was made of the Dalai Lama's demise. The old monk disguised himself as the Great Fifth and appeared occasionally at ceremonies dressed in concealing vestments. Although the Chinese eventually suspected that they had been deceived, Sangye Gyatso managed to consolidate the Dalai Lama's rule and finish the Potala palace before announcing the death of the Fifth and the imminent succession of the Sixth Dalai Lama in 1695. Some historians hold that the regent was greedy and ambitious, whilst others see him as fulfilling the programme of the Fifth and serving the interests of the line of Dalai Lamas. In view of the enigmatic brilliance of his mentor, it may be that he and the Fifth Dalai Lama planned this course of action in advance of the Fifth's death.

A new Mongol alliance used the Sixth Dalai Lama's unusual behaviour as an excuse to declare him an impostor – an accusation firmly rejected by Tibetans then and now. Marching into Lhasa, Lhapsang Khan of the Qoshot Mongols killed Sangye Gyatso and captured the Sixth Dalai Lama. He was sent to Peking to meet the Manchu emperor in 1706 but he died under mysterious circumstances while on the way. Many believe that Lhapsang Khan had arranged for his assassination. However that may be, Lhapsang Khan imposed his own candidate on the throne of Lhasa, but though he remained there for a decade, he was not accepted. When the Manchus invaded Lhasa in 1720 and pushed the Mongols out of Tibet permanently, the true Seventh was installed. Although neither the Great Fifth nor the First Panchen Lama nor the regent Sangye Gyatso could prevent the confusion and turbulence of the early 1700s, the unquestioned firmness of the institution of the Dalai Lamas is testimony to the brilliance of their work. Of the silver tombs of the Dalai Lamas outside the Potala, that of the Fifth has always been the most deeply venerated.

Events ensured that the Fifth Dalai Lama would be remembered by historians as an accomplished statesman. He himself, however, placed greater emphasis on cultivation of the Bodhisattva Path and the development of meditation and universal compassion integral to it. Having become proficient in the four levels of *tantra*, all of which require initiation by a *guru*, he wrote numerous works to assist meditators involved in the lower *tantras*, that is, the first three levels. Though there are practices which involve no symbols, the *sutra* and *tantra* traditions are bridged by a *yoga* of symbols, a means of transforming consciousness through meditation by a disciplined use of symbols that has been called Deity Yoga. The symbols invoked include detailed visualizations and specific *mantras* which transform intellectual understanding of the *sutras* into immediate cognition of aspects of oneself as corresponding to aspects of the cosmos. These practices lead, under the watchful eye of the *guru*, to the highest *yoga tantras*, such as the *Heruka* and *Kalachakra tantras*, but they remain suitable for daily practice throughout a lifetime, regardless of the level of attainment in meditation. Recognizing the importance of right beginnings, the Fifth Dalai Lama wrote a number of texts to give direction in the practice of meditation.

In "*A Meditation Upon Orange Manjushri*", the Fifth Dalai Lama made obeisance to Tsong-Kha-Pa as the embodiment of Manjushri, the Bodhisattva of Wisdom. Reminding the disciple to begin by taking refuge in the Three Jewels – Buddha, Dharma and Sangha – by generating *bodhichitta,* the altruistic thought of Enlightenment, and by contemplating the immeasurable thoughts of love, compassion, joy and equanimity, he instructed the disciple to visualize an unfolding set of symbols:

At my heart is my mind in the shape of an egg, its point upwards. Inside the egg on a full moon disc is an orange letter DHIH, from which an infinite amount of light emits. It fills the whole of my body, purifying all my negativities and removing all my obscurations accumulated since beginningless time. The light rays then leave through my pores and become offerings to the Buddhas and Bodhisattvas. The lights then become offerings for the Buddhas and Bodhisattvas, thereby delighting them. This causes the blessings of the body, speech and mind of these holy beings to dissolve into light that destroys the darkness of ignorance of all sentient beings, thus placing them in wisdom's illumination.

The rays then re-collect into the syllable DHIH. It changes into light, my ordinary perception and my clinging thereto vanish, and I emerge as the Venerable Manjushri, orange in colour, with one face and two arms.

My right hand brandishes a Sword of Wisdom in the space above me. At my heart between the thumb and ring fingers of my left hand I hold the stem of an utpala lotus. Upon its petals in full bloom by my left ear rests a volume of the Prajnaparamita Sutra.

I sit in full lotus posture and am adorned with precious ornaments for my head, ears, throat and shoulders, as well as bracelets and anklets. I am draped in a flowing mantle and skirt of exquisite silks; my hair is tied up in five knots and coils anticlockwise. Bearing an entrancing and serene smile, I sit amidst a mass of light radiating from my body. The letter OM marks the crown of my head, AH my throat, and HUM my heart.

HUM emits rays of light that invite the Wisdom Beings from the inconceivable mansion of their own pure lands. They resemble the Manjushri described above and are surrounded by hosts of Buddhas and Bodhisattvas.

JAH HUM BAM HOH: they absorb into me and thus we become one.

Having completed this visualization, culminating in a union of consciousness with the vision it invokes, mental offerings are made to Manjushri, who is conceived as a graceful youth of beautiful speech.

> O Manjushri, I make obeisance to your mind
> Wherein is illuminated the entire tapestry of the
> myriad objects of knowledge.
> It is a tranquil ocean of unfathomable profundity,
> Of immeasurable breadth, boundless like space itself.

The disciple then visualizes a *yantra* which contains a *mantra* of sacred syllables. They are imagined to contain collectively every level of wisdom attained by Buddhas, Bodhisattvas, *shravakas*, Pratyeka Buddhas and "the wise and learned masters of all the Buddhist and non-Buddhist traditions". This universality of inclusion is matched at the end of the meditation period by an equally universal aspiration:

> By the virtue of this practice, may I soon
> Accomplish the powerful attainments of Manjushri,
> And then may I lead all beings without exception
> To that same supreme state.

The imagery of this *yoga* of symbols saturates the mind, yet its richness of forms has nothing to do with fantasy or pleasant dreamlike states. Its precision in every detail is rooted in a profound and arcane knowledge of colours, sounds and numbers, their correspondences and their permutations.

In *"The Fasting Practice of Eleven-Faced Avalokiteshvara"*, the meditation follows a pattern similar to that of *"A Meditation Upon Orange Manjushri"*, with the addition of a fast and the taking of precepts. The Fifth Dalai Lama warned that the practice must be taken seriously – a fast means a total fast and vows are not to be taken lightly. Noting that there were many "propounders of a false type of fasting retreat" who did not clearly distinguish between *sutra* and *tantra* or even between Mahayana and Hinayana, he pointed out that the intimate interrelation of all things should not be an excuse for confusing them. If distinct entities are muddled together, the correspondences between them and their connections with various states and aspects of consciousness are lost. Regarding those who teach facile methods, he laughed, "They, upon surveying the suffering of the six types of beings, proceed to count radishes as things having minds". He emphasized the importance of being guided by a preceptor and of studying the works of great scholars, including those of the Second Dalai Lama.

The force and beauty of his *"Sadhana Focussing on the Bodhisattva Maitreya"*, Buddha of love and futurity, included a meditation which invoked the spirit of Maitreya in one's consciousness.

> Having developed the supreme *bodhichitta,*
> I will take care of all sentient beings as my guests;
> I will follow the excellent ways of the Bodhisattvas;
> For the sake of all beings,
> I will attain Enlightenment.

Once the mind is purged, purified, collected and one-pointed, the meditator visualizes Maitreya:

> In the sphere of emptiness, my own mind appears as a yellow syllable MAIM, from which light radiates. It pleases the Enlightened Ones by bringing them offerings. Then it purifies the negative karma and obscurations of all sentient beings. The light collects back into the MAIM, which transforms into the syllable

PAM. This in turn transforms into a lotus marked by AH. This AH becomes a moon cushion, on top of which I arise as three-faced Arya Maitreya. My main face is yellow, saffron-like in colour. My right face is black, and my left, white. Each face has three eyes; each is peaceful and smiles. My dark hair is tied up in a knot. The first two of my four hands are at my heart, in the mudra expressing the turning of the Wheel of Dharma. My lower right hand is in the mudra of Supreme Generosity, and my lower left hand holds a fragrant dark-yellow flower. I am adorned by eight precious ornaments: head ornaments, ear-rings, a neckband, armbands, bracelets, anklets, shoulder-belts, and long crystal necklaces. Heavenly silks cover the upper half of my body, and I wear a panchalika skirt. A full moon is my backrest, for I am seated in the Sattvasana, in the centre of a halo of light. My forehead is marked by the syllable OM, my throat by AH, my heart by HUM. At my heart stands a yellow MAIM on a moon-disc. It radiates light, inviting the Wisdom Beings, who are similar to myself, from their actual abodes: VAJRA SAMAJAH, JAH HUM RAM HOH: They merge and become non-dual with me.

The offering made in this *sadhana* on Maitreya included an invocation which represents the spiritual confidence and selfless service that marked the Life and labours of the Great Fifth:

> *The fire of Great Love burns the fuel of anger,*
> *The light of Wisdom clears the darkness of ignorance.*
> *I bow down to you, King of the Dharma,*
> *Abiding in Tushita, who protects all beings.*

*Hermes*, October 1986
Elton Hall

# THE SEVENTH DALAI LAMA

*The higher you climb in Samsara, the higher the cliff where*
    *you perch;*
*The more the possessions you own, the tighter you are*
    *bound.*
*The dearer someone is held by you, the greater the chance*
    *he will hurt you;*
*The faster you conquer your foes, the faster their numbers*
    *increase. . . .*

*Therefore no position in the world*
*Is worth the effort of gaining it.*
*Renounce that which only weighs you down:*
*The unburdened mind is joy supreme.*

*The highest of aims is to follow this path:*
*Body, speech and mind kept stainless with pure self-*
    *discipline.*
*Mind in samadhi, both blissful and clear,*
*And wisdom, seeing the reality of every situation.*

The Seventh Dalai Lama

When Lobsang Khan invaded Lhasa in 1705 and seized the Sixth Dalai Lama, he unleashed forces beyond his comprehension and control. He slew the regent Sangye Gyatso, took the Dalai Lama to the Manchu emperor of China and placed a monk of his own choice in the Potala. Just before leaving under armed escort for China, the Sixth Dalai Lama gave a farewell message to his people:

> White bird in the sky,
> Lend me but one great wing
> That I too may soar eastward.

> Soon I shall return from Lithang,
> And return your wing to you.

After he died on the road to China, some said that he was assassinated, but others held that he had seated himself in the posture of meditation and consciously abandoned his body to seek another. The Tibetan people, faced with these events, readily rejected Lobsang Khan's choice for the throne of Lhasa and happily accepted the news that the Seventh Dalai Lama had been born in Lithang, just as his predecessor had promised.

Gyalwa Kalsang Gyatso was born in 1708 in Lithang near the Tubchen Jampa Ling Monastery in the Amdo region of eastern Tibet. His luminous intelligence and profound spiritual inclination were evident almost from the moment of his birth. When he was four years old he received a vision of Buddha surrounded by the sixteen *arhants,* and in the following year he had a vision of Tsong-Kha-Pa, who instructed him to take up his duties in central Tibet. Although he preferred to study and meditate in seclusion, he followed the dictates of his *dharma* and involved himself in the turmoil of the world. At the age of six he placed himself under Ngawang Lobsang Tempa, who became his Teacher, and within a year he yielded to requests to offer an Avalokiteshvara *mandala* initiation. So rapidly did his study of the *sutras* and the *tantras* progress that by his eighth year he was invited to visit and bless monasteries all over eastern Tibet. He travelled to Kumbum, the great monastery founded by the Third Dalai Lama at the site of Tsong-Kha-Pa's birth, and there he sat on the Dalai Lama's throne and gave discourses to a large assemblage of monks.

While at Kumbum, Gyalwa Kalsang Gyatso shaved his head and received ordination as a monk. Placing himself under Chuzang Nomohan, he took up an intense study of Buddhist dialectics, the doorway to Buddha's five great themes. He studied Dharmakirti for *pramana,* right thought and perception; Maitreya and Asanga for *prajnaparamita,* perfection of wisdom; Nagarjuna, Aryadeva and Chandrakirti for *madhyamika,* the Middle Way doctrine of *shunyata* or the Void; Vasubandhu for metaphysics; and Gunaprabha for *vinaya* or monastic discipline. Having immersed himself in the *sutras* and the *tantras*, taken all the vows of a monk and mastered both dialectics and the broad divisions of Buddhist teaching, Gyalwa Kalsang Gyatso turned his attention to Lhasa.

In 1717 the Dzungar Mongols invaded Tibet with the declared aim of deposing the pretender and placing the Seventh Dalai Lama on the throne. They succeeded in entering Lhasa, killed Lobsang Khan and removed his pretender to the throne. But they could not make good on their promise to install the true Dalai Lama, for he had come under the 'protection' of the Manchu emperor. When the Dzungars subsequently began to loot the temples and houses of Lhasa, the Tibetans looked to the Chinese for assistance. In 1720 K'ang Hsi invaded Tibet, drove the Dzungars out and oversaw the enthronement of the Seventh Dalai Lama. The price of this service was the Chinese foothold he established in Tibet. In 1720 Gyalwa Kalsang Gyatso was welcomed into the sacred city as the Seventh Dalai Lama. He proceeded to the Great Temple, where he discoursed to an enormous number of monks and lay people. Then he went to the Potala, where he was greeted by Lobsang Yeshe, the Second Panchen Lama, and received ordination at his hands. In keeping with the tradition founded by the Fifth Dalai Lama, he declared his desire to study under the Panchen Lama and submitted to his discipline.

Since Lhasa had become peaceful when the Dzungars had been driven out and the Seventh Dalai Lama entered the city, the Chinese withdrew their military forces and established diplomatic relations with the Dalai Lama's government. For the next few years the Seventh Dalai Lama studied under the Panchen Lama and other illustrious teachers. First, he took up Tsong-Kha-Pa's *Lamrim chenmo,* the exposition of the stages of the Path, and listened to the Panchen Lama's discourses on it. In addition, he received initiations into the *Vajrabhairava Tantra* and learnt the highest forms of *Yoga Tantra.* Then he moved to Drepung Monastery, where he reviewed all that he had learnt in logic and studied Dharmakirti's *Seven Treatises on Pramana,* as well as Nagarjuna's texts, the works of the

Madhyamika school and Tsong-Kha-Pa's commentaries. Returning to Lhasa, he was ordained by the Panchen Lama and assumed the full authority of his office. Despite his onerous duties as the Dalai Lama, he spent long periods of time within the sanctity of the Tushita Chamber of the Potala, where the Panchen Lama gave him numerous initiations into the *Guhyasamaja* and *Heruka Tantras*, along with Tsong-Kha-Pa's Teachings concerning them. He also devoted a great deal of time to *Abhidharma* metaphysics.

In 1727 the Seventh Dalai Lama's father was involved in political intrigues that led to brief civil strife between factions of the aristocracy. By the time the Chinese arrived in Lhasa, the capital was calm, but their suspicion that the Dalai Lama had been involved – a conclusion for which there is no evidence – induced them to send him into exile for seven years. Rather than succumb to defeatism or despair, he seized this opportunity to enter upon a retreat accompanied by excellent teachers and to intensify his study and meditation. He visited various monastic communities and discoursed on the Teachings of Buddha, Tsong-Kha-Pa and previous Dalai and Panchen Lamas. Concluding his exile with a grand tour of central Tibet, he returned to the Potala amidst a joyous welcome and began to give ordination to neophytes. He requested that the Panchen Lama return to Lhasa and sit at his side, but the old monk declined because of fragile health. Once the Dalai Lama had ordered affairs in Lhasa, he made the hard journey to Tashilhumpo Monastery to be with his chief teacher. There the two companions in wisdom and selfless service had daily conversations, and the Dalai Lama studied the Panchen Lama's *Direct Path* and looked after his Teacher's needs. The great monasteries of Tibet sought his presence, however, and in time the Dalai Lama was compelled by his office to travel to Drepung, Sera and a host of other centres. When the Second Panchen Lama died in 1737, the Dalai Lama mourned his loss but continued to travel, teach and initiate monks while waiting for the Panchen Lama's reappearance.

Once Palden Yeshe, the Third Panchen Lama, was old enough to make his will known, he asked for instruction from the Dalai Lama.

Effortlessly, the two companions renewed their friendship and reversed their roles. The Third Panchen Lama showed the same profound reverence for the Seventh Dalai Lama that the Seventh had shown for the Second Panchen Lama. Despite his devotion to meditation and study, the Dalai Lama became increasingly active in later life. In addition to tutoring the young Panchen Lama, he regularly visited monasteries to teach, preach, reform and initiate. Although the Chinese had placed Phola, a powerful military officer, in Lhasa after the revolt of 1727, the Dalai Lama had quietly reorganized and strengthened the Tibetan government. He did not challenge Phola, but he gradually made him irrelevant to the administration of Tibet.

When Phola died, his son, Gyurma Namgyal, an impulsive man who had witnessed the subtle divestment of Phola's authority, sought to restore by force of arms the power of the office he inherited. A new revolt broke out and the Manchus sent an army into Lhasa, but, by the time they arrived, total order had been restored and all issues had been settled by the Dalai Lama himself. Embarrassed by their over-reaction, the Chinese realized that the Dalai Lama was better able to govern Tibet than any agent they might select, and so his temporal authority was accepted and the army withdrew. Though remembered as the most scholarly of the Dalai Lamas, the Seventh was also an adept in meditation and an able ruler.

He persuaded one of his teachers to gather and master materials on the *Kalachakra Tantra*, especially everything Tsong-Kha-Pa had written and taught concerning it. Synthesizing all that could be found, he restored the great *Kalachakra* initiation, which intimates the mysteries of Shamballa. He established the Kashag, a cabinet of ministers to oversee the operations of government, and reorganized the departments of state. He also built the most famous landmark in Lhasa after the Potala, the Norbulingka or Jewel Park summer palace. The procession of the Dalai Lama from the one to the other became the central festival of the Tibetan year, during which the population greeted their spiritual guide and temporal ruler with joyous abandon. When the Seventh Dalai Lama died in 1757, he left a legacy that survived more than a century of vicissitudes and aided the Thirteenth Dalai Lama in his efforts to restore the political dignity and spiritual vitality of Tibet.

The Seventh Dalai Lama was beloved in his lifetime, and his amazing knowledge of the scriptures was matched by his deep spiritual insight. Once when he performed the *Vajrabhairava Tantra* for a thousand monks, flowers fell from the clear sky and advanced practitioners of meditation witnessed the manifestation of mystical forces. Despite his extensive travels from monastery to monastery, he found time to compose spiritual songs and poems. When he visited Ganden, founded by Tsong-Kha-Pa, he was overcome by reverential feeling and poured out a profusion of songs. His attainments won the respect of spiritual Teachers of all lineages, and his natural humility and simplicity of life endeared him to his subjects. Among the common people he was remembered as the Lama who never forgot them. If he recognized the face of a peasant from his village or from some town he had visited, he would invite him into the Potala or Norbulingka Palace for tea and a brief discourse on *Buddhadharma*. To every monk he gave the advice he offered to the young Third Panchen Lama when his period of study had ended:

> Listen to and study the vast ocean of scriptures, just as did the incomparable master Lama Tsong-Kha-Pa, until you gain a profound understanding of the intent of Buddha. Then you should listen well to the special oral transmission teachings on the *sutras* and *tantras* and draw a direct experience of them into your heart. Finally, you should generate the thought of turning the Wheel of Dharma for the benefit of living beings near and far.

In a poem which he wryly called a "dry log of a thing", the Seventh Dalai Lama indicated the immense seriousness of the spiritual Path. Bowing to Tsong-Kha-Pa, he taught:

> Most wondrous is this opportunity found but once,

This foundation with eight freedoms and ten
endowments.
Yet it is impermanent, like a rainbow,
For who can be certain that even today
Consciousness will not leave his body?
We die, young and old alike, and in the end,
Who meets not with death?

Noting the abyss between the illusory search for happiness in a transient world and the behests of Buddha's teaching, he deplored the delusion of people in general:

Practice of the ten virtues is the fuel of sandalwood,
But today people burn black coals of vulgarity.
Meaningless transient pleasures deceive the masses,
And divert their faces from things of lasting joy.

In language reminiscent of the *Dhammapada* and the *Udanavarga*, he expressed horror at the myriad ways the same delusion creeps unchecked into every effort to live the spiritual life:

"Suffering is the method of attaining liberation", they say,
And they don the robes and talk religion.
But even while they preach, five poisons rule their minds.
Qualities they feign and faults they hide:
Corruption flourishes everywhere, it would seem.

The Seventh Dalai Lama was revered for his gentleness and kind-heartedness, but he was neither sentimental nor compromising. Encouraging every sincere aspirant, he had no sugary words for those who deluded themselves about their spiritual progress or sought to impress others:

"Whatever I see is beheld in the light of *shunyata*", they say,
Yet they cannot bear the slightest upsets and become like
lost owls
In inner fires of explosive frustration.
Theirs is not the path to freedom.

It is impossible, the Seventh Dalai Lama taught, to find one's way unaided when one's own thinking can betray one's best aspirations. Yet help cannot be taken at random without the likelihood of being misled by others just as blind as oneself:

> Therefore the root of every accomplishment
> Depends on correctly following a *guru,*
> A spiritual friend.
> Rely upon a perfected teacher,
> One of control, peace of mind and every excellence.

If one is blest with the good fortune of fruitful guidance from a true spiritual friend, one has to practise faithfully what one has been taught. Even though the Seventh Dalai Lama knew all the major *Tantras,* he did not advise aspirants to focus upon them. The basis for any assault on the deceptions of consciousness and illusions of the world is ethical thought and action, not fragmentary flashes of insight or sombre rituals:

> Subdue attachment and aversion
> And generate an attitude moist with love
> That looks on all with delight.
> Develop compassion that wishes to see
> All beings freed from misery.
> Develop the special attitude that carries
> The weight of the welfare of the world.

The effort to shed delusion and shun attachment is not conducted only in respect to others. Besides reorienting oneself in relation to the world, learning to speak and act on a radically different basis from that recommended by the worldly, one has to confront one's mental dynamics as well:

> Work day and night on the elephant of the unaware mind.
> Strike it with sharp hooks
> Of attention, mindfulness and negations of negativity.
> Guard self-discipline as you would the pupils of your eyes.

The inner and outer practices which lead towards spiritual emancipation and universal compassion are summed up in the six *paramitas: dana* or kindly generosity, *shila* or calm self-control, *kshanti* or serene patience, *virya* or steadfast perseverance in meditation and service, *dhyana* or uninterrupted meditation, and *prajna* or transcendental wisdom:

> Think, "Now that I have a human mind,
> And have tasted the unsullied Dharma,
> Embraced in the fatherly compassion of a spiritual guide,
> May I practise well and generate
> Never-ending joy in the flow of consciousness."

For the Seventh Dalai Lama, the Bodhisattva Path is the only means worth thinking about or considering. Treading this Path of several stages demands a tremendous effort of self-development, but never for the sake of self, however subtly conceived. The only thought which is fundamental enough to be at once the essence of consciousness, the mode of Bodhisattvic thinking and the means to its own fruition is *bodhichitta*, the seed of wisdom- consciousness. In a poem he declared:

> The sole thought on everyone's side,
> The precious mind aiming at Enlightenment as the
>     way to further the world,
> Was seen by Buddha to be
> The highest Spiritual means.

*Bodhichitta*, "the elixir which transforms gross beings into Buddhas", is the innermost secret of spiritual alchemy. The world could not contain its qualities if they were all made manifest simultaneously, and not even Buddha tried to describe "the ocean of beneficial effects of *bodhichitta*".

Although he was esteemed for his immense erudition and dialectical skill, the Seventh Dalai Lama wrote verses which are startling in their simplicity and subtlety. In a poem written to help an old monk prepare for death, he said:

> When comes the time to carry

> The load of life through death's door,
> One can take neither relatives, friends, servants
>     nor possessions.
> Attached mind is animal mind:
> Abandon attachment.
> The limitless beings around us,
> Parents who have kindly nurtured us,
> Are creatures seeking only happiness:
> Cultivate altruistic mind.

In the middle of a complex song dealing with the multitudinous tricks the ignorant deploy to support a false sense of 'I', he addressed the problem of bridging meditation and practice:

> During meditation, keep the mind as unobstructed as
>     space;
> After meditation, regard the flow of events as a
>     rainbow.
> Thus the things which seduce the world
> Are seen to be insubstantial hallucinations.

And in the same poem he suggested the vital connection between causality and *shunyata,* the voidness of all things:

> Just as a reflected image clearly appears
> When a man holds his face to a mirror,
> All things are radiantly manifest and void.
> For that reason cause and effect are unfailing.

Just as the kindly and compassionate manner of the Seventh Dalai Lama was accompanied by an uncompromising insistence that spiritual life is the only issue that compels human concern, so too his humility and spiritual severity were wedded to bright humour. Many of his poems were written at the request of monks, and he added colophons which made fun of his efforts in ways that illuminated some important truth of the moment. Having just conveyed the enormous effort needed to transcend the ego, he signed himself, "the lazy Buddhist monk Gyalwa Kalsang Gyatso". When a great monk asked for a second poem, he received a beautiful text, to which was appended the note: "This work contains nothing not found in the song I wrote for him earlier, but because he persistently asked for another, I wrote it to silence his constant requests." Thereby he added a small, significant lesson about asking for spiritual teachings.

Subtlety of thought, delicacy of feeling and resilience in action marked the Seventh Dalai Lama's life. A man of meditation and action, imbued with probing compassion and profound devotion, he left a radiant record of his life in his poems and songs. The quintessence of his Teaching, repeatedly tested in his own life, may perhaps be found in his short *"Three Meditations"*, written for a hermit:

> *If one does not sow the seed*
> *Of appreciation for a perfect guru,*
> *The tree of power is not germinated.*
> *With undivided mind entrust yourself.*
>
> *Human life is rare and precious,*
> *Yet, if not inspired by thoughts of death,*
> *One wastes it on materialism.*
> *Be ready to die at any moment.*
>
> *All living beings have been our mothers,*
> *Three circles of suffering always binding them.*
> *Ignoble it would be not to repay them,*
> *Not to strive to attain Enlightenment.*

*Hermes*, November 1986
Elton Hall

# THE SEVENTH PANCHEN LAMA

*With one-pointedness sustain the clear realization that not even an atom of all the phenomena of* samsara *and* nirvana *– the ego, the aggregates, mountains, houses, tents and so forth – exists in and of itself. Know that all are merely imputed designations. This is the yoga of contemplative equipoise which is like space. Following the attainment of this condition, realize that all objects of perception are by nature false, not really existent, since they depend for their appearance on cause and circumstance. This is the* yoga *of illusoriness. When, relying on these two* yogas, *contemplative equipoise is joined by the bliss of well-disciplined mind and body, which is drawn out by the power of analysis, one attains intense, profound insight.*

Tenpe Nyim
*Three Principles of the Path*

The death of the Seventh Dalai Lama, a monk of deep meditation and vast erudition, heralded the end of Tibet's efflorescence as a spiritual culture. Faithful to the spirit of Tsong-Kha-Pa's mysterious work and to the brilliant statesmanship and religious guidance of the Great Fifth, he had heroically faced hostile forces which sought to control Tibet. Preserving the lines of spiritual instruction and the sanctity of his office, he restored the temporal authority of the Dalai Lama and fixed the pattern of Tibetan government which persisted until the exile of the Fourteenth Dalai Lama in 1959. The Eighth Dalai Lama, leaving much of the administration of daily affairs to others, pursued a scholarly and contemplative life. Unfortunately, events destroyed the peaceful conditions forged by the Seventh Dalai Lama, and the resulting disasters were as much due to Tibetans as to outsiders.

In 1768 Prithivi Narayan, the ruler of Gurkha, a minor principality west of the Nepal valley, invaded the kingdoms of

Patan, Katmandu and Bhadgaon (Bhaktapur) and seized the whole valley. Shortly thereafter he conquered Jumla and Mustang and invaded parts of Western Tibet without encountering resistance from either Lhasa or Beijing. A few years later, the Sixth Panchen Lama, renowned for his wisdom and insight, yielded to the urgent and frequent invitations of the Manchu emperor to visit Beijing. He made the arduous journey to China in 1779 and was received with high honours. He used the goodwill generated by his presence in Beijing to press for the autonomy of the Dalai Lama's government, but he died in 1780 before he could achieve his aims. His brother, Tenpe Nyima, became the Seventh Panchen Lama, and in accordance with the Sixth Panchen Lama's testament, he was given total control of Tashilhumpo's enormous wealth. A second brother, who had become a high-ranking monk in the Karmapa Order in Nepal, claimed a share of these resources for himself. When Tenpe Nyima refused to recognize the claim, his brother prevailed on the willing Gurkhas to invade Tibet.

In 1792 the Gurkhas sacked Tashilhumpo, the sacred seat of the Panchen Lama. This affront to China's largely symbolic suzerainty and the high esteem in which Tenpe Nyima was held by the emperor compelled the Chinese to launch a massive retaliatory force which eventually drove the Gurkhas back into Nepal. Although the Seventh Panchen Lama was restored to his throne, the Chinese forced upon the Gurkhas a peace which recognized Tibet as having a special and subordinate relationship to China. Neither the Dalai Lama nor the Tibetan government was consulted in this arrangement, and though the Chinese were not in a position to face resistance to the treaty, it marked the end of Tibet's autonomous dealings with the rest of the world. Tibet withdrew behind its borders, adopted a xenophobic attitude and eventually became the 'forbidden land' which inspired romantic novelists in the late nineteenth century.

When the Eighth Dalai Lama died in 1804, the Chinese attempted to alter the traditional methods of discovering his reincarnation by introducing a lottery amongst the most promising candidates. The

Tibetans rejected the idea, and after some intense encounters, the Ninth Dalai Lama was recognized by Tibetans and Chinese alike. He lived only ten years, and during that time Tibet was governed by a regent. When his successor died in his twentieth year, a number of Tibetans came to suspect foul play. The Eleventh and Twelfth Dalai Lamas also died just about the time they were to assume full spiritual and temporal authority. Although historians have tended to look for Chinese machinations in these untimely deaths, the fragmentary evidence available suggests otherwise. Tibetans themselves disagree regarding the role of the regents in this rapid succession of Dalai Lamas. Some suspect poison in every case, and there is some evidence for this point of view, particularly in the light of similar attempts made on the Thirteenth Dalai Lama. Others understand these deaths as the result of karma, holding that Tibetans had so completely failed to honour the work of Tsong-Kha-Pa and the Fifth Dalai Lama that they had made it impossible for their successors to survive for long in the polluted land.

The last strong Manchu emperor, Ch'ien Lung, died in 1799, and though the dynasty survived for more than a century, internal rebellion and foreign intrigues weakened its capacity to influence affairs far from the capital. The regents at Lhasa were quick to grasp the significance of this change in Manchu fortunes and they sought to take advantage of it, but their power lasted only so long as the Dalai Lama was a minor. Tenpe Nyima lived through most of this tumultuous period, and as the obscuration of the office of Dalai Lama continued through a series of incarnations, he found himself increasingly the effective representative of Tibetan spiritual unity. Ruling from Tashilhumpo, which remained essentially independent of Lhasa, he acted as the spiritual head of the whole country. While he was careful to do nothing to weaken the prestige of the Dalai Lamas, he sought to remain faithful to the precepts of his predecessors and to avoid being ensnared in the politics of Lhasa. The skill with which he carried out his difficult duties won the profound respect of the Tibetan people and the Chinese government. When he died in 1853, a quarter of a century before the birth of the Thirteenth Dalai Lama, many Tibetans thought that the light had finally gone out of Tibet.

Despite the onerous duties imposed on the Seventh Panchen Lama by time and circumstance – the restoration of Tashilhumpo, governing all the Gelukpa monasteries, ministering to the people and preserving the sacred lineages against internal disintegration – he was a man of meditation and contemplation. For him, all truth could be found in the Teaching of Buddha, and the greatest representative of that Teaching was Tsong-Kha-Pa. He wrote extended commentaries on short works of Tsong-Kha-Pa meant to be taken as root texts. These brief poems encompass the *Bodhidharma* in a form which is as easy to memorize as it is difficult to understand. A monk who had memorized a root text could contemplate it wherever he went and during any activity, and he could turn to a commentary for advice on how to translate the spirit of the text into an unfolding series of meditative practices. In his commentary on Tsong-Kha-Pa's Three Principles of the Path, the Seventh Panchen Lama provided a complete programme for meditation centred on the principles of renunciation, *bodhichitta* and right view.

The aspirant to this form of meditation begins by carefully preparing himself and the place for meditation – cleaning the room, installing some suitable object of devotion, making a pure offering and assuming a posture of meditation. The meditator then takes the fourfold refuge:

> I go for refuge to the Guru.
> I go for refuge to the Buddha.
> I go for refuge to the Dharma.
> I go for refuge to the Sangha.

He imagines light and nectar streaming from the objects of refuge to heal and purify all beings. Placing himself under the beneficent protection of the Three Jewels – Buddha, Dharma and Sangha – he seeks to arouse *bodhichitta* through renunciation.

Through whatever merit I have gained
By *dana, shila, kshanti, virya, dhyana* and *prajna,*
May I attain Buddhahood for the sake of all living beings.

He then imagines a great assembly of *lamas* and deities gathered around Buddha. Their light enters into his being, purifies it and passes into the world for the sake of all beings. Perceiving in the mind's eye a glorious rain of nectar which falls upon living beings and purifies them, he beholds the objects of refuge dissolving into light which in turn dissolves into Tsong-Kha-Pa, who becomes a brilliant light in the place between the eyebrows.

The aspirant should next imagine his *guru* in the form of Tsong-Kha-Pa, seated on a cushion of sun and moon and lotuses.

> Each hand holds the stem of a blue lotus. Upon the blossoming blue lotus at his right shoulder, the wisdom of all the Buddhas is embodied in the form of a flaming sword. Its light fills the world and the flame that blazes from its tip consumes all ignorance. Upon the blossoming blue lotus at his left shoulder is a volume of the Prajnaparamita Sutra, the mother of all Buddhas of past, present and future. On its sapphire pages are glowing letters of burnished gold, from which shine rays of light, clearing away the ignorance of living beings. These letters are no mere shapes; they are the clear tones of the stages on the Path and of the final goal. They proclaim the way of acting for the benefit of all living beings.

Vajradhara is discerned seated in the heart of Buddha, and Buddha is seated in the heart of Tsong-Kha-Pa. He is enthroned on a rainbow, along which are ranged great teachers. Two beams of light radiate from his heart, the right bearing the lineage of Maitreya, which represents *mahakaruna,* universal compassion, and the left carrying the lineage of Manjushri, which represents the profound wisdom of *shunyata,* the Void.

Once the meditator is firmly fixed in this condition of consciousness, he performs the sevenfold act of worship, in which he makes offerings, acknowledges his wrongdoing in mind and body, welcomes every virtuous activity, requests the Buddhas to turn the wheel of Dharma, petitions all teachers to remain in the world and offers any merit gained to all living beings. Having offered a mandala and invoked the Great Teachers, he is ready to begin the two phases of meditation – contemplation of the teachings and complete meditation. Beginning with an unconditioned recognition that all one has received comes from one's *guru*, one seeks to honour what one can never repay by assimilating the three principles of the Path.

> To obtain Buddhahood, it is necessary to learn method and wisdom. The guiding principle of method is *bodhichitta*, and the guiding principle of wisdom is right view. To engender *bodhichitta* and right view, you must renounce *samsara*. . . . The guiding principle of method, by which the *rupakaya* is attained, is the accumulation of merit. The key, root and essence of all accumulation of merit is *bodhichitta*. The guiding principle that is the cause of attaining the *dharmakaya*, mind of Buddha, is accumulation of wisdom. The key, root and essence of all wisdom is right view. Thus all the keys of the path are included within renunciation, *bodhichitta* and right view. This is the teaching which Manjushri gave to Tsong-Kha-Pa, King of Dharma.

In conjunction with this teaching one should dwell upon the fact that Opportunity for real meditation comes only when one lays down an ethical foundation for practice, takes up the *paramitas* and offers both to all living beings.

To begin to accomplish the ends set out, one has to meditate on universal suffering, which is the quintessence of *samsara*, the world of appearance and delusion. So long as one finds some aspects of *samsara* enjoyable, one has failed to penetrate its fundamental nature. Only through a realization of its root nature will one engender the motivation for emancipation which sustains a pilgrim on the Bodhisattva Path. Renunciation of the wiles of *samsara* is only part of the task set for the aspirant. One has to make a positive effort to arouse *bodhichitta*, beginning with the cultivation of equanimity. By thinking of some individual who has neither helped nor harmed one, towards whom one feels neither attraction nor aversion, and by consciously vowing to have equanimity towards all living beings, one begins to develop *bodhichitta*. One then thinks of the most attractive individual one knows or can imagine and repeats the exercise.

> I will be free from attachment and aversion; I will not feel close to some and help them, while feeling distant from others and harming them. I will learn to have equanimity towards all living beings. Lamas and gods, enable me to do this.

Finally, one should contemplate some individual who is exceedingly unattractive to oneself and consciously make the same invocation. When one has done all this to some degree, one should deliberately extend the same line of thought to all beings, known and unknown, visible and invisible.

Equanimity is the basis for meditating upon the seven steps to arouse *bodhichitta*. The first step involves asking the question "Why are all living beings my relatives?" One should consider the fact that, since there is no beginning to *samsara*, there is no beginning to one's births in some form or another. Since one has taken birth innumerable times, all living beings may have been one's mother at one or another time. One is related over time to all that exists, and since time is an aspect of *samsara* and ultimately an illusion, one should bring awareness of this universal relatedness into the present moment. Doing so will profoundly affect the way one conducts oneself with others. When one has realized the truth of universal relationship, one should undertake the second step, meditation upon the self-sacrificial *dana* or loving kindness one's mother showered upon one. In light of universal interdependence, one can gradually extend one's gratitude to all beings for the kindness of which one has been a beneficiary. The third step involves thinking again of beings towards whom one is impartial, attracted or feels revulsion. Knowing that each individual has shown great kindness to one at some time, one should respond with *dana* and recognize that differences which presently exist are the consequences of karma.

These three steps constitute a prolonged meditation upon what one has received and they aim to engender gratitude. The fourth step turns from what one has received to what one should want to give in return. An individual can never fully repay all beings in one life or even in many, but he can nurture a profound longing to help them free themselves from *samsara* and suffering. He will begin to awaken the positive dimension of the Bodhisattva vow, pledging himself to serve others in thought, word and deed. Such thoughts move naturally to the fifth step, which is the radiation of love towards all beings. As an exercise, one can begin by extending love in one's mind to those close to one, then to those towards whom one is attracted, then towards those one dislikes and finally towards all beings.

The sixth step involves meditation upon *mahakaruna,* supreme compassion for all beings. When one can engender an authentic current of compassion, one can then take a vow to help redeem all beings from the trammels of delusion. The seventh step is meditation upon *bodhichitta* itself. In doing so, one should think:

> I do not know where I am going. How can I establish even one living being in Buddhahood? Even *shravakas* and Pratyeka Buddhas can do but little for human beings and cannot ground them in Buddhahood. It is only the perfect Buddha who can lead beings to full Enlightenment. Therefore, I shall aim for nothing less for the sake of all beings. *Gurus* and gods, enable me to do this.

To the degree that one awakens *bodhichitta,* one can perform the activities of the Bodhisattva. One should make *bodhichitta* one's sole motivation and practise the six *paramitas* from that standpoint. This effort works alchemically on one's own nature and radiates outwardly through the world. During meditation, one consciously works on oneself; between periods of meditation, one should seek to put the *paramitas* into practice in relation to others. In doing so, one makes use of the three doors – body, speech and mind – by exercising beneficent control over what passes through them. Rather than remaining a deluded victim who victimizes others in turn, one begins to become a compassionate influence in the world. Whatever the activity – sleeping, eating, bathing or speaking to others – one conjoins the activity to *bodhichitta* and transmutes the endless round of action and reaction into a gradual process of emancipation. In healing oneself, one ministers to others without imposition or visible action.

This vast cycle of meditation reaches its conclusion in meditation upon right view, which centres on the knot of the personal ego. Meditation on the phenomenal ego – the sense of self as it is experienced from moment to moment – is limited and not ultimately helpful. One has to meditate upon the innate ego, the source of the phenomenal 'I'. It is the sense of self which persists through sleep, which abides in the heart and which reacts to blame and injustice against oneself. Once innate egoism is identified, one can use four keys to dispel its grip on consciousness. The first key is a careful analysis of how one perceives the innate 'I'. Although it seems to persist amidst changes in states of consciousness and external conditions, it is never wholly separated from the transient *skandhas* or aggregates – form, feeling, limited perception, conditioned activities and conditional consciousness. Recognizing the dependency of this 'I' upon the conditions it claims to stand beyond, one can negate it.

The second key requires logical clarity: either the innate ego is the same as or different from the five *skandhas*. Once one has clearly decided which option is exclusively true, one can use the last two keys. If one is convinced that the 'I' is the same as the *skandhas*, then one can use the third key which denies true sameness. If the innate ego is identical with the *skandhas*, then either there are five coexisting egos – one for each *skandha* – or the five *skandhas* are really a single unified aggregate. A little reflection will show that both alternatives are absurd. If, however, the 'I' is taken to be different from the aggregates, the fourth key is used to deny true diversity. If the 'I' is different from the *skandhas*, it should be analysable. Any one of the aggregates can be indirectly identified by removing the other four. Removal of all five should reveal the innate ego. But this cannot be done. The 'I' which claims to be independent and seems to be dependent is, in fact, non-existent. If one focusses on this truth in one-pointed meditation, the core delusion of a deep-seated personal ego will be dissolved gradually. From the standpoint of realization, one comes to recognize the unreality of all manifest existence; from the standpoint of perception, one beholds *shunyata,* the Void. When these two standpoints are held together in one-pointed meditation, one achieves the meditation of equipoise like space. Having gained that, *samsara* will appear as a magical illusion.

Although the cycle of meditation is undertaken by the aspirant to the Bodhisattvic Path on his own, he understands its stages through his *guru's* instruction. The magnificent panoply of symbols remains a sealed book to the disciple until his teacher opens it for him by explanations which fit the symbols to his particular nature. When he begins to assimilate what is gleaned in meditation, the invisible benediction of the *guru* guides him at every moment. This Presence reminds the disciple that the effort he puts forth is not for himself alone but for the sake of all sentient beings. As one's meditation draws to a close, one should offer all that has been accomplished to the welfare of living beings. Relying on the *guru's* grace and guidance, one gives all credit to him. The final dedication which brings the cycle of meditation to a close might be taken as the motto of the life of the Seventh Panchen Lama, who sought in harsh and hostile conditions to serve all beings with compassion and integrity:

> I dedicate the pure white virtue here accomplished
> That I might support the Dharma of teaching and
>     understanding,
> And fulfil all the wishes and deeds

Of the Buddhas and Bodhisattvas of past, present and future.

———

*Holding the body, head and neck erect, motionless and firm, gazing at the tip of his nose, without peering round about him;*

*With self serene, devoid of fear, firm in the vow of continence (brahmacharivrata), controlling the mind, with thought fixed on Me, he should sit yoked in devotion to Me as the Supreme.*

*Thus, ever yoked to the Supreme Self the yogin whose self is restrained from going outward attains to peace (shanti) abiding in Me, gaining the Supreme Bliss of nirvana.*

Shri Krishna
*Bhagavad Gita VI.13-15*

**OM**

*Hermes*, December 1986
Elton Hall

# ESOTERIC BUDDHISM

In consequence of a book with this title having been written by A. P. Sinnett, much controversy and inquiry has arisen, on the one hand, as to what Esoteric Buddhism is and on the other, as to whether there be any such thing.

The term as it has been used since the Theosophical Society began to be the means of bringing the sublime philosophies of the East before a large body of students, is held to refer to some hitherto hidden knowledge or explanation of the laws governing the evolution of the universe.

While there is in fact an Esoteric Buddhism, some other name for the book referred to might have been perhaps better, because the student speedily finds that there is no essential difference between Esoteric Buddhism and Esoteric Brahmanism, although as a matter of history, the Brahmans drove the Buddhists out of India several hundred years after the death of Buddha.

If the title selected had been "Esoteric Brahmanism," it would have done just as well.

## THE ESOTERIC DOCTRINE

In briefly considering the matter then, it must be understood that we are not confined solely to Buddhism but to what would be more properly called the "Esoteric doctrine," which underlies Brahmanism and Buddhism alike. And it should also be well understood that much that is now called "Esoteric" by us, has been long known in India and cannot therefore be properly said to be Esoteric.

Very much as the secret meaning of the Hebrew *Bible* has been plainly before the eyes of all in what is known among the rabbins as the Kabalah, so this Esoteric doctrine has been buried in the Indian scriptures for ages under many allegories, the key to which has been held by the Brahmans, the priests of India, and they, like the priests of other religions, have kept that key to themselves or thrown it away.

A very good illustration of this may be found in the story of Draupadi, who is said to have been the wife of all the five Pandu brothers at the same time, as related in the great epic poem of the Aryans, the *Mahabharata.* This is taken as proof by many prominent orientalists of the existence of polyandry in India at that period.

The key to the story is found in the Indian psychological system, which locates in the human body five vital centers. The union of these centers is in this system said to take place when a man has become completely master of himself and is called the marriage of Draupadi with the five Pandus, as those vital centers are the Pandus.

In the *Bhagavad-Gita,* translated by Edwin Arnold under the title of *The Song Celestial,* the entire doctrine called Esoteric Buddhism may be found; and this book is held in the highest esteem by both Brahmans and Buddhists. The reason why this doctrine has not been long ago apparent to us is because of the extremely narrow way in which all Indian psychology and philosophy has hitherto been regarded, with the aid of such eminent authority as Max Muller.

## A KEY TO ESOTERICISM EXISTS

It has been said above that the *Bhagavad-Gita* contains all of this Esoteric doctrine, but while such is the case it cannot be found in its entirety without the key. That key was deliberately suppressed at the time of the driving out of the Buddhists from India when the Pauranikas, or those who followed the ancient Puranas, were desirous of concealing the similarity between Buddhism and Brahmanism.

The missing key is said to be contained in a work three times as bulky as the *Mahabharata,* and to have been carried away by the Buddhist Initiates; and the tradition now claims that in Ceylon at the Kandy Temple is a copy. It is from this key that whatever is new in Mr. Sinnett's book has been taken, although it is improbable that he was aware of that fact.

## WHENCE THE UNIVERSE ?

Most orthodox Aryans believe that the universe came out of something, while a few say that it came out of nothing. The Esoteric doctrine reconciles these by saying that that *something is no thing*. The particular sect which holds to the coming out of nothing is known as the Madhyamika, and is not numerous.

The exoteric Indian philosophies, call the Universe, Brahma, consisting of (Sat) absolute existence, (Chit) absolute intelligence and (Ananda) absolute bliss, with two other divisions called (Nama) name and (Rupa) form.

The Esoteric doctrine does not content itself with a mere metaphysical juggling with these terms, but goes to the length of claiming to explain the method of universal evolution and the hidden things in nature. This of course includes declarations in regard to the state of the soul of man preceding birth and his condition and course after death.

## THE COURSE OF EVOLUTION

As to the course of evolution, it is said, as far as our solar system is concerned, that there are seven planets corresponding to a seven fold division of man's nature which are necessary to carry out the process. This earth is one of these and the other planets known to astronomy are not necessarily a part of that portion of the process so far given out.

In these this earth is the turning point where the soul of man begins its conscious career.

## HOW KARMA WORKS

Here, after having passed through all forms of animate and inanimate life he begins to come consciously under the operation of the law of Karma, which is a law demanding complete compensation for every act, word and thought, and which results in removing the idea of the possibility of a vicarious atonement; and here he is born over and over again, reaping in each life the exact results due to him from the life preceding, and being therefore at any one instant of time the exact product or resultant of all his previous lives and experiences. So that these two doctrines of Karma and Rebirth, are interwoven one with the other.

After death the real man – the ego – goes to what the Christians call Heaven, and which in the East is called Devachan. The words of the *Bhagavad-Gita* will best enunciate this. In Chapter VI, Arjuna asks,

> "Whither O Krishna , doth the man go after death, who although he be endowed with faith, hath not obtained perfection in his devotion?"

To which Krishna replied:

> "His destruction is found neither here nor in the world above. A man whose devotions have been broken off by death, *having enjoyed for an immensity of years the rewards of his virtues in the regions above,* is at length born again. . . . Being thus born again he resumes in his new body the same habit he had before acquired and the same advancement of the understanding and here he begins again his labor (where he left it off)."

## HEAVEN IS DEVACHAN BETWEEN REBIRTHS

This law applies to all, righteous or not, and the period of rest which is had in Devachan is the exact length of time the spiritual energy stored up in earth life will last. The length of time one stays in Devachan has been put by one or two English writers at fifteen hundred years, but this is erroneous, for the stay there depends in each particular instance upon the application of the immutable law to the facts of that case.

The Devachanic period is the great resting spell for all, and is one of the means provided by Nature for preventing a total degradation. During that state the Ego acquires some goodness for the next earth life, and when the Ego of a man who had before been extremely wicked is reborn, the new personality has to feel the consequences of all the evil done in that preceding life but comes to the task with the aid of the good influences of the rest in Devachan.

## "RACES" VIEWED THEOSOPHICALLY

The doctrine does not leave out of view the different races of men, but in this instance the word "races" must be extended in its meaning so that it includes not merely a few varieties, such as ethnologists now admit, but gathers several of those varieties into one class.

Those races were developed as man himself developed different senses and different uses for them, and as the necessity for each race ceased, that race gradually almost disappeared, leaving now on earth only a few examples of each. In this way each ego had to pass successively through all the great races with their offshoots and being in every case subject to the law that it could not pass on to any new race until the one to which it belonged had finished its course and become converted into another.

This law is capable of modification in the case of adepts – sometimes called Mahatmas – who by the use of another law are able to rise above the limitations to which the ordinary man is subject.

The different races come and go, according to this doctrine, for enormous periods of time and all forms of life and nature pass and repass, until the hour arrives when the universal dissolution takes place. This dissolution is called the end of the Manvantara, and the name for it is *Pralaya*.

## PRALAYA AND REBIRTH OF THE UNIVERSE

The succeeding chaotic period is known as the night of Brahma and is said to be as long as the Day, each lasting one thousand ages. When the night ends then all manifested nature begins again to appear as before, the evolutionary process commencing with nebulous matter or fire mist which cools gradually into various planets and stars where come forth forms of life.

Each world is held to be subject in its own small way to the law governing the outbreathing and inbreathing of the whole, just as man has his own pralaya each night in sleep and his great, or Maha pralaya, at death. So it follows that while in one solar system a minor pralaya had covered all with night, other systems might be perfecting their evolution, until the Maha pralaya when the whole manifested universe of Brahma comes to an end. From this follows the doctrine held by some Indian pandits, that Brahma containing potentially all manifested nature – or manifestable nature – *converts* itself into the Universe, and in no case creates anything but leaves all to be regularly evolved.

Much detail, very necessary for a proper understanding of the subject, has been omitted, but even from this inadequate view of only a portion of the Esoteric Doctrine, it will be seen that it is one which has a perfect scheme of evolution where both spirit and matter are given their proper places.

*Theosophical Forum*, October 1934
W.Q. Judge

# TIBETAN TEACHINGS

## A LONG-DELAYED PROMISE FULFILLED

*They who are on the summit of a mountain can see all men; in like manner they who are intelligent and free from sorrow are enabled to ascend above the paradise of the Gods; and when they there have seen the subjection of man to birth and death and the sorrows by which he is afflicted, they open the doors of the immortal.*

– From the *Tched-du brjod-pai tsoms* of the BKAH-HGYUR

In the January number of the *Theosophist* for 1882, we promised our readers the opinions of the Venerable Chohan-Lama – the chief of the Archive-registrars of the libraries containing manuscripts on esoteric doctrines belonging to the Ta-loï and Tashu-hlumpo Lamas Rim-boche of Tibet – on certain conclusions arrived at by the author of *Buddha and Early Buddhism*. Owing to the brotherly kindness of a disciple of the learned Chohan, than whom no one in Tibet is more deeply versed in the science of esoteric and exoteric Buddhism, we are now able to give a few of the doctrines which have a direct bearing on these conclusions. It is our firm belief that the learned Chohan's letters, and the notes accompanying them, could not arrive at a more opportune time. Besides the many and various misconceptions of our doctrines, we have more than once been taken severely to task by some of the most intelligent Spiritualists for misleading them as to the real attitude and belief of Hindus and Buddhists as to "spirits of the departed." Indeed, according to some Spiritualists "the Buddhist belief is permeated by the distinctive and peculiar note of modern Spiritualism, the presence and guardianship of departed spirits," and the Theosophists have been guilty of misrepresenting this belief. They have had the hardihood, for instance, to maintain 'that this "belief in the intervention of departed human spirits" was anathema maranatha in the East, whereas it is "in effect, a permeating principle of Buddhism."

What every Hindu, of whatever caste and education, thinks of the "intervention of departed spirits" is so well known throughout the length and breadth of India that it would be loss of time to repeat the oft-told tale. There are a few converts to modern Spiritualism, such as Babu Peary Chand Mittra, whose great personal purity of life would make such intercourse harmless for him, even were he not indifferent to physical phenomena, holding but to the purely spiritual, subjective side of such communion. But, if these be excepted, we boldly reassert what we have always maintained: that there is not a Hindu who does not loathe the very idea of the reappearance of a departed "spirit" whom he will ever regard as impure; and that with these exceptions no Hindu believes that, except in cases of suicide, or death by accident, any spirit but an evil one can return to earth. Therefore, leaving the Hindus out of the question, we will give the ideas of the Northern Buddhists on the subject, hoping to add those of the Southern Buddhists to them in good time. And, when we say "Buddhists," we do not include the innumerable heretical sects teeming throughout Japan and China who have lost every right to that appellation. With these we have nought to do. We think but of Buddhists of the Northern and Southern Churches – the Roman Catholics and the Protestants of Buddhism, so to say.

The subject which our learned Tibetan correspondent treats is based on a few direct questions offered by us with a humble request that they should be answered, and the following paragraphs from *Buddha and Early Buddhism*:

> "I have dwelt somewhat at length on this supernaturalism, because it is of the highest importance to our theme. Buddhism was plainly an elaborate apparatus to nullify the action of evil spirits by the aid of good spirits operating at their highest potentiality through the instrumentality of the corpse or a portion of the corpse of the chief aiding spirit. The Buddhist temple, the Buddhist rites, the Buddhist liturgy, all seem based on this one idea that a whole or portions of a dead body was necessary.

What were these assisting spirits? Every Buddhist, ancient or modern, would at once admit that a spirit that has not yet attained the Bodhi or spiritual awakenment cannot be a good spirit. It can do no good thing; more than that, it must do evil things.

"The answer of Northern Buddhism is that the good spirits are the Buddhas, the dead prophets. They come from certain 'fields of the Buddhas' " to commune with earth.

## Our learned Tibetan friend writes:

"Let me say at once that monks and laymen give the most ridiculously absurd digest of the Law of Faith, the popular beliefs of Tibet. The Capuchin Della Penna's account of the brotherhood of the 'Byang-tsiub' is simply absurd. Taking from the Bkah-hgyur and other books of the Tibetan laws some literal descriptions, he then embellishes them with his own interpretation. Thus he speaks of the fabled worlds of 'spirits,' where live the 'Lha, who are like gods'; adding that the Tibetans imagine 'these places to be in the air above a great mountain, about a hundred and sixty thousand leagues high and thirty-two thousand leagues in circuit; which is made up of four parts, being of crystal to the east, of the red ruby to the west, of gold to the north, and of the green precious stone – lapis lazuli – to the south. In these abodes of bliss they – the Lha – remain as long as they please, and then pass to the paradise of other worlds.'

"This description resembles far more – if my memory of the missionary-school-going period at Lahoula does not deceive me the 'new Jerusalem coming down from God out of heaven' in John's vision – that city which measured 'twelve thousand furlongs,' whose walls were of 'jasper,' the buildings of 'pure gold,' the foundations of the walls 'garnished with all manner of precious stones' and 'the twelve gates were twelve pearls' – than the city of the Jang-Chhub either in the Bkah-hgyur or in the ideas of the Tibetans. In the first place, the sacred canon of the Tibetans, the Bkah-hgyur and Bstan-hgyur, comprises one thousand seven hundred and seven distinct works – one thousand and eighty-three public and six hundred and twenty-four secret volumes –

the former being composed of three hundred and fifty and the latter of seventy-seven folio volumes.

"Could they even by chance have seen them, I can assure the theosophists that the contents of these volumes could never be understood by anyone who had not been given the key to their peculiar character, and to their hidden meaning.

"Every description of localities is figurative in our system; every name and word is purposely veiled; and a student, before he is given any further instruction, has to study the mode of deciphering, and then of comprehending and learning the equivalent secret term or synonym for nearly every word of our religious language. The Egyptian enchorial or hieratic system is child's play to the deciphering of our sacred puzzles. Even in those volumes to which the masses have access, every sentence has a dual meaning, one intended for the unlearned, and the other for those who have received the key to the records.

"If the efforts of such well-meaning, studious and conscientious men as the authors of *Buddhist Records of the Western World*, and *Buddha* and *Early Buddhism* – whose poetical hypotheses may be upset and contradicted, one by one, with the greatest ease – resulted in nought, verily then, the attempts of the predecessors and successors of the Abbés Huc, Gabet and others must prove a sorry failure; since the former have not and the latter have, an object to achieve in purposely disfiguring the unparalleled and glorious teachings of our blessed master, Shakya Thub-pa.

"In the *Theosophist* for October, 1881, a correspondent correctly informs the reader that Gautama the Buddha, the wise, 'insisted upon initiation being thrown open to all who were qualified.' This is true; such was the original design put for some time in practice by the great Sang-gyas, and before he had become the All-Wise. But three or four centuries after his separation from this earthly coil, when Asoka, the great supporter of our religion, had left the world, the Arhat initiates, owing to the secret but steady opposition of the Brâhmans to their system, had to drop out of the country one by one and seek safety beyond the Himalayas. Thus, though popular Buddhism did not spread in Tibet before the seventh century, the Buddhist initiates of the mysteries and esoteric system of the Aryan Twice-born, leaving their motherland, India, sought refuge with the pre-Buddhistic ascetics; those who had the Good Doctrine, even before the days of Shâkya-Muni. These ascetics had dwelt beyond the Himâlayan ranges from time immemorial. They are the direct successors of those Âryan sages who, instead of accompanying their Brâhman brothers in the pre-historical emigration from Lake Manasarovara across the Snowy Range into the hot plains of the Seven Rivers, had preferred to remain in their inaccessible and unknown fastnesses. No wonder, indeed, if the Âryan esoteric doctrine and our Arahat doctrines are found to be almost identical. Truth, like the sun over our heads, is one; but it seems as if this eternal truism must be constantly reiterated to make the dark, as much as the white, people remember it. Only that truth may be kept pure and unpolluted by human exaggerations – its very votaries betimes seeking to adapt it, to pervert and disfigure its fair face to their own selfish ends – it has to be hidden far away from the eye of the profane. Since the days of the earliest universal mysteries up to the time of our great Shâkya Tathâgata Buddha, who reduced and interpreted the system for the salvation of all, the divine Voice of the Self, known as Kwan-yin, was heard but in the sacred solitude of the preparatory mysteries.

"Our world-honoured Tsong-kha-pa closing his fifth Damngag reminds us that 'every sacred truth, which the ignorant are unable to comprehend under its true light, ought to be hidden within a triple casket concealing itself as the tortoise conceals his head within his shell; ought to show her face but to those who are desirous of obtaining the condition of Anuttara Samyak Sambodhi' – the most merciful and enlightened heart.

"There is a dual meaning, then, even in the canon thrown open to the people, and, quite recently, to Western scholars. I will now try to correct the errors – too intentional, I am sorry to say, in the case of the Jesuit writers. No doubt but that the Chinese and Tibetan Scriptures, so-called, the standard works of China and

Japan, some written by our most learned scholars, many of whom – as uninitiated though sincere and pious men – commented upon what they never rightly understood, contain a mass of mythological and legendary matter more fit for nursery folklore than an exposition of the Wisdom Religion as preached by the world's Saviour. But none of these are to be found in the canon; and, though preserved in most of the Lamasery libraries, they are read and implicitly believed in only by the credulous and pious whose simplicity forbids them ever stepping across the threshold of reality. To this class belong *The Buddhist Cosmos*, written by the Bonze Jin-ch'an, of Pekin; *The Shing-Tao-ki*, or 'The Records of the Enlightenment of Tathagata,' by Wang-Puh, in the seventh century, *The Hi-shai Sûtra*, or 'Book of Creation,' various volumes on heaven and hell, and so forth – poetic fictions grouped around a symbolism evolved as an after-thought.

"But the records from which our scholastic author, the monk Della Penna quotes – or I should rather say, misquotes – contain no fiction, but simply information for future generations, who may, by that time, have obtained the key to the right reading of them. The 'Lha' of whom Della Penna speaks but to deride the fable, they who 'have attained the position of saints in this world,' were simply the initiated Arhats, the adepts of many and various grades, generally known under the name of Bhanté or Brothers. In the book known as the *Avatamsaka Sûtra*, in the section on 'the Supreme Âtman – Self – as manifested in the character of the Arhats and Pratyeka Buddhas,' it is stated that 'Because from the beginning, all sentient creatures have confused the truth, and embraced the false; therefore has there come into existence a hidden knowledge called Alaya Vijnâna.' 'Who is in the possession of the true hidden knowledge?' 'The great teachers of the Snowy Mountain,' is the response in *The Book of Law*. The Snowy Mountain is the 'mountain a hundred and sixty thousand leagues high.' Let us see what this means. The last three ciphers being simply left out, we have a hundred and sixty leagues; a Tibetan league is nearly five miles; this gives us seven hundred and eighty miles from a certain holy spot, by a distinct road to the west. This becomes as clear as can be, even in Della Penna's further description, to one who has but a glimpse of the truth. 'According to their law,' says that monk, 'in the west of this world, is an eternal world, a paradise, and in it a saint called Ho-pahme, which means "Saint of Splendour and Infinite Light." This saint has many distinct "powers," who are all called "chang-chüb",' which – he adds in a footnote – means 'the spirits of those who, on account of their perfection, do not care to become saints, and train and instruct the bodies of the reborn Lamas, so that they may help the living.'

"This shows that these presumably dead 'chang-chubs' are living Bodhisatwas or Bhanté, known under various names among Tibetan people; among others, Lha or 'spirits,' as they are supposed to have an existence more in spirit than in flesh. At death they often renounce Nirvâna – the bliss of eternal rest, or oblivion of personality – to remain in their spiritualized astral selves for the good of their disciples and humanity in general.

"To some Theosophists, at least, my meaning must be clear, though some are sure to rebel against the explanation. Yet we maintain that there is no possibility of an entirely pure 'self' remaining in the terrestrial atmosphere after his liberation from the physical body, in his own personality, in which he moved upon earth. Only three exceptions are made to this rule:

"The holy motive prompting a Bodhisatwa, a Sravaka, or Rahat to help to the same bliss those who remain behind him, the living; in which case he will stop to instruct them either from within or without; or, secondly, those who, however pure, harmless and comparatively free from sin during their lives, have been so engrossed with some particular idea in connection with one of the human mâyâs as to pass away amidst that all-absorbing thought; and, thirdly, persons in whom an intense and holy love, such as that of a mother for her orphaned children, creates or generates an indomitable will fed by that boundless love to tarry with and among the living in their inner selves.

"The periods allotted for these exceptional cases vary. In the first case, owing to the knowledge acquired in his condition of

Anuttara Samyak Sambodhi – the most holy and enlightened heart – the Bodhisatwa has no fixed limit. Accustomed to remain for hours and days in his astral form during life, he has power after death to create around him his own conditions, calculated to check the natural tendency of the other principles to rejoin their respective elements, and can descend or even remain on earth for centuries and millenniums. In the second case, the period will last until the all-powerful magnetic attraction of the subject of the thought – intensely concentrated at the moment of death – becomes weakened and gradually fades out. In the third, the attraction is broken either by the death or the moral unworthiness of the loved ones. It cannot in either case last more than a lifetime.

"In all other cases of apparitions or communications by whatever mode, the 'spirit' will prove a wicked 'bhuta' or 'ro-lang' at best – the soulless shell of an 'elementary.' The 'Good Doctrine' is rejected on account of the unwarranted accusation that 'adepts' only claim the privilege of immortality. No such claim was ever brought forward by any eastern adept or initiate. Very true, our Masters teach us 'that immortality is conditional,' and that the chances of an adept who has become a proficient in the Alaya Vijñana, the acme of wisdom, are tenfold greater than those of one who, being ignorant of the potentialities centered within his Self, allows them to remain dormant and undisturbed until it is too late to awake them in this life. But the adept knows no more on earth, nor are his powers greater here than will be the knowledge and powers of the average good man when the latter reaches his fifth and especially his sixth cycle or round. Our present mankind is still in the fourth of the seven great cyclic rounds. Humanity is a baby hardly out of its swaddling clothes, and the highest adept of the present age knows less than he will know as a child in the seventh round. And as mankind is an infant collectively, so is man in his present development individually. As it is hardly to be expected that a young child, however precocious, should remember his existence from the hour of his birth, day by day, with the various experiences of each, and the various clothes he was made to wear on each of them, so no 'self,' unless that of an adept having reached Samma-Sambuddha – during which an illuminate sees the long series of his past lives throughout all his previous births in other worlds – was ever able to recall the distinct and various lives he passed through But that time must come one day. Unless a man is an irretrievable sensualist, dooming himself thereby to utter annihilation after one of such sinful lives, that day will dawn when, having reached the state of absolute freedom from any sin or desire, he will see and recall to memory all his past lives as easily as a man of our age turns back and passes in review, one by one, every day of his existence."

We may add a word or two in explanation of a previous passage, referring to Kwan-yin. This divine power was finally anthropomorphized by the Chinese Buddhist ritualists into a distinct double-sexed deity with a thousand hands and a thousand eyes, and called Kwan-shai-yin Bodhisatwa, the Voice-Deity, but in reality meaning the voice of the ever-present latent divine consciousness in man; the voice of his real Self, which can be fully evoked and heard only through great moral purity. Hence Kwanyin is said to be the son of Amitabha Buddha, who generated that Saviour, the merciful Bodhisatwa, the "Voice" or the "Word" that is universally diffused, the "Sound" which is eternal. It has the same mystical meaning as the Vâch of the Brâhmans. While the Brahmans maintain the eternity of the Vedas from the eternity of "sound," the Buddhists claim by synthesis the eternity of Amitabhâ, since he was the first to prove the eternity of the Self-born, Kwan-yin. Kwan-yin is the Vâchîshvara or Voice-Deity of the Brahmans. Both proceed from the same origin as the Logos of the neo-platonic Greeks; the "manifested deity" and its "voice" being found in man's Self, his conscience; Self being the unseen Father, and the "voice of Self" the Son; each being the relative and the correlative of the other. Both Vâchîshvara and Kwan-yin had, and still have, a prominent part in the Initiation Rites and Mysteries in the Brâhmanical and Buddhist esoteric doctrines.

We may also point out that Bodhisatwas or Rahats need not be adepts; still less, Brâhmans, Buddhists, or even "Asiatics," but simply holy and pure men of any nation or faith, bent all their lives on doing good to humanity.

## DOCTRINES OF THE HOLY "LHA"

"The forms under which any living being may be reborn, are six-fold. The highest class are the Lha, 'spirits, highest beings, gods'; they rank next to the Buddhas, and inhabit the six celestial regions. Two of these regions belong to the earth; but the four others, which are considered as superior mansions, lie in the atmosphere, far beyond the earth."

"As a consequence of premature decease, the 'Bardo' is prolongated. This is the middle state between the death and the new rebirth, which does not follow immediately, but there exists an interval which is shorter for the good than for the bad." (Emil Schlagintweit, *Buddhism in Tibet*.)

The notes that follow are compiled. or rather translated, as closely as the idiomatic difficulties would permit, from Tibetan letters and manuscripts, sent in answer to several questions regarding the western misconceptions of Northern Buddhism or Lamaism. The information comes from a Gelung of the Inner Temple – a disciple of Bas-pa Dharma, the Secret Doctrine.

"Brothers residing in Gya-P-heling – British India – having respectfully called my master's attention to certain incorrect and misleading statements about the Good Doctrine of our blessed Phag-pa Sang-gyas – most Holy Buddha – as alleged to be carried on in Bhod-Yul, the land of Tibet, I am commanded by the revered Ngag-pa to answer them. I will do so, as far as our rules will permit me to discuss so sacred a subject openly. I can do no more, since, till the day when our Pban-chhen-rin-po-chhe shall be reborn in the lands of the P-helings – foreigners – and, appearing as the great Chom-dën-da, the conqueror, shall destroy with his mighty hand the errors and ignorance of ages, it will be of little, if of any use to try to uproot these misconceptions."

A prophecy of Tsong-ka-pa is current in Tibet to the effect that the true doctrine will be maintained in its purity only so long as

Tibet is kept free from the incursions of western nations, whose crude ideas of fundamental truth would inevitably confuse and obscure the followers of the Good Law. But, when the western world is more ripe in the direction of philosophy, the incarnation of Pban-chhen-rin-po-chhe – the Great Jewel of Wisdom – one of the Teshu Lamas, will take place, and the splendour of truth will then illuminate the whole world. We have here the true key to Tibetan exclusiveness.

Our correspondent continues:

> "Out of the many erroneous views presented to the consideration of our master, I have his permission to treat the following: first, the error generally current among the Ro-lang-pa – spiritualists – that those who follow the Good Doctrine have intercourse with, and reverence for, Ro-lang-ghosts – or the apparitions of dead men; and, secondly, that the Bhanté – Brothers – or 'Lha,' popularly so-called – are either disembodied spirits or gods."

The first error is found in *Buddha and Early Buddhism*, since this work has given rise to the incorrect notion that spiritualism was at the very root of Buddhism. The second error is found in the *Succinct Abstract of the Great Chaos of Tibetan Laws* by the Capuchin monk Della Penna and the accounts given by his companions, whose absurd calumnies of Tibetan religion and laws written during the past century have been lately reprinted in Mr. Markham's *Tibet*.

> "I will begin with the former error," writes our correspondent. "Neither the Southern nor Northern Buddhists, whether of Ceylon, Tibet, Japan or China, accept western ideas as to the capabilities and qualifications of the 'naked souls.'

> "For we deprecate unqualifiedly and absolutely all ignorant intercourse with the Ro-lang. For what are they who return? What kind of creatures are they who can communicate at will objectively or by physical manifestation? They are impure, grossly sinful souls, 'a-tsa-ras'; suicides; and such as have come to

premature deaths by accident and must linger in the earth's atmosphere until the full; expiration of their natural term of life.

"No right-minded person, whether Lama or Chhipa – non-Buddhist – will venture to defend the practice of necromancy, which, by a natural instinct has been condemned in all the great Dharmas – laws or religions – and intercourse with, and using the powers of these earth-bound souls is simply necromancy.

"Now the beings included in the second and third classes – suicides and victims of accident – have not completed their natural term of life; and, as a consequence, though not of necessity mischievous, are earth-bound. The prematurely expelled soul is in an unnatural state; the original impulse under which the being was evolved and cast into the earth-life has not expended itself – the necessary cycle has not been completed, but must nevertheless be fulfilled.

"Yet, though earth-bound, these unfortunate beings, victims whether voluntary or involuntary, are only suspended, as it were, in the earth's magnetic attraction. They are not, like the first class, attracted to the living from a savage thirst to feed on their vitality. Their only impulse – and a blind one, since they are generally in a dazed or stunned condition – is, to get into the whirl of rebirth as soon as possible. Their state is that we call a false Bar-do – the period between two incarnations. According to the karma of the being – which is affected by his age and merits in the last birth – this interval will be longer or shorter.

"Nothing but some overpoweringly intense attraction, such as a holy love for some dear one in great peril, can draw them with their consent to the living; but by the mesmeric power of a Ba-po, a necromancer – the word is used advisedly, since the necromantic spell is Dzu-tul, or what you term a mesmeric attraction – can force them into our presence. This evocation, however, is totally condemned by those who hold to the Good Doctrine; for the soul thus evoked is made to suffer exceedingly, even though it is not itself but only its image that has been torn or stripped from itself to become the apparition; owing to its premature separation by violence from the body, the 'jang-khog' – animal soul – is yet heavily loaded with material particles – there has not been a natural disintegration of the coarser from the finer molecules – and the necromancer, in compelling this separation artificially, makes it, we might almost say, to suffer as one of us might if he were flayed alive.

"Thus, to evoke the first class – the grossly sinful souls – is dangerous for the living; to compel the apparition of the second and third classes is cruel beyond expression to the dead.

"In the case of one who died a natural death totally different conditions exist; the soul is almost, and in the case of great purity, entirely beyond the necromancer's reach; hence beyond that of a circle of evokers, or spiritualists, who, unconsciously to themselves, practise a veritable necromancer's Sang-nyag, or magnetic incantation. According to the karma of the previous birth the interval of latency – generally passed in a state of stupor – will last from a few minutes to an average of a few weeks, perhaps months. During that time the 'jang-khog' – animal soul – prepares in solemn repose for its translation, whether into a higher sphere – if it has reached its seventh human local evolution – or for a higher rebirth, if it has not yet run the last local round.

"At all events it has neither will nor power at that time to give any thought to the living. But after its period of latency is over, and the new self enters in full consciousness the blessed region of Devachan – when all earthly mists have been dispersed, and the scenes and relations of the past life come clearly before its spiritual sight – then it may, and does occasionally, when espying all it loved, and that loved it upon earth, draw up to it for communion and by the sole attraction of love, the spirits of the living, who, when returned to their normal condition, imagine that it has descended to them.

"Therefore we differ radically from the western Ro-lang-pa – spiritualists – as to what they see or communicate with in their circles and through their unconscious necromancy. We say it is but the physical dregs, or spiritless remains of the late being; that which has been exuded, cast off and left behind when its finer particles passed onward into the great Beyond.

"In it linger some fragments of memory and intellect. It certainly was once a part of the being, and so possesses that modicum of interest; but it is not the being in reality and truth. Formed of matter, however etherealized, it must sooner or later be drawn away into vortices where the conditions for its atomic disintegration exist.

"From the dead body the other principles ooze out together. A few hours later the second principle – that of life – is totally extinct, and separates from both the human and ethereal envelopes. The third – the vital double – finally dissipates when the last particles of the body disintegrate. There now remain the fourth, fifth, sixth and seventh principles: the body of will; the human soul; the spiritual soul, and pure spirit, which is a facet of the Eternal. The last two, joined to, or separated from, the personal self, form the everlasting individuality and cannot perish. The remainder proceeds to the state of gestation – the astral self and whatever survived in it of the will, previous to the dissolution of the physical body.

"Hence for any conscious action in this state are required the qualifications of an adept, or an intense, undying, ardent and holy love for someone whom the deceased leaves behind him on earth; as otherwise the astral ego either becomes a 'bhûta' – 'ro-lang' in Tibetan – or proceeds to its further transmigrations in higher spheres.

"In the former case the Lha, or 'man-spirit,' can sojourn among the living for an indefinite time, at his own pleasure; in the latter the so-called 'spirit' will tarry and delay his final translation but for a short period; the body of desire being held compact, in proportion to the intensity of the love felt by the soul and its unwillingness to part with the loved ones.

"At the first relaxation of the will it will disperse, and the spiritual self, temporarily losing its personality and all remembrance of it, ascends to higher regions. Such is the teaching.

None can overshadow mortals but the elect, the 'Accomplished,' the 'Byang-tsiub,' or the 'Bodhisatwas' alone – they who have penetrated the great secret of life and death – as they are able to prolong, at will their stay on earth after 'dying.' Rendered into the vulgar phraseology, such overshadowing is to 'be born again and again' for the benefit of mankind."

If the spiritualists, instead of conferring *the* power of "controlling" and "guiding" living persons upon every wraith calling itself "John" or "Peter," limited the faculty of moving and inspiring a few chosen pure men and women only to such Bodhisatwas or holy initiates – whether born as Buddhists or Christians, Brahmans or Mussulmans on earth – and, in very exceptional cases, to holy and saintly characters, who have a motive, a truly beneficial mission to accomplish after their departure, then would they be nearer to the truth than they are now.

To ascribe the sacred privilege, as they do, to every "elementary" and "elemental" masquerading in borrowed plumes and putting in an appearance for no better reason than to say: "How d'ye do, Mr. Snooks?" and to drink tea and eat toast, is a sacrilege and a sad sight to him who has any intuitional feeling about the awful sacredness of the mystery of physical translation, let alone the teaching of the adepts.

Further on Della Penna writes:

" 'These chang-chüb – the disciples of the chief saint – have not yet become saints, but they possess in the highest degree five virtues – charity, both temporal and spiritual, perfect observance of law, great patience, great diligence in working to perfection, and the most sublime contemplation.' "

We would like to know how they could have all these qualities, especially the latter – trance – were they physically dead!

"These chang-chüb have finished their course and are exempt from further transmigrations; passing from the body of one Lama to that of another; but the Lama {meaning the Dalai-Lama} is always endowed with the soul of the same chang-chüb, although he may be in other bodies for the benefit of the living to teach them the Law, which is the object of their not wishing to become saints, because then they would not be able to instruct them. Being moved by compassion and pity they wish to remain chang-chüb to instruct the living in the Law, so as to make them finish quickly the laborious course of their transmigrations. Moreover, if these chang-chüb wish, they are at liberty to transmigrate into this or other worlds, and at the same time they transmigrate into other places with the same object.

"This rather confused description yields from its inner sense two facts: first, that the Buddhist Tibetans – we speak of the educated classes – do not believe in the return of the departed spirits, since, unless a soul becomes so purified upon earth as to create for itself a state of Bodhisat-hood – the highest degree of perfection next to Buddha – even saints in the ordinary acceptation of the term would not be able to instruct or control the living after their death; and, secondly, that, rejecting as they do the theories of creation, God, soul – in its Christian and spiritualistic sense – and a future life for the personality of the deceased, they yet credit man with such a potentiality of will, that it depends on him to become a Bodhisatwa and acquire the power to regulate his future existences, whether in a physical or in a semi-material shape.

"Lamaists believe in the indestructibility of matter, as an element. They reject the immortality, and even the survival of the *personal* self, teaching that the *individual* self alone – *i.e.*, the collective aggregation of the many personal selves that were represented by that One during the long series of various existences – may survive. The latter may even become eternal – the word eternity with them embracing but the period of a great cycle – eternal in its integral individuality, but this may be done only by becoming a Dhyan-Chohan, a 'celestial Buddha,' or what a Christian Kabbalist might call a 'planetary spirit' or one of the Elohim; a part of the 'conscious whole,' composed of the aggregate intelligences in their universal collectivity, while Nirvâna is the 'unconscious whole.' He who becomes a Tong-pa-nyi – he who has attained the state of absolute freedom from any desire of living personally, the highest condition of a saint – exists in non-existence and can benefit mortals no more. He is in 'Nipang' for he has reached the end of 'Thar-lam,' the path to deliverance, or salvation from transmigrations. He cannot perform Tul-pa – voluntary incarnation, whether temporary or life-long – in the body of a living human being; for he is a 'Dang-ma,' an absolutely purified soul. Henceforth he is free from the danger of 'Dal-jor,' human rebirth; for the seven forms of existence – only six are given out to the uninitiated – subject to transmigration have been safely crossed by him. 'He gazes with indifference in every sphere of upward transmigration on the whole period of time which covers the shorter periods of personal existence,' says the *Book of Khiu-ti.*

"But, as 'there is more courage to accept being than non-being, life than death,' there are those among the Bodhisatwas and the Lha – 'and as rare as the flower of udambara are they to meet with' – who voluntarily relinquish the blessing of the attainment of perfect freedom, and remain in their personal selves, whether in forms visible or invisible to mortal sight – to teach and help their weaker brothers.

"Some of them prolong their life on earth – though not to any supernatural limit; others become 'Dhyan-Chohans,' a class of the planetary spirits or 'devas' who, becoming, so to say, the guardian angels of men, are the only class out of the seven-classed hierarchy of spirits in our system who preserve their personality. These holy Lha, instead of reaping the fruit of their deeds, sacrifice themselves in the invisible world as the lord Sang-gyas – Buddha – did on this earth, and remain in Devachan – the world of bliss nearest to the earth."

*Lucifer*, September, October, 1894
H. P. Blavatsky

# REINCARNATIONS IN TIBET

So little is known by Europeans of what is going on in Tibet, and even in the more accessible Bhootan, that an Anglo-Indian paper – one of those which pretend to know, and certainly discuss every blessed subject, whether they really know anything of it or not – actually came out with the following bit of valuable information:

> It may not be generally known that the Deb Raja of Bhootan, who died in June last, but whose decease has been kept dark till the present moment, probably to prevent disturbances, is our old and successful opponent of 1864-65 . . . .

> *The Bhootan Government consists of a spiritual chief, called the Dhurm Raja, an incarnation of Buddha (?!!) who never dies* – and a civil ruler called the Deb Raja in whom is supposed to centre all authority.

A more ignorant assertion could hardly have been made. It may be argued that "Christian" writers believe even less in Buddha's reincarnations than the Buddhists of Ceylon, and, therefore, trouble themselves very little, whether or not they are accurate in their statements. But, in such a case, why touch a subject at all? Large sums are annually spent by Governments to secure old Asiatic manuscripts and learn the truth about old religions and peoples, and it is not showing respect for either science or truth to mislead people interested in them by a flippant and contemptuous treatment of facts.

On the authority of direct information received at our Headquarters, we will try to give a more correct view of the situation than has hitherto been had from books. Our informants are firstly – some very learned lamas; secondly – a European gentleman and traveller, who prefers not to give his name; and thirdly – a highly educated young Chinaman, brought up in America, who has since preferred to the luxuries of worldly life and the pleasures of Western civilization, the comparative privations of a religious and contemplative life in Tibet. Both of the two last-named gentlemen are Fellows of our Society, and the latter – our "Celestial" Brother – losing, moreover, no opportunity of corresponding with us. A message from him has been just received *via* Darjeeling.

In the present article, it is not much that we will have to say. Beyond contradicting the queer notion of the Bhootanese Dharma Raja being "an incarnation of Buddha," we will only point out a few absurdities, in which some prejudiced writers have indulged.

It certainly was never known – least of all in Tibet – that the spiritual chief of the Bhootanese was "an incarnation of Buddha, who never dies." The "Dug-pa[1] or Red Caps" belong to the old Nyang-na-pa sect, who resisted the religious reform introduced by Tsong-kha-pa between the latter part of the fourteenth and the beginning of the fifteenth centuries. It was only after a lama coming to them from Tibet in the tenth century had converted them from the old Buddhist faith so strongly mixed up with the Bhon practices of the aborigines – into the Shammar sect, that, in opposition to the reformed "Gyelukpas," the Bhootanese set up a regular system of reincarnations. It is not Buddha though, or "Sang-gyas" – as he is called by the Tibetans. who incarnates himself in the Dharma Raja, but quite another personage, one of whom we will speak about later on.

Now what do the Orientalists know of Tibet, its civil administration, and especially its religion and its rites? That, which they have learned from the contradictory, and in every case imperfect statements of a few Roman Catholic monks, and of two or three daring lay travellers, who, ignorant of the language, could scarcely be expected to give us even a bird's-eye view of the

---

[1] The term "*Dug-pa*" in Tibet is deprecatory. They themselves pronounce it "Dûg-pa" from the root to "bind" (religious binders to the old faith): while the paramount sect – the Gyeluk-pa (yellow caps) – and the people, use the word in the sense of "Dug-pa" *mischief*-makers, *sorcerers*. The Bhootanese are generally called Dug-pa throughout Tibet and even in some parts of Northern India. – ED.

country. The missionaries, who introduced themselves in 1719, stealthily into Lhassa,[2] were suffered to remain there but a short time and were finally forcibly expelled from Tibet. The letters of the Jesuits – Desideri, and Johann Grueber, and especially that of Fra della Penna, teem with the greatest absurdities.[3] Certainly as superstitious, and apparently far more so than the ignorant Tibetans themselves, on whom they father every iniquity, one has but to read these letters to recognize in them that spirit of *odium theologicum* felt by every Christian, and especially Catholic missionary for the "heathen" and their creeds; a spirit which blinds one entirely to the sense of justice. And when could have been found any better opportunity to ventilate their monkish ill-humour and vindictiveness than in the matter of Tibet, the very land of mystery, mysticism and seclusion? Beside these few prejudiced "historians," but five more men of Europe ever stepped into Tibet. Of these, three – Bogle, Hamilton and Turner – penetrated no farther than its borderlands; Manning – the only European who is known to have set his foot into Lhassa[4] – died without revealing its secrets, for reasons suspected, though never admitted, by his only surviving nephew – a clergyman; and Csaimo de Korais, who never went beyond Zanskar, and the lamasery of Phag-dal.[5]

---

[2] Out of twelve Capuchin friars who, under the leadership of Father della Penna, established a mission at Lhassa, nine died shortly after, and only three returned home to tell the tale. (See *Tibet*, by Mr. Clements R. Markham.)

[3] See Appendix to *Narratives of the Mission of George Bogle to Tibet*. By Clements R. Markham, C. B., F. R. S., Træbner & Co., I London. – ED.

[4] We speak of the present century. It is very dubious whether the two missionaries Huc and Gabet ever entered Lhassa. The Lamas deny it. – ED.

[5] We are well aware that the name is generally written *Pugdal*, but it is erroneous to do so. "Pugdal" means nothing, and the Tibetans do not give meaningless names to their sacred buildings. We do not know how Csaimo de Korais spells it, but, as in the case of *Pho-ta-la* of Lhassa loosely spelt "Potala" – the lamasery of Phaug-dal derives its name from Phaug-pa (Phag – eminent in holiness, Buddha-like, spiritual; and *pha-man*, father) the title of "Awalokiteswara," the Boddhisatwa who incarnates himself in

The regular system of the Lamaistic incarnations of "Sang-gyas" (or Buddha) began with Tsong-kha-pa. This reformer is not the incarnation of one of the five celestial Dhyans, or heavenly Buddhas, as is generally supposed, said to have been created by Sakya Muni after he had risen to Nirvana, but that of "Amita," one of the Chinese names for Buddha. The records preserved in the Gôn-pa (lamasery) of "Tda-shi Hlum-po" (spelt by the English *Teshu Lumbo*) show that Sang-gyas incarnated himself in Tsongkha-pa in consequence of the great degradation his doctrines had fallen into. Until then, there had been no other incarnations than those of the five celestial Buddhas and of their Boddhisatwas, each of the former having created (read, overshadowed with his spiritual wisdom) five of the last-named – there were, and now are in all but thirty incarnations – five Dhyans and twenty-five Boddhisatwas. It was because, among many other reforms, Tsong- kha-pa forbade necromancy (which is practiced to this day with the most disgusting rites, by the Bhons – the aborigines of Tibet – with whom the Red Caps, or Shammars, had always fraternized), that the latter resisted his authority. This act was followed by a split between the two sects. Separating entirely from the Gyelukpas, the Dugpas (Red Caps) – from the first in a great minority – settled in various parts of Tibet, chiefly its borderlands, and principally in Nepaul and Bhootan. But, while they retained a sort of independence at the monastery of Sakia-Djong, the Tibetan residence of their spiritual (?) chief Gong-sso Rimbo-chay, the Bhootanese have been from their beginning the tributaries and vassals of the Dalai-Lamas. In his letter to Warren Hastings in 1774, the Tda-shi Lama, who calls the Bhootans "a rude and ignorant race," whose "Deb Rajah is dependent upon the Dalai-Lama," omits to say that they are also the tributaries of his own State and have been now for over three centuries and a half. The Tda-shi Lamas were always more

---

the Dalai Lama of Lhassa. The valley of the Ganges where Buddha preached and lived, is also called "Phaug-yul," the holy, spiritual land; the word *phag* coming from the one root – Phau or Phâ being the corruption of Fo – (or Buddha) as the Tibetan alphabet contains no letter F. – ED.

powerful and more highly considered than the Dalai-Lamas. The latter are the creation of the Tda-shi Lama, Nabang-Lob-Sang, the sixth incarnation of Tsong-kha-pa – himself an incarnation of Amitabha, or Buddha. This hierarchy was regularly installed at Lhassa, but it originated only in the latter half of the seventeenth century.[6]

In Mr. C. R. Markham's highly interesting work above noticed, the author has gathered every scrap of information that was ever brought to Europe about that *terra incognita*. It contains one passage, which, to our mind, sums up in a few words the erroneous views taken by the Orientalists of Lamaism in general, and of its system of perpetual reincarnation especially. "It was, indeed," it reads, "at about the period of Hiuen-Thsang's journey, that Buddhism first began to find its way into Tibet, both from the direction of China and that of India; but it came in a very different form from that in which it reached Ceylon several centuries earlier. Traditions, metaphysical speculations, and new dogmas, had overlaid the original Scriptures with an enormous collection *of* more recent revelation. Thus Tibet received a vast body of truth, and could only assimilate a portion for the establishment of popular belief. Since the original Scriptures had been conveyed into Ceylon by the son of Asoka, it had been revealed to the devout Buddhists of India that their Lord had created the five Dhyani or celestial Buddhas, and that each of these had created five Boddhisatwas, or beings in the course of attaining Buddha-hood. The Tibetans took

---

[6] Says Mr. Markham in *Tibet* Ap. XVII *Preface*): "Gedun-tubpa, another great reformer, was contemporary with Tsong-kha-pa, having been born in 1339, and dying in 1474" (having thus lived 135 years). He built the monastery at Teshu Lumbo (Tda-shi Hlum-po) in 1445, and it was in the person of this perfect Lama, as he was called, that the system of perpetual incarnation commenced. He was himself the incarnation of Boddhisatwa Padma Pani and on his death he relinquished the attainment of Buddhahood that he might be born again and again for the benefit of mankind. . . . When he died, his successor was found as an infant by the possession of certain divine marks.

firm hold of this phase of the Buddhistic creed, and their distinctive belief is that the Boddhisatwas continue to remain in existence for the good of mankind by passing through a succession of human beings from the cradle to the grave. This characteristic of their faith was gradually developed, and it was long before it received its present form;[7]  but the succession of incarnate Boddhisatwas was the idea towards which the Tibetan mind tended from the first." At the same time, as Max Müller says: "The most important element of the Buddhist reform has always been its social and moral code, not its metaphysical theories. That moral code, taken by itself, is one of the most perfect which the world has ever known; and it was this blessing that the introduction of Buddhism brought into Tibet." (p. XIV, *Introduction*.)

The "blessing" has remained and spread all over the country, there being no kinder, purer-minded, more simple or sin-fearing nation than the Tibetans, missionary slanders notwithstanding.[8] But

---

[7] Its "present" is its *earliest* form, as we will try to show further on. A correct analysis of any religion viewed but from its popular aspect, becomes impossible – least of all Lamaism, or esoteric Buddhism as disfigured by the untutored imaginative fervour of the populace. There is a vaster difference between the "Lamaism" of the learned classes of the clergy and the ignorant masses of their parishioners, than there is between the Christianity of a Bishop Berkeley and that of a modern Irish peasant. Hitherto Orientalists have made themselves superficially acquainted but with the beliefs and rites of popular Buddhism in Tibet, chiefly through the distorting glasses of missionaries which throw out of focus every religion but their own. The same course has been followed in respect to Sinhalese Buddhism, the missionaries having, as Col. Olcott observes in the too brief Preface to his *Buddhist Catechism*, for many years been taunting the Sinhalese with the "puerility and absurdity of their religion" when, in point of fact, what they speak of is not orthodox Buddhism at all. Buddhist folklore and fairy stories are the accretions of twenty-six centuries. – ED.

[8] The reader has but to compare in Mr. Markham's *Tibet* the warm, impartial and frank praises bestowed by Bogle and Turner on the Tibetan character and moral standing and the enthusiastic eulogies of Thomas

yet, for all that, the popular Lamaism, when compared with the real esoteric, or Arahat Buddhism of Tibet, offers a contrast as great as the snow trodden along a road in the valley, to the pure and undefiled mass which glitters on the top of a high mountain peak.[9] A few of such mistaken notions about the latter, we will now endeavour to correct as far as it is compatible to do so.

Before it can be clearly shown how the Bhootanese were forcibly brought into subjection, and their Dharma Raja made to accept the "incarnations" only after these had been examined into, and recognized at Lhassa, we have to throw a retrospective glance at the state of the Tibetan religion during the seven centuries which preceded the reform. As said before, a Lama had come to Bhootan from Kam – that province which had always been the stronghold and the hot-bed of the "Shammar" or Bhon rites[10] – between the ninth and tenth centuries, and had converted them into what he called Buddhism. But in those days, the pure religion of Sakya Muni had already commenced degenerating into that Lamaism, or

---

Manning to the address of the Dalai-Lama and his people, with the three letters of the three Jesuits in the *Appendix*, to enable himself to form a decisive opinion. While the former three gentlemen, impartial narrators, having no object to distort truth, hardly find sufficient adjectives to express their satisfaction with the Tibetans, the three "men of God" pick no better terms for the Dalai-Lamas and the Tibetans than "their devilish *God the Father*" . . . "*vindictive* devils" . . . "fiends who know how to dissemble," who are "cowardly, arrogant, and proud" . . . "dirty and immoral," &c.,& c., &c., all in the same strain for the sake of truth and Christian charity! – ED.

[9] As Father Desideri has it in one of his very few correct remarks about the lamas of Tibet, "though many may know how to read their mysterious books, not one can explain them" – an observation by-the-bye, which might be applied with as much justice to the Christian as to the Tibetan clergy. (See App. *Tibet* p. 306). – ED.

[10] The Shammar sect is not, as wrongly supposed, a kind of corrupted Buddhism, but an offshoot of the Bhon religion – itself a degenerated remnant of the Chaldean mysteries of old, now a religion entirely based upon necromancy, sorcery and sooth-saying. The introduction of Buddha's name in it means nothing. – ED.

rather fetichism, against which four centuries later, Tsong-kha-pa arose with all his might. Though three centuries had only passed since Tibet had been converted (with the exception of a handful of Shammars and Bhons), yet esoteric Buddhism had crept far earlier into the country. It had begun superseding the ancient popular rites ever since the time when the Brahmins of India, getting again the upper hand over Asoka's Buddhism, were silently preparing to oppose it, an opposition which culminated in their finally and entirely driving the new faith out of the country. The brotherhood or community of the ascetics known as the *Byangtsiub* – the "Accomplished" and the "Perfect" – existed before Buddhism spread in Tibet, and was known, and so mentioned in the pre-Buddhistic books of China as the fraternity of the "great teachers of the snowy mountains."

Buddhism was introduced into Bod-yul in the beginning of the seventh century by a pious Chinese Princess, who had married a Tibetan King,[11] who was converted by her from the Bhon religion into Buddhism, and had become since then a pillar of the faith in Tibet, as Asoka had been nine centuries earlier in India. It was he who sent his minister – according to European Orientalists: his own brother, the first Lama in the country – according to Tibetan historical records – to India. This brother minister returned "with the great body of truth contained in the Buddhist canonical Scriptures; framed the Tibetan alphabet from the Devanagri of India, and commenced the translation of the canon from Sanskrit – which had previously been translated from Pali, the old language of Magadha – into the language of the country." (See Markham's *Tibet*.)[12]

---

[11] A widely spread tradition tells us that after ten years of married life, with her husband's consent she renounced it, and in the garb of a nun – a *Ghelung-ma*, or "Ani," she preached Buddhism all over the country, as, several centuries earlier, the Princess Sanghamitta, Asoka's daughter, had preached it in India and Ceylon. – ED.

[12] But, what he does not say (for none of the writers, he derives his information from, knew it) is that this Princess is the one, who is believed

Under the old rule and before the reformation, the high Lamas, were often permitted to marry, *so as to incarnate themselves in their own direct descendants* – a custom which Tsong-kha-pa abolished, strictly enjoining celibacy on the Lamas. The Lama Enlightener of Bhootan had a son whom he had brought with him. In this son's first male child born after his death the Lama had promised the people to reincarnate himself. About a year after the event – so goes the religious legend – the son was blessed by his Bhootanese wife with triplets, all the three boys! Under this embarrassing circumstance, which would have floored any other casuists, the Asiatic metaphysical acuteness was fully exhibited. The spirit of the deceased Lama – the people were told – incarnated himself in all the three boys. One had his *Om*, the other his *Han*, the third – his *Hoong*. Or, (Sanskrit): *Buddha* – divine mind, *Dharma* – matter or animal soul, and *Sangha* – the union of the former two in our phenomenal world. It is this pure Buddhist tenet which was degraded by the cunning Bhootanese clergy to serve the better their ends. Thus their first Lama became a *triple* incarnation, three Lamas, one of whom – they say – got his "body," the other, his "heart" and the third, his "word" or wisdom. This hierarchy lasted with power undivided until the fifteenth century, when a Lama named Duk-pa Shab-tung, who had been defeated by the Gyelukpas of Gay-don Toob-pa,[13] invaded Bhootan at the head of his army of monks. Conquering the whole country, he proclaimed himself their first Dharma Raja, or Lama Rimbochay – thus starting a third "Gem" in opposition to the two Gyelukpa "Gems." But this

---

to have reincarnated herself since then in a succession of female Lamas or Rim-ani – precious nuns. Durjiay Pan-mo of whom Bogle speaks – his Tda-shi Lama's half-sister – and the superior of the nunnery on the Lake Yam-dog-ccho or Piate-Lake, was one of such reincarnations. – ED.

[13] The builder and founder of Tda-shi Hlum-po (Teshu-lumbo) in 1445: called the "Perfect Lama," or Panchhen – the precious jewel from the words – *Pan-chhen* great teacher, and "Rim-bochay" priceless jewel. While the Dalai-Lama is only Gyalba Rim bochay, or "gem of kingly majesty," the Tda-shi Lama of Tzi-gadze is Panchhen Rimbochay or the *Gem of Wisdom and Learning.* – ED.

"Gem" never rose to the eminence of a Majesty, least of all was he ever considered a "Gem of Learning" or wisdom. He was defeated very soon after his proclamation by Tibetan soldiers, aided by Chinese troops of the Yellow Sect, and forced to come to terms. One of the clauses was the permission to reign spiritually over the Red Caps in Bhootan, provided he consented to reincarnate himself in Lhassa after his death, and make the law hold good forever. No Dharma Raja since then was ever proclaimed or recognized, unless he was born either at Lhassa or on the Tda-shi Hlum-po territory. Another clause was to the effect that the Dharma Rajas should never permit public exhibitions of their rites of sorcery and necromancy, and the third that a sum of money should be paid yearly for the maintenance of a lamasery, with a school attached where the orphans of Red-caps, and the converted Shammars should be instructed in the "Good Doctrine" of the Gyelukpas. That the latter must have had some secret power over the Bhootanese, who are among the most inimical and irreconcilable of their Red-capped enemies, is proved by the fact that Lama Duk-pa Shab-tung was reborn at Lhassa, and that to this day, the reincarnated Dharma Rajahs are sent and installed at Bhootan by the Lhassa and Tzi-gadze authorities. The latter have no concern in the administration save their spiritual authority, and leave the temporal government entirely in the hands of the Deb-Rajah and the four Pân-lobs, called in Indian official papers *Penlows*, who in their turn are under the immediate authority of the Lhassa officials.

From the above it will be easily understood that no "Dharma Raja" was ever considered as an incarnation of Buddha. The expression that the latter "never dies" applies but to the two great incarnations of equal rank – the Dalai and the Tda-shi Lamas. Both are incarnations of Buddha, though the former is generally designated as that of Avalokiteswara, the highest celestial Dhyan. For him who understands the puzzling mystery by having obtained a key to it, the Gordian knot of these successive reincarnations is easy to untie. He knows that Avalokiteswara and Buddha are one as Amita-pho[14] (pronounced *Fo*) or Amita-Buddha is identical with the former. What the mystic doctrine of the initiated "Phag-pa" or "saintly men" (adepts) teaches upon this subject, is not to be revealed to the world at large. The little that can be given out will be found in a paper on the "Holy Law" which we hope to publish in our next.

*Theosophist*, March, 1882
H.P. Blavatsky

---

[14] In Tibetan *pho* and *pha* – pronounced with a soft labial breath-like sound – means at the same time "man, father." So *pha-yul* is native land: *pho-nya*, angel, messenger of good news: *pha-me*, ancestors, &c.,& c.

# THE SOUL OF TIBET

Many of us were deeply moved by the tragic happenings in Tibet which led to the dramatic escape and exile of the Dalai Lama. Here was a harmless, happy people, with a distinctive culture and a traditional society totally different from that existing anywhere else in the world. To some of us this society seemed to be an archaic survival, an anachronism in the modern world, a "theocratic" system which Europe had rejected long before the Enlightenment and the French Revolution. And yet, in spite of all our attempts to label Tibet, many of us had a feeling of deference towards a religious culture that we could not claim to understand. Despite all the travellers' tales, the many volumes written by scholars and by people interested in Tibet, we still felt that the essential truth had not been told, that perhaps it never could be told by anybody inside that remote and close-knit community to anyone outside it. A few of us went so far as to follow Burke's maxim: "We must venerate where we cannot understand." But even the most insensitive of persons, willing to write off Tibet and dismiss its traditions, had somewhere deep down in his mind a sense of not knowing what he was talking about.

All of us, ranging from the troubled sceptic to the ardent admirer and even to the believer – all of us felt that there had taken place a sudden confrontation, unprecedented in history, between a way of life centred on spiritual concerns – which could be criticized in terms of modern criteria but none the less had a radiant integrity of its own – and the crude forces of aggression and the destructive passions of politics which are all too familiar in the outside world. It seemed as though Tibet was a test case: can a spiritual tradition survive if it does not arm itself against aggressors who are ruthless, who care nothing for the tradition they are prepared to tear apart or for the culture they are willing to destroy in the name of modernization? This is a question which still troubles many of us.

The Dalai Lama is fortified by his faith that in the end Tibetan tradition, embodied in the way of life of which he is the custodian and the conscience, will survive, will even eventually triumph. He is also convinced that, as time goes on, more and more people will come to see that Tibet has a profound political and spiritual significance for us. Elementary human rights have been flagrantly violated by aggressors among a people who were not linked with any foreign power, who were not involved in any sense in the cold war or giving cause for offence to any neighbouring nation.

Here, then, is a test case of the vindication of human rights, and the Dalai Lama pins his hopes on people everywhere who think about this, who read the reports of the International Commission of Jurists, who seriously try to get some idea of the implications, for a people such as the Tibetans, of the desecration of their monasteries and hamlets, and of a stable religious and social order in need of internal reform. His Holiness feels that if men continue to be silent about Tibet they will be betraying their very humanity.

We find that on the political plane the issue has been so sharply and squarely stated that it ultimately touches upon those fundamental decencies which make life meaningful. But, also, the Dalai Lama is convinced that the tragedy of Tibet has a spiritual significance and a meaning even for those who are not primarily interested in Buddhist tradition. Even for them it must appear tragic that there should have been this brutal interference with the beliefs of a gentle and tolerant people. Do the virtues of tolerance and civility for which Europe fought so hard, and which were finally enshrined in the seventeenth century – do these virtues mean nothing to people who may not necessarily share in the beliefs of the Tibetans?

The Dalai Lama speaks with a faith and confidence akin to that of the Encyclopaedists, the great humanists and the religious prophets, and it would be wonderful for any of us to get something of this faith. How this could be translated into immediate political action is a question which is not a matter for casual discussion. Although nowhere more than in England was there an immediate response in the way of sympathy and material support for the Tibetans in their plight, yet already, in a short time, many people even there have begun to take the subjugation of Tibet for granted, and sometimes to talk as though the Tibetan cause were wholly lost. The Dalai Lama has spoken very warmly about England as the leading spiritual and cultural centre of the whole of Europe. He thought that the British Government, more than any other Government in the West, was aware of the historical background of Tibet and the implications of all that had happened. He also felt that the admirable work of the Tibet Society in England was a pointer to the kind of sympathy and support which could be fruitful.

It is indeed distressing that we should come across the feeling that Tibet is a lost cause, an irretrievable tragedy, and that perhaps the time has come to write Tibet's epitaph. Some of us are keen to do what we can for the refugees and to assist the Dalai Lama, while still regarding the cause of Tibet, at least in a political sense, as hopeless. This feeling of hopelessness is unwarranted but perfectly understandable in our time. Whatever we may feel about the legitimacy of the survival of the Tibetan way of life, we are all affected by the tremendous increase in historicism, determinism and fatalism in the modern world, and especially in our own century, even though we instinctively condemn these attitudes when they are couched in their crudest Marxist form. Many of us think that there is something irreversible about the process of modernization, something titanic and totally irresistible about the Industrial Revolution, the march of science and technology. We consequently feel that when any country, but especially a country with an archaic society and a simple economy, with a monastic culture and old-fashioned ideas of government, comes up against a modern aggressor, be he communist or anyone else, the traditional system must necessarily give way to the forces of modernization.

When the British entered Tibet at the time of the famous Younghusband Expedition, and even earlier – going back to the emissary sent out in the eighteenth century – there was a willing recognition that Tibet was no worse for being different. It is Britain, more than any other power that has moved out into far places, which has preserved that due respect for differing cultures and traditions which comes naturally to a people steeped in a traditional culture that has set a high value upon tolerance and the acceptance of diversity. The British failed in the assimilation of people who were racially and culturally different, but they were able to play a protective role in many areas of the world where they were in power. Even in countries where they unwittingly launched the process of modernization they had doubts and reservations; they were never too certain that this was the universal panacea.

But when a country such as Tibet comes into violent contact with fanatical believers in the gospel of material progress and ruthless modernization, can it survive? If we are convinced it cannot, then we can do no more than merely deplore the actual methods used by the Chinese, which indeed are ghastly. And here we have the cruel paradox of modernization introduced by methods which take us right back to the Middle Ages, methods which beggar description. Sickening details of the heinous things that are being done in Tibet in the name of modernization are to be found in the objective reports prepared by the International Commission of Jurists.

Are we going to be content with deploring the pace, the cost, the pains and the ruthlessness of this compulsory modernization? Has not the time come for us to re-assess our high valuation of the very process of modernization? If we do this, we shall become less inclined to accept without question the notion that it is inevitable and unavoidable in every part of the world. We may even come to distrust the dogmatism or fatalism with which people declare Tibet to be a lost cause.

If we wish to appreciate the significance of Tibet, we must not merely have second thoughts about the blessings and inevitability of modernization but also discard at least one version still in vogue of the doctrine of Progress. No doubt the idea of progress is an ancient one, derived from several sources of the Western tradition, different from the cyclical views of history of the East, but it assumed a wholly new form in the last sixty years. All the early apostles of progress – Herder, Kant, Condorcet, Renouvier – regarded it mainly as a moral concept, an ethical ideal towards which modern man was moving. Renouvier clearly condemned the deterministic notion of progress. There is, after all, no religious warrant for the belief that the Kingdom of God will inevitably appear on earth in the foreseeable future. There is no scientific proof for the belief that technological and scientific developments will necessarily ensure better social relations, happier and more harmonious human relationships. There is no economic basis, either, for the belief in indefinite and automatic expansion.

But none of these doubts entered sixty years ago into the minds of those who took the permanency of their political universe for granted. Then, for the first time, as a result of the Darwinian theory of evolution, a new and specious form of the doctrine of progress came into being: the idea of inevitable, automatic, cumulative and irreversible progress achieved purely through technological inventions, economic betterment and the raising of living standards. This idea, although it was powerfully attacked and rejected by several leading thinkers and writers in Europe, still lingers on in people's minds even if they disavow it. This lingering latter-day notion of progress is a serious obstacle to our appreciation of the significance of Tibet.

If we look at Tibet with this idea in our minds, there is no chance of our really understanding it. Tibetans have lived in a land rich in mineral resources but refused to develop them because they believed that this would be an unnecessary and undesirable interference with the soil. These are people willing to spend a significant proportion of their meagre earnings upon the maintenance of a vast number of monasteries; a people completely happy to accept that the only education available to them (and it was generally available in Tibet) was an essentially religious education. It is true that those who did not wish to become monks went to these ancient monastic universities and got some kind of secular learning, but not what we would today call secular learning.

They might acquire a little knowledge of elementary mathematics, indigenous medicine, traditional arts and crafts and practical skills. But how could such people be fitted into any scale of values we might have?

It is not going to be easy for "progressive" people to seize on the true significance of Tibet, and to realize that they are confronted not just by helpless exiles pleading for sympathy but by a moral challenge to many assumptions they normally would not question. As the Dalai Lama has said in his book *My Land and My People,* one cannot understand Tibet if one has no feeling for religion.

What is religion to the Dalai Lama, to Tibetans?

Religion, he says in his book, has got everything to do with the mental discipline, the peace of mind, the calm and poise, the inner equanimity achieved by any human being, which is bound to show in his daily life. The Dalai Lama says explicitly that religion is not a matter of merely going into retreats and monasteries. No doubt when this is done it has its value, but religion is not a matter of outward profession or formal observance. His Holiness does not even use the word "Buddhism" with anything like a sectarian sound. He is simply not interested in making claims of any sort. Religion means for him something quite different from what it means to almost all of us in the modern world. For him, and for the Tibetans, religion means what it meant in Carlyle's definition – the beliefs by which a man really lives from day to day, not the beliefs to which he merely gives verbal or even mental assent.

The Tibetan view of religion is indeed something totally different from our ordinary response to religious as opposed to secular thought. How many of us really believe that even more important than material advancement and the utilitarian criterion of physical pleasure, is the possession of priceless truths concerning the numerous inhibitions and tendencies which afflict the human psyche and of which we have hardly any definite and exact knowledge? If we do believe this, we will be prepared to approach in a spirit of humility the thousands of Buddhist texts in Tibet that came from India, Nepal and China. Tibet is a repository of the real wisdom of the East – a much abused phrase. It has been the home of thousands upon thousands of manuscripts, scrolls, and volumes in which we have not only profound spiritual truths but also examples of a highly developed system of logic and dialectics that was primarily put to a metaphysical and a religious use but which in itself provides a unique discipline to the mind. Tibet has no parallel in this sphere. Of course, no one would admit that he does not care for logical processes. But how much thought do we give simply to perfecting the art of enquiry and disputation? How much time do we give to evolving a technique of constructive discussion? Do we really know how it is possible to resolve the apparently contrary standpoints of relative truths in religion and philosophy and our human relationships?

This technique was highly developed in Tibet. It was founded upon the doctrine of what the Dalai Lama calls the Dual Truth: the distinction between a Platonic archetype of absolute truth, which is unknown to mortal man but can always be held up as an ultimate ideal, and the relative truth every human being embodies, acquired purely by reference to his own experience. We have here the basis of an epistemology which in its higher flights enters into mysticism and metaphysics, but which at the same time is firmly grounded in undogmatic empiricism. The resulting attitude of mind enshrines the belief that a man can only speak authentically in the name of the experience he himself has had. That is why to the Dalai Lama and to the Tibetans it would be irrelevant what one calls oneself or how one is labelled, and this is as true on the political as on the religious plane.

It is simply not possible for people who rely largely on their own direct experience to make a general issue out of Communism or to generalize about the Chinese, though they have had to suffer acutely from acts of aggression performed by particular people calling themselves Communists and Chinese. This does not mean that they are "soft" on Communism or blind to the developments in China, but it is a generally shared attitude to life in Tibet – a willing recognition of the inherent worth and true measure of any man, as well as of his stature as a soul, manifested through his acts and gestures, his face, his smile, his total self. There is also an immediate recognition of the evil, separative tendencies in all of us which cause violence, but with this recognition there is a spontaneous compassion for the evil-doer. It is quite literally possible, in the case of Tibetans, for thousands upon thousands of people to say, in their daily lives, "Lord Buddha, forgive him for he knows not what he does." The doctrine of renunciation, of universal salvation and collective welfare, a doctrine embodied in the ideal figure of the Bodhisattva, is meaningful to the ordinary man in Tibet. It is not just a mysterious truth to which a chosen few have privileged access. It is significant that the Dalai Lama in his book does not wish to make special claims on behalf of Gautama the Buddha. He casually states that the Buddha is one of a thousand Buddhas. But this makes no difference to the inward gratitude and profound reverence that he has for the Buddha as the transmitter and exemplar of truths that have become part of the way of life of millions of people in the world.

So the very idea of renunciation is absorbed into the consciousness of ordinary people: the idea that a man reveals himself by the extent to which he can shed what he has, and not by how much he acquires. This is an idea which we might put under the label of Christian charity, or Buddhist compassion, or something else – but the fact of the matter is that modern society is founded, as William Morris saw, upon the opposite principle. It is only in the modern world with its shallow moral values that the very spirit of acquisitiveness has given us a new and dominant criterion of judgment, so that we feel if a person acquires more and more of this or that – be it degrees or titles, wealth, or property shares, fame or influence – he is worthy of admiration and imitation. He may at best use his assets in the service of some exclusive cause. It is very difficult for a man to pretend that he is acquiring something for the sake of the whole of humanity; it is not so difficult to pretend that he is acquiring something for the sake of a particular nation, or group – to identify his own personal ambition with a narrow conception of collective self-interest. And we all know how easy it is indeed for us to say that we wish to get ahead for the sake of our children and our families. But once the acquisitive instinct becomes deep-rooted, there takes place a total transvaluation of values – something that is so subtly pervasive that we do not notice the resulting corruption in our natures and in the society to which we belong.

Once this happens, inevitably we begin to set up new idols and false gods. We gradually come to abandon the heroic ideal as well as the very notion of intrinsic value and merit. The heroic ideal which was precious to the Greeks and to the ancient Indians has been applied by the Tibetans to the unseen odyssey of the human soul. We cannot easily imagine what it means to live by the idea that an individual can by his self-discipline dare all, that the world is a place of probation, that he does not have to take what does not belong to him, that he can take freely from nature and put his own talents to a use that may compel admiration and evoke emulation but dispenses with the cruder forms of competition and conflict. This heroic ideal, which even in its worldly form did so much good to Europe and to England even as late as the nineteenth century, has gone – some feel for good.

In Tibet, then, there have been large numbers of people who were shown a technique of creative thinking based upon the doctrine of the Dual Truth, a technique perfected by lamas in the great monasteries of Drepung and Sera. Among the Tibetan people the doctrine of renunciation, as opposed to the notion of personal salvation, is deeply rooted, more than anywhere else even in the East. In India, the original home of the Buddha, the doctrine of *Moksha* or *Mukti* , the quest for personal salvation, became so deeply rooted for centuries that it engendered a selfish individualism, a subtle kind of spiritual isolationism. As a result, most people are not wedded to a living ideal of renunciation, although it is to be found in the Indian scriptures. But this ideal did mean, and has continued to mean, a very great deal to a large mass of people in Tibet. So here is a claim to uniqueness that we may make on behalf of the Tibetans, though they have no interest in making any claims to uniqueness, unlike people less deeply rooted in their cultures and religions.

This is not the occasion to go into all the Tibetan beliefs. The moral values that flowed from their system of beliefs were richly reflected in their daily lives, despite their human failings. Many visitors to Tibet in the course of centuries were much struck by the gentleness, humility, humour and dignity of the people, such as they had not seen anywhere else. These endearing qualities were combined with the rare virtue of intense devoutness to which there is no parallel, as was freely admitted even by the missionaries who went to Tibet. Tibetans are men of quiet faith, but also men of cheerful simplicity; not men of words, not men obsessed with the idea of personal development or any activity that merely enhances the ego. These men were constantly retreating within, training themselves to meditate and to maintain peace of mind in daily life, preparing themselves for the tests that are brought to light by intense suffering. It is not then surprising that the Dalai Lama should now say in effect: "This is the hour of our trial, this is the time when we must show our faith." In his book he extols the creed of *ahimsa* or non-violence and salutes Gandhi as the greatest man of the age.

This does not mean that the Dalai Lama has no use whatever for the small but brave Tibetan army. He recognizes, as indeed any person who believes in the Dual Truth must, that while we must keep clearly before our minds the unadulterated ideal, we must also be prepared to allow others to show their courage and their integrity in differing ways – each human being in a sense being a law unto himself. This is implicit in the very notion of the doctrine that each person has to find out his own way and his own sphere of duty. In his book the Dalai Lama's plea is somewhat like this: "This is our great moment of trial; we have had such moments in our history, but more than ever before we are being tested in our capacity to endure immeasurable suffering with courage and compassion. We must show our willingness to speak the truth until men may hear it in all quarters of the globe, but at the same time preserving, with deliberate intention, freedom from hatred of the people responsible for our suffering." Almost everyone who reads the Dalai Lama's book will be deeply moved by the last paragraph, in which he clearly conveys this spirit of detachment, non-retaliation and of active compassion. At the same time he does not flinch throughout the book to state courageously what is at stake.

Mr. Hugh Richardson has pointed out, in his excellent book *Tibet and Its History*, that although one may deplore the blunder committed by the Indian Government in its handling of the entire Tibetan question in 1950 – in allowing itself to be mesmerized by the word "suzerainty" while not laying down the full implications of the word "autonomy" – it has at least atoned, if atonement were possible, by doing all it can, freely and generously, for the Tibetan refugees. And yet not enough could be done by any Government. Other Governments gave money – Australia and England, initially, and some assistance has also come from other countries. The scale of the problem is so vast, however, that unless we can organize effective international action to provide the material basis for the scattered community of Tibetans outside Tibet, we will not really be doing our bit for Tibet.

All this only refers to the sheer physical survival of an uprooted community. But is this all that will be left of the old Tibet? Is it not possible that ancient Tibet may rise again? In India, or perhaps elsewhere? Or will there be several little Tibets? We are here faced with large questions, and it is because these occur at the most practical level that it has been necessary to look a little at Tibetan values and beliefs. In rendering elementary assistance to these Tibetans we must not forget that it is also our duty to help them to maintain their spiritual independence and the integrity of their way of life.

Of course, the eminent monks who have come from Tibet and who represent the efflorescence of the Tibetan tradition do not need to be cushioned and protected. But what of the children? Mr. Christmas Humphreys, in two lectures which he gave in London, spoke with very great feeling about the problem of the Tibetan children, who are now beginning to receive Tibetan education but are being approached on every side by swarms of missionaries. The very idea is repellent – of children being looked upon simply as religious cannon-fodder, and actually being approached, not because their souls are to be saved (for which of us is going to fall for that kind of self-deception?), but just so that the egotistical claims of some people may be statistically fulfilled to their own satisfaction. If the whole world were to become Catholic or Protestant or Communist, the outcome would only be that we should find the largest number of lapsed Catholics or Protestants or Communists in world history. The idea of formal conversion is absurd and even irreligious, and now there is a real danger that many of these Tibetan children would be the hapless victims.

In the past we have been given subtle distortions of Tibetan thought. The remarkable Englishmen who visited Tibet, from Bogle to Gould – men like Sir Charles Bell – wholly responded to Tibet, as they might respond to the classical culture of Europe. Lesser men who did not know any better were merely interested in stressing the oddities and peculiarities of Tibetan beliefs, without adequate understanding or spiritual insight. A great deal was written about the ritual dances, about necromancy and polyandry and other such intriguing practices. No attempt was made to distinguish the crude and the vulgar, the debased and the distorted (which exist in every religious tradition) from the pure and the sublime aspects of Tibetan religion.

In his book, the Dalai Lama draws attention to the wholly false picture often given of "Lamaism" in Tibet, implying that Buddhist tradition in Tibet is something totally different from elsewhere. On the contrary, when they left India, the original and primeval Buddhist teachings took root in Tibet. This can be verified by reference to innumerable texts which have never left Tibetan soil until recently with the dramatic flight of the Dalai Lama. The Dalai Lama says in his book that no one today can say he really understands Buddhist philosophy unless he studies these Tibetan texts.

The Dalai Lama's book also clears up some other common misconceptions about Tibet. He readily concedes that there were social abuses in the old system, but refers to the programme of reform begun by the previous Dalai Lama and which he himself tried to continue. In any case, the existence of social abuses and pseudo-religious practices in Tibet does not lend any real justification for the Chinese conquest or for present attempts to Christianize Tibetan refugee children and alienate them from their traditional culture. If we are at all sensitive to the best in Tibetan tradition and recognize the importance of preserving its integrity intact, then we could do a real service to Tibet by raising our voices against the Westernization of Tibetan children.

Meanwhile, the Dalai Lama, characteristically, does not complain but looks ahead. For him there is still much to be done. Countless Tibetan refugees need practical assistance. The cause of Tibet must continue to be raised at the United Nations; it must secure the active support of an increasing number of people and their Governments. At the same time, he realizes that the suppression of religious life and thought in Tibet itself may result in a steady diffusion of Buddhist teaching throughout the world. In India itself, for the first time in many centuries, Hindu and Buddhist are drawing together, an event of great significance. It is as though Judaism and Christianity really drew together without people from one religion being converted to the other. It is as though for the first time Protestants were really prepared to learn from the Catholics, and Catholics prepared to learn from the Reformation. Of course, the renewal of the Hindu-Buddhist tradition is now only in its early, seminal phase, but it could eventually produce a rich harvest. The Dalai Lama himself may move about from one end of the country to the other, reaffirming once again, in the homeland of the Buddha, the simple and profound truths that he preached on Indian soil. The soul of Tibet will survive, and therefore we cannot despair of the survival of Tibet, in that ultimate sense.

But we dare not despair of the survival of Tibet even in the more worldly and ephemeral sense as long as Tibetan resistance continues and men respond to the claims of conscience, as long as we can still take a long view of history and smile at the inordinate pretensions of messianic systems, and as long as people retain their faith that truth must triumph and justice will prevail.

The Royal Society, London
June 13, 1962

*Hermes*, February 1976
Raghavan Iyer

# THE MAHAMUDRA OF VOIDNESS

*Thou has to study the voidness of the seeming full, the fullness of the seeming void. O fearless Aspirant, look deep within the well of thine own heart, and answer. Knowest thou of Self the powers, O thou perceiver of external shadows?*

*If thou dost not – then art thou lost.*

*For, on Path fourth, the lightest breeze of passion or desire will stir the steady light upon the pure white walls of Soul. The smallest wave of longing or regret for Maya's gifts illusive, along Antaskarana – the path that lies between thy Spirit and thy self, the highway of sensations, the rude arousers of Ahankara – a thought as fleeting as the lightning flash will make thee thy three prizes forfeit the prizes thou hast won.*

*For know, that the ETERNAL knows no change.*

*The Voice of the Silence*

True meditation upon emptiness depends upon a fullness of preparation through a series of stages of moral practice. Without proper preparation, authentic insight into the nature of voidness (*shunyata*) is impossible. It matters not how long this preparation takes; it must be honest and genuine, devised by each human being according to his or her own individual karmic agenda. Otherwise it is impossible to launch seriously into meditation, to enter into it with an inward assurance that one will never abandon it. Even after one has entered the path leading to *dhyana*, one will, inevitably, experience difficulties. Yet one's very presence upon that path must be based upon an immutable resolve. One's preparation for deep meditation upon emptiness must be rooted in a commitment that is irreversible, inalienable and irrevocable.

In Tibetan Buddhism this arduous course cf preparation is understood as a necessary precondition for a further and even more fundamental transformation of consciousness that is the fruition of meditation upon emptiness. This quintessential transformation of consciousness is conveyed in a text composed by the First Panchen Lama as a *mahamudra*. His teaching, first written down in the sixteenth century, derives from a series of oral instructions transmitted by Tsong-Kha-Pa, the founder of the Gelukpa Order in the fourteenth century. These teachings are said to have been received by Tsong-Kha-Pa ultimately from Manjushri, one of the Dhyani Bodhisattvas and an emanation from one of the Dhyani Buddhas. The First Panchen Lama crystallized an oral tradition around a central Teaching which he called a *mahamudra*.

According to a contemporary commentary upon this Teaching delivered by Geshe Rabten, a religious counsellor to the present Dalai Lama, a *mahamudra* may be understood as a great seal symbolizing an immutable realization of voidness. When one enters into a formal agreement, as in signing a contract, one puts down one's name or seals a document. Everyone knows what this means in statutory law. It is sacred and irrevocable. It is firm and binding. So, too, in a deeper and spiritual sense, one may seal one's entire consciousness irreversibly upon the path of *dhyana* – meditation. Ultimately, this is a direct subjective experience of voidness. Yet as Geshe Rabten's commentary points out, this fundamental transformation of consciousness cannot come about except as the sequel to a long and difficult period of preparation through moral practice, mental development and preliminary exercises in meditation. Even these, as set forth in the *Sutra Yana* teachings of Tibetan Buddhism, require resolves, vows and the development of an unshakeable determination that once one has begun upon this path, no matter what the difficulties, one will seek to become increasingly honest with oneself and strive ever harder to overcome them.

One must be committed in advance not to become infatuated with one's own difficulties, but rather to see beyond them and to persevere in one's course of self-induced and self-devised inner growth. As in all of Buddha's teachings, the only authentic basis of such resolve is a motivation to heal the suffering of humanity. Every time one is inclined to falter upon this path, one should think of the pain of human beings and the misery of human ignorance. Thinking of one's own share in the world's pain, one may realize one's obligation to lessen the burden of the world. To think about this deeply and in detail is to find the motivation necessary to carry on and to persist in a heroic search for deep meditation and the realization of truth or *satya*.

The primary means of preparation for the *mahamudra* meditation is taking refuge in the Buddha, the Dharma and the Sangha. As soon as one directs one's mind towards the supreme compassion and enormous sacrifice of Gautama Buddha and the entire Host of Bodhisattvas, one is filled with a tremendous purifying strength. By thinking of these beings, who have attained to the state of supreme enlightenment solely for the sake of humanity, one can gain the energy and strength to form an irreversible resolve. Thus all efforts at meditation should begin with an adoration of predecessors, a rejoicing in their very existence and in the reality of their deeds and their living presence. To this joyous practice each individual may bring devotion and an undivided seriousness entirely of his or her own choice. Thinking of the meaning of one's own life in relationship to the meaning of the lives of all, and in relation to the world's pain and need, one may contemplate the great work of the Bodhisattvas, inserting one's own resolve into the broader mission of building a rainbow bridge between the Host of Dhyanis and the world of Myalba. Taking refuge in the triple gem, one can find the courage in oneself to try to aid the earth with all its plight and pain, caused ultimately by a fundamental alienation from the true Self, an ignorance of the true destiny of humanity.

It is not possible to take refuge in the Buddha, the Dharma and the Sangha without prostrating oneself before their clearly visualized presence. In his commentary on the *mahamudra*, Geshe Rabten recommends performing one hundred thousand such prostrations, and acknowledges that even these may not be enough to bring about the necessary purification. In the East, physical prostration before objects of veneration comes naturally because of a pervasive sense of the sacred and heartfelt sentiments of gratitude towards ancestors and benefactors of every kind. But in the West, physical prostration is not something that everybody can readily undertake. It may come naturally, but one had better not simulate it, force it or fake it. Nonetheless, mental prostrations, an inward humility, and the surrendering of the personal will and the judgemental mind can be of great benefit. Nothing but good can come to a human being through the surrender of a divided and treacherous heart. The total prostration of one's being, as enjoined by Krishna in the fourth chapter of the *Bhagavad Gita*, is an essential mental posture preparatory for true meditation.

The Tibetan texts lay down for monks a series of *mantrams* to be chanted. As Geshe Rabten explains, the set of recitations and visualizations revolving around *vajrasattva* is intended to assist in the elimination of negative tendencies. This aspect of the *mahamudra* preparation is of particular significance to individuals who have yet to master the discipline and momentum of a mendicant. *Vajrasattva* represents the embodiment of the power of purification of all the Buddhas. Whilst Tibetan tradition lays down for monks specific modes for visualizing *vajrasattva* and specific *mantrams* to be chanted, these details are inappropriate and unnecessary for lay individuals outside the tradition. What is of crucial importance is to bring to bear from within oneself the purifying power of the Buddha-nature upon the whole assemblage of one's unholy modes of thought, feeling and will. There are, in every human being, a myriad such elements in a state of interconnection. These negative tendencies no doubt arose in former lives, and if they are not extinguished in this life, they will have their fruition in future lives of pain and suffering. The entire assemblage should be acknowledged so as to create a mental posture of total honesty.

To enter the Path, one must be free of all self-deception. Otherwise, as the Sutras teach, one will be arrested from further progress and thrown back from further growth. Such devices as prostration and chanting are intended to help one confront all one's errors, especially those that may have caused pain to other beings and which were avoidable, occasions when one knew better and yet acted wickedly. Purification in preparation for the path leading to meditation requires that all of these must be confronted. They must be collected together, brought to the forefront of one's attention, and then burnt out at the very root. Their force of persistence must be destroyed through a resolve in relation to the future and an honest recognition of their effects upon others.

This is, no doubt, a difficult practice and must be repeated again and again. Whichever purificatory chants one selects – whether it be from *The Voice of the Silence*, the *Bhagavad Gita* or *The Jewel in the Lotus* – these must all be taken as means that are helpful in confronting what is called the *papapurusha* – the assemblage of sins. It is this hideous aggregate of negative tendencies that forms the basis, at the moment of death, of the *kama rupa*. On average, it will take some one hundred and fifty years for this form to disintegrate. But if it is more tenacious, owing to a life of self-deception, dishonesty and spiritual pretension, it can last much longer, emitting a foul odour and precipitating crimes and even murders, recognized and unrecognized, on this earth. After-death consequences involving the *kama rupa* pertain to a plane of effects, but what one does in life pertains to the causal plane of human consciousness. If one is not vigilant, one may be gestating the energies that become powerfully coagulated into a tenacious *kama rupa*. All such entities are based, in Buddhist theory, upon the force of self-grasping, bound up with the false imputation of inherent existence to the personal ego. Naturally, the presence of such entities putrefying and disintegrating over many centuries throws an oppressive pall over humanity that puts a tremendous brake upon the aspirations of every single human being. Yet this should not be allowed to become a subject of fascination or speculation. Rather, one should recognize one's own liability to contribute to astral pollution and so one should resolve to purify oneself and one's emanations.

In describing the preparation for *mahamudra* meditation, Geshe Rabten compares these negative tendencies to seeds. It is as if one wished to build a beautiful building, but could not do so without preparing clean ground for its foundations. Before laying the foundations, one must clear away rocks and weeds, cleansing the ground of all obstructions and removing seeds that spring up and interfere with the building. At the same time, this work of purification must be coupled with the collection of materials that will be helpful in setting up the foundations. In the long run, one's fundamental attention must be directed towards the constructive end of serving universal enlightenment. There is little or no essential interest in the obstructions and tendencies that come in the way of the release of this higher motivation. All these tendencies can be classified into certain broad types which are, in the end, both banal and boring. Most of them have to do with attraction and aversion, anger and pride, greed and delusion, and, above all, a false conception of the self. Owing to this false conception of a fake ego, reinforcing it through unconscious habit and semi-conscious patterns of reaction, a persistent aggregate of tendencies has originated.

Instead of becoming preoccupied with the melodramatic history of this aggregate of tendencies, one should merely note them as they arise and mark them for elimination. They will inevitably appear when one starts to engage in meditation, and one should note them only with a view to removing them through the setting up of counter-tendencies drawn from positive efforts to visualize spiritual strengths. Hence the connection, in the Tibetan practice, between the visualization of *vajrasattva* and the elimination of negative tendencies. Each individual must learn to select the appropriate counter-forces necessary to negate the particular strong negative tendencies that arise. In drawing upon these counter-forces from within, one will discover that one can bring to one's aid many an element in one's own being that can serve to one's spiritual advantage. Every human being has a number of elements which represent a certain ease, naturalness, decency and honesty as a human being. Sometimes there is a debilitating tendency to overlook these or take them for granted. The spiritual path requires a progressively heightened degree of self-awareness. One should give oneself full credit for whatever positive tendencies one has, whether they have to do with outward energies on the physical plane, mental energies, moral tenacity or metaphysical insight. In order to find that in oneself which can work in one's favour, and can help in counteracting negative tendencies, one should engage in regular recitation and frequent reflection upon sacred scriptures. Thus one will discover points of resonance in one's individual karmic inheritance that can help release purifying energies flowing from the ideation of Buddhas and Bodhisattvas.

If this practice is going to prosper, one must bring to it a moral insight rooted in an understanding of metaphysics. The mind must be focussed upon general ideas. One must reflect upon the relationship of insight and compassion. Insight is not merely intellectual, but rather arises through the recognition of what skill in action means in specific contexts. Insight involves a perception of how wisdom is reflected within action, and which can come about only through a deep reflection upon the process of how such insight is released. On the other side, before one can truly generate a conscious current of compassion, one must create a state of calm abiding. One must find out one's resources and potentials for calmness and for generating the maximum field of patience, peacefulness, gentleness and steadfastness. Then one must combine in practice one's capacity for calmness with one's capacity for discerning what is essential. Inevitably, this will involve a protracted study lasting over lifetimes, and include enquiry into the fundamental propositions of *Gupta Vidya*, the study of karma and the study of what Buddhist thought refers to as the chain of dependent origination.

In essence, this entire course of study is aimed at bringing about a meta-psychological encounter with a false view of the self that must be confronted and dispelled. Ultimately, this complex matter goes to the core of the *mahamudra* meditation. But at a preliminary level and in the course of preparation for that meditation, one must come to grips with the confused notion of oneself that is identified with bodily desire, proclivities towards pleasure and avoidance of pain. At subtler levels one must confront one's conception of oneself that is bound up with the entire chaotic series of thoughts, all of which have particular histories and form associative chains of memory that have been built up over lifetimes of indulgence. All take a variety of forms and leave discernible tracks, all are connected with certain fantasies, wishes, hopes and expectations. They are designated in various ways in different analytic traditions, but always at the root there is the protean force of self-grasping. It is not easy either to confront or to abandon, and hence *The Voice of the Silence* warns that even when one is very close to attaining *dhyana*, one may be completely disrupted by a sudden eruption of self-grasping.

> "Ere the gold flame can burn with steady light, the lamp must stand well guarded in a spot free from all wind." Exposed to shifting breeze, the jet will flicker and the quivering flame cast shades deceptive, dark and ever-changing, on the Soul's white shrine.
>
> And then, O thou pursuer of the truth, thy Mind-Soul will become as a mad elephant, that rages in the jungle. Mistaking forest trees for living foes, he perishes in his attempts to kill the ever-shifting shadows dancing on the wall of sunlit rocks.
>
> Beware, lest in the care of Self thy Soul should lose her foothold on the soil of Deva-knowledge.
>
> Beware, lest in forgetting SELF, thy Soul lose o'er its trembling mind control, and forfeit thus the due fruition of its conquests.
>
> Beware of change! For change is thy great foe. This change will fight thee off, and throw thee back, out of the Path thou treadest, deep into viscous swamps of doubt.
>
> *The Voice of the Silence*

This passage from *The Voice of the Silence* refers primarily to an extremely high state of consciousness and an advanced stage along the Path. It refers to a point at which the very core of self-grasping must be let go. Long before one has earned the privilege of such an archetypal confrontation with the false self, one will have to win many minor skirmishes with the force of self-grasping. For this purpose, *The Voice of the Silence* gives a specific recipe that is indispensable. It is emphasized in every authentic spiritual tradition and it is central to the New Cycle and the Aryanization of the West. It is put in terms of the metaphor of the mango fruit. One must become as tender as the pulp of the mango towards the faults of others, feeling with them their suffering and pain. Yet one must also learn to be as hard as the mango stone towards one's own faults. One must give no quarter to excuse-making or shilly-shallying. Instead, one must fully accept what one thinks to be one's own particular pain, while recognizing that it is, at its core, nothing but a manifestation of delusive self-grasping.

The mango metaphor sums up all the elements involved in the preparation for deep *dhyana* – continuous uninterrupted meditation. Geshe Rabten points to a specific preparatory exercise called "taking and giving", which is a beautiful and profound instantiation of the mango metaphor. One begins by visualizing all the ignorance and all the suffering of the world. Then one must consciously take in with every inhalation of breath everything that is ugly, unsatisfactory, violent and disturbing. For the purpose of understanding and contemplation, the world's mess may be thought of as sticks of fuel burning with a thick black smoke. One must inhale this dense black smoke and let it flow through one's body, permeating every nerve and cell, penetrating to the centre of one's heart, where it destroys all traces of self-concern. Then as one exhales, one should visualize sending out light-energy towards all beings, acting through one's positive tendencies and serving to eliminate their sufferings.

This exercise of taking and giving should be conjoined with one's adoration and prostration before the Buddhas and before one's *Ishtaguru*. Indeed, *Guru Yoga* is the fifth and quintessential element of the preparation for *mahamudra* meditation. One may, at first, contemplate the *Ishtaguru* as a drop of light, or, at a more advanced stage, one may actually contemplate the essential form of the *Ishtaguru* in the space before one's mind. It is implicit in the very conception of the *Ishtaguru* that the individual must choose whichever form of contemplation will be most beneficial. Once a choice is made, however, it is crucial that one persistently and with full fidelity bring the distracted mind back, again and again, to the object of its contemplation. The test of this devotion is that one will find a deepening, and yet spontaneous, longing to be of service to others. More and more, one's motivation will be that the black smoke of human ignorance and suffering should pass through oneself and become converted, through persistence in *dhyana,* into a healing light that will radiate, brightening and helping the lives of others. In other words, one will become an instrument through which a great sacrifice is made consciously, a channel through which a great redemptive force can proceed. At that point, of course, there can be no separative self.

One must have become like an alabaster vase, pure and radiant, a translucent sphere mirroring the Dhyanis through *dhyana*. In the act of choosing one's *Ishtaguru* or *Ishtadevata* – whether it be under the form of Buddha or Krishna or some other Avatar – one will in fact have entered the ray of a particular Dhyani. One will have activated the potentiality of a Fohatic circuit through which may be drawn the beneficent energies of the entire Host of Dhyanis. One will infallibly recognize this because one's body and mind will be greatly lightened. So free does one become from any dependence upon anything outside that one can subsist upon the food of meditation. This is an extremely high stage which cannot be attained and maintained except by individuals who have early made the great renunciation spoken of in *The Voice of the Silence.*

Every neophyte can approach the threshold of that path and gain an intuition of that exalted condition. The entire practice of the *paramitas* at every level – cycling from *dana* through *virya* to *dhyana* and gaining a glimpse of *prajna* and coming back to the foundation of boundless charity in *dana* – will bring about an inevitable loosening and lightening of the tendency to grasp, to crave and even to think of oneself as separate from other beings. The entire preparatory course of the *paramitas* is summed up in Mahatma

Gandhi's mantramic phrase: one reduces oneself to a zero. In mystical terms, one becomes a sphere of light.

As one treads the difficult path towards the *dhyana* haven of pure, uninterrupted meditation, one is sure to encounter distractions. According to Geshe Rabten, these may be broadly classified into two types that always work in one or another of two directions. On the one hand, distractions may work as a kind of excitement. On the other, they may operate as a kind of sinking or slackening. With either type, one is liable to become over-active and therefore agitated, and so lose concentration through exaltation in one's happiness or joy or sense of release, or one is likely to get sluggish, drowsy, enfeebled, and thereby lose the power of concentration. These two dangers will combine, recurring again and again. Everyone, therefore, must find out where his or her propensities lie. Different individuals at different times will be more or less liable to become distracted from a current of meditation by excitement or by sluggishness. If one tends to get distracted by excitement, it is suggested that one not close one's eyes during the practice of meditation, but rather keep them open and focussed upon a form that is representative of the object of meditation. Yet, if one is liable to get sluggish and fall prey to sinking, then one may benefit by focussing attention on the navel and taking one's breath from below. Different suggestions will be applicable to different people; in the end, propensities towards distractions are only significant in relation to a process of learning by trial and error.

As with all efforts to purify one's moral practice, the effort to establish a non-distracted mind must begin with a contemplation of the possibilities of a state of perfected meditation. In Tibetan tradition the state of mental quiescence needed for true meditation is represented by myriad analogies. Thus, for example, the clear cognitive nature of the mind may be represented by the image of the sun ablaze in a cloudless sky. There is light and luminosity throughout the field of the mind, giving a supreme clarity to all its operations. There is a simultaneous omnidirectional transmission of light, and, in relation to concentration on any specific object, there is a sharpening of the contours of existence and a heightened alertness to details in the phenomenal world. The cloudlessness signifies an absence of obstruction and confusion of the cognitive nature of the mind, but also a total suffusion of the mind by the overarching, refulgent light of the sun. As Geshe Rabten explains, this analogy represents the nature of the mind as clear cognition, and though it is not to be confused with a realization of the mind's ultimate nature as voidness, it is an authentic intimation of the future course of the *mahamudra* meditation.

Another analogy, perhaps more applicable to the situation of aspirants who are just beginning the practices leading to *dhyana*, is the sureness of the eagle soaring through the sky. The eagle glides gracefully through the sky, ascending without apparent effort, and only periodically flapping its wings. The gliding state represents the absorption of the mind in the object of meditation. The flapping of the wings represents the use of the analytic faculty to dispel a temporary distraction. Whilst it will be necessary in the initial stages to employ the analytic mind to confront and dispel a great variety of distractions, one should steadily move towards the ideal of an eagle's soaring flight. One must advance from a state that is essentially one of great distraction to a steady state, in which one may remain undistracted for relatively long periods of time. Then, when distracting thought currents arise, whether they involve excitation or sinking, they may be noticed, confronted and mastered without breaking the course of meditation any more than the eagle's flight is broken by a single flapping of its wings. In meditation one's basic concern is with the graceful glide, the smooth ascent, movement towards the One.

If one is able to take the standpoint that all human history is a series of successes and failures in preparation for meditation and for initiation into the Mysteries, one may understand that the seemingly burdensome accumulation of history is nothing but the collective residues of a series of over-reactions to distractions in meditation. Confronted honestly, the entire pseudo-drama of history is nothing but a mass of excuses for the inability to maintain concentration. Thus, if one truly wants to effect a fundamental transformation in consciousness so that one becomes incapable of falling back from the true path of *dhyana,* one must be willing to carry out the full course of preparation for that transformation. One must begin by honestly taking stock of oneself and learning to engage in a sufficient degree of self-surrender of the will, through humility, devotion, adoration and prostration, so that one may begin to attune oneself to the higher chords of one's being. Once one begins seriously to meditate, one may begin to visualize the meaning of a harmonic balance within oneself. Whether one pictures oneself as a fish swimming in the ocean of wisdom or as an eagle soaring in the heavens of light, one's emphasis must be upon developing a continuous current of meditative practice. One must develop those spontaneous reflexes whereby one confronts and dispels distracting thoughts without fascination or excess, bringing the mind back again to the main focus of attention. This must be done again and again at first, and one should never underestimate the tremendous effort involved in the beginning.

Every honest student of the path intimated in *The Voice of the Silence* will understand these difficulties. But a point must come in the practice of *dhyana* when there is a taste of the flow of uninterrupted contemplation, when there is a lightening of the load, when tension disappears – including the tension of striving – and when it becomes easier, subtler and more discriminating. Losing preoccupation with oneself, one begins to forget even the meditating self, and so becomes more aware of the vast, boundless expanse into which one proceeds. One will still be far from the summits of meditation and the accomplishment of the true *mahamudra,* whereby one permanently sets aside the bonds of delusion, but one will have embarked upon the authentic preparation for real meditation and sensed thereby the boundlessly buoyant life of the spirit.

*Hermes,* May 1985
Raghavan Iyer

# THE FORWARD IMPULSE

*Each class of Creators endows man with what it has to give: the one builds his external form; the other gives him its essence, which later on becomes the Human Higher Self owing to the personal exertion of the individual.... Where there is no struggle, there is no merit. Humanity, "of the Earth earthy", was not destined to be created by the angels of the first divine Breath: therefore they are said to have refused to do so, and man had to be formed by more material creators.... The first humanity...was a pale copy of its progenitors; too material, even in its ethereality, to be a hierarchy of gods; too spiritual and pure to be MEN, endowed as it is with every negative (Nirguna) perfection. Perfection, to be fully such, must be born out of imperfection, the incorruptible must grow out of the corruptible, having the latter as its vehicle and basis and contrast.*

*The Secret Doctrine*, ii 95
H.P. Blavatsky

Since that which is absolute and real is boundless and inexhaustible, no realized degree of perfection by beings in any world or system of worlds can be considered as the final terminus. In every theatre of spiritual evolution there are some beings who represent the serene fulfilment of the impulse to growth from a prior period of evolution. There will be many others who must still struggle towards maturation and perfection. There will also be a few who represent the forward impulse of spiritual evolution, moving far beyond any degree of realized perfection ever known before. Like bright stars radiating from invisible centres in space, their hearts are centred upon unmanifest eternal wisdom, which they transmit and transmute into fresh opportunities for growth for every struggling being around them. Self-luminous with theurgic wisdom and therapeutic compassion, these are the *Agnishvatta Pitris*, the Promethean Asuras who light up self-consciousness in human beings when the moment is right.

Before this sacred hour can strike, preparatory work must take place, guided by those intermediate hosts of fecund intelligences that represent realized degrees of perfection from the past. These are the efflorescent Suras, the pantheons of ethereal gods, who are mentally passive in relation to the possibilities of the future but still able to form and furnish the needed vestures of lower hosts of struggling monads. The substantial difference between the Suras and Asuras may be seen as the enormous difference between passive goodness or negative perfection, and the heroic capacity, which is quintessentially human, to take existing forms and inspire authentic spiritual creativity. All heroic strength arises out of this magical power of the majestic light of divine self-consciousness. It is the rare ability to see that which does not exist and the creative capacity to make real that which has never been realized before, but has ever subsisted in the latent realm of Eternal Ideation. This remarkable ability to bring the Unmanifest to bear upon the active realm of manifestation is the extraordinary gift of higher self-consciousness. It is the talismanic gift of creative courage that characterizes the *Agnishvatta Pitris*.

Self-consciousness enables them to become skilful transmitters of the divine light of supersensuous ether in a world of grossly differentiated matter. They have developed the infallible capacity to sift and select, to concentrate to the exclusion of other things, and the dialectical ability to analyse and reduce to basic elements what is otherwise nebulous and diffuse. These are distinct faculties that all human beings possess to some degree, but are rarely understood because rarely considered. All too often, people imagine that these potent faculties are to be used for making final judgements about the world, for fattening the predatory *kama rupa* and buttressing the insecure self. In reality, however, they exist solely for the sake of spiritual freedom. The seminal gifts of the *Agnishvatta Pitris* repose in the human mind for the sake of self-conscious mastery over the chaotic kingdom of inherited vestures.

Thus, any viable conception of perfectibility requires a sensitive, scrupulous care for the undeniable imperfections of flawed materials in the lunar vestures. These may be vitally affected if a vigilant individual generates fresh patterns of thought or feeling that can work like alchemy. It is certainly possible to change the polarity and quality of the life-atoms in the vestures by increasing the porosity of the elementals that comprise them. This is a creative and courageous task, and it can be carried out only if one faces the facts. One must always scrutinize and settle one's karmic accounts. One must be ever willing to look honestly where one really stands in relation to the moment of death. One must see through and beyond entire realms of appearances and so take a moral stand based on general principles. One must derive their deeper meanings and apt applications within the sacred sphere of one's duty. In short, one must cultivate one's own garden of Eden or Gethsemane.

This Promethean stance in relation to one's own spiritual evolution is crucial to the entire Theosophical philosophy of growth. It is supported by the ancient teaching, which was intuited by Leibniz, that every monad has inherent within it the potency of All-Force. Given typically truncated views of human nature, this is seldom understood by most human beings. As Mahatma K.H. explained in the last century:

> The great difficulty . . . lies in the liability to form more or less incomplete mental conceptions of the working of the one element, of its inevitable presence in every imponderable atom, and its subsequent ceaseless and almost illimitable multiplication of new centres of activity without affecting in the least its own original quantity.

He then intimated that from the beginning of a long sequence of manvantaric cycles, centred on a single point in abstract Space, proceeding through the development of a series of globes replete with genera, species and classes of beings, there is no loss of the original force or life-essence during the protracted evolution of their derivatives.

> The force there is not transformed into something else . . . but with each development of a new centre of activity from *within* itself multiplies *ad infinitum* without ever losing a particle of its

nature in quantity or quality. Yet acquiring as it progresses something plus in its differentiation. This "force" so-called shows itself truly indestructible but does *not* correlate and is *not* convertible . . . but rather may be said to *grow* and *expand* into "something else" while neither its own potentiality nor being are in the least affected by the transformation.

The extraordinary energy in the One Element, when correctly understood in relation to a complex doctrine of emanation, is capable of endless reproduction, expansion and innovation without taking away anything from that which was in the beginning. Since the ultimate ground of the One Element is inherently boundless and beyond all perceptible limitation, the entire process of differentiation leaves intact the whole potential in the impartite essence of that which was in the beginning.

The poet's observation that in love, "to divide is not to take away", is a profound intuition of a fundamental law of Nature which applies to all its operations, from the formation of worlds to the transformations of atoms. This supreme law of cosmic Eros (Fohat) governs all the processes whereby the one Universal Element differentiates to form manifest Nature, with its incredibly complex diversity of systems. In this recondite doctrine of recurring emanation there is a hidden continuity between that which was potentially present at the beginning and that which is fully developed at the end of any cycle. What is vital for alert human beings to realize, and what was so crucial to the Leibnizian doctrine, is that the monad contains within it this potent force of growth and development. But this seminal force cannot be separated from the whole, even in the name of spiritual individuation. It is not merely appropriate to any particular monad, but is itself all-potent on the plane of the One Element. Naturally enough, this force must be intelligently applied to the vast spectrum of possibilities within which the individual monad has to confront its own perceptions and apperceptions. Applying this mind-boggling idea to the monadic wave, working from the *devas* right down to the critical mineral kingdom, and onward and upward to the highest perfected human being, one can see that there is an incredible range and at the same time an extraordinary continuity. Always and everywhere this supreme principle of growth is at work, sustaining a myriad of processes of unfoldment and development, reform and regeneration.

In terms of human principles, this ubiquitous force of growth is objectively correlative with the Atma-Buddhic monad, the uncompounded thinking element that is the very essence of higher *Manas*. *Manas* itself may be thought of as a flame from the fire of *Mahat*. In man this flame is surrounded by dense smoke. That which is all-potent on the higher planes is obscured on the lower planes by inferior forces. That which is an extremely refined vibration on the higher planes, capable there of self-maintenance and perpetual motion, will be eclipsed when inserted into a context of harsher and grosser vibrations. This accounts for the tremendous gap in human beings between what they can touch and experience in deep sleep and what they can express in waking life. To understand this it is necessary to gain a dynamic sense of balance between the activation, on the deeper plane of ideation, of the all-potent force, and the dialectical difficulties of realizing its fullness in everyday life. To tap the noumenal power of growth in the human monad is to draw away from the so-called attraction of the lower realm of desire and become irradiated by the light of *Atman*. One must not fall prey to any false sense of obligation to express one's deepest thoughts or attempt to convince others. That will only serve to ensure disappointment, and it will never contribute to any significant improvement in the human condition.

Here one may profit from the teachings of the *Tao Te Ching*. Taoism emphasizes a cool appreciation of the eternal interplay of light and shadow, and also the importance of minimizing manifestation, expression and interference with others. To gain spiritual buoyancy in the realm of ideation, it is necessary to let go of that which weighs one down. This is not something that can be done all at once, but rather must be made a regular practice. As one contemporary philosopher puts it, one must initiate a *"samadhi* shift". Most individuals are so caught up in the fickle ego that they become tense and strained, like the child in Aesop's fable who caught the fox. Instead, one should appropriately pause and let go. If one is in a mad hurry to get somewhere and has a flat tire, one should not fret and fume, but pause to look around, shifting attention to that which has nothing to do with oneself. If nothing else, one can always look up at the sky, which, as Emerson said, is the great purifier. This is a kind of *samadhi* shift into a realm of ego-free experience. Once one has let go, released all tension, one can achieve much more and with much greater ease. One can begin to enjoy the world from a non-egocentric standpoint, seeing it through the eyes of children or old people, of strangers or friends. To see the world in ways that go beyond one's tyrannical ego is to restore, if only for a moment, some awareness of one's vast potential for growth and timely self-correction.

To sustain and make more continuous this noetic awareness, it is necessary to have a clear philosophical conception of the different modes of manifestation of the universal power of growth. All the animal and vegetable kingdoms possess this immense power of growth; indeed, they could not exist without it. Nevertheless, it exists in them in an instinctual mode quite different from that relevant to thinking beings, to moral agents and responsible choosers. *Gupta Vidya* expresses this constellation of skills in terms of sets of fires constituting the principles of Man and Nature.

> Man needs four flames and three fires to become one on Earth, and he requires the essence of the forty-nine fires to be perfect. It is those who have deserted the Superior Spheres, the Gods of Will, who complete the Manu of illusion. For the "Double Dragon" has no hold upon the mere form. It is like the breeze where there is no tree or branch to receive and harbour it. It cannot affect the form where there is no agent of transmission (Manas, "Mind") and the form knows it not.

> *The Secret Doctrine*, ii 57

Through this arcane doctrine of the three fires, the Occult Catechism expresses something of the extraordinary subtlety of the dynamic relationship between the higher and lower planes of existence. These three fires correspond to three sets of entities: gods, Asuras and human beings. In manifestation, however, there must be material ancestors or lunar Pitris before there can be cognitively self-conscious beings. These are responsible for the projection in ethereal matter of human beings in form. When they also have got the gifts that come from the higher classes of gods and Asuras, they become human beings in mind. The three fires are the solar fire of the gods, the electric fire of the Pitris, and the fire by friction of the Asuras. These three fires cannot be understood through mere physical analogies, but must be understood through deep meditation, through the subtle interplay of idea and image in the realm of creative imagination. Indeed, this alchemical process is itself intimately connected with the Hermetic awakening to self-conscious awareness of these three higher fires. Thus, it is difficult to convey the eternal light of the *Atman,* the sempiternal light of universal *Buddhi* or the supernal light of pure self-consciousness to contemporary human beings, in whom the three higher principles are merely an overbrooding presence.

In most human beings, *Manas* itself is only very partially incarnated, because all attention is given to the external sensory world, to eating and drinking, to the clamorous wants of the physical body, to getting and spending. People seem only too willing to become servants, sadly enslaved to the legions of lunar and sidereal elementals that occupy the lower quaternary. When human beings have thoughtlessly enlisted themselves in the service of these insatiable elementals – and making all their tortuous cerebration utilitarian, centred upon a furtive and shadowy personal ego – they cannot be given any meaningful conception of the real subjective life of the true man of meditation in whom *Atma, Buddhi* and higher *Manas* are fully active. It is no wonder that most human beings have some intense experience of higher conscious activity only in deep sleep or in *devachan.* In the latter condition, it is solely the presence of the solar element of *Manas* that makes it a positive state of perception for the disembodied monad. In deep sleep and *devachan,* the involuntary absence of the ego-centred lunar *manas* permits the activation of these higher powers of perception.

Clearly, the common difficulty in releasing the creative potential for growth lies in the absurd way so many people identify themselves wholly or largely with the shadowy psycho-physical vestures. This is, in fact, a direct inversion and costly misappropriation of the quintessential and defining principle of man – *Manas.* How one employs the creative mind in thinking of oneself is a potent talisman and, according to Shankara, the chief key to both bondage and liberation. In the wondrous cosmogony of the *Puranas,* Brahma is said to create by thinking of himself as the father of the world. As H.P. Blavatsky noted,

> This *thinking of oneself* as this, that, or the other, is the chief factor in the production of every kind of psychic or even physical phenomena. The words "whosoever shall say to this mountain be thou removed and cast into the sea, and *shall not doubt . . .* that thing will come to pass", are no vain words. Only the word "faith" ought to be translated by WILL. Faith without Will is like a windmill without *wind* – barren of results.

*Ibid,* 59

The capacity to think constructively of oneself is intimately connected with the mysterious power of *Kriyashakti,* and is crucial to the gaining of self-conscious immortality. Without vainly attempting to pry into arcane mysteries, anyone may begin to draw upon this sovereign power through mystic meditation. One may take the sublime portrait of the Self-Governed Sage – associating it, if one wishes, with an actual statue or picture – and think of the resplendent qualities of the Silent Sage, adoring and apprehending them, assimilating them in one's heart and mind. Thus can one actively and deliberately undertake a subtle process of transformation in one's own astral sphere.

The true aim of this esoteric practice of self-transformation is to engender the priceless seed of *bodhichitta,* which in the bloom of enlightenment becomes the Self-Governed Sage. By meditating upon, by adoring, by even thinking of oneself in relation to the Self-Governed Sage – intensely, persistently and with unconditional will, heart and mind – one may gestate the embryonic Bodhisattva in oneself. So it is that in the Deity Yoga of Tibetan Buddhism, detailed rules for meditation and purification are given in relation to the meticulous consecration of the field, the mandala, the magnetic sphere and the central image upon which the rapturous meditation is based. All are integral parts of a systematic discipline which can only be helpful if used with the assured guidance of an accredited    guru,    with    an    authentic    spiritual    lineage *(Guruparampara).*

In Deity Yoga, or indeed in any such arduous practice, it is vitally important to understand at some level the abstruse notion of voidness, of omnipresent Akashic Space. One must have the proven capacity, philosophically, to make real to oneself transcendental and absolute abstractions. As soon as one can do this, one becomes intensely aware of the tremendous richness, the unbounded potency, existing within metaphysical Space and also, therefore, within any enveloping matrix of ideation, even within one's own imperfect vestures. As one gains this sacred awareness, one will become effortlessly able to bring down the ineffable light of intense concentrated adoration. This is an extremely high and difficult practice, and certainly much too sacred to be spoken about. But if one truly thinks about it, and truly determines to do it for the highest motives, there is no looking back.

Until this point is reached, the neophyte must patiently engage in a long and arduous course of preparation, probation and purification, seeking to gain at least conceptual clarity with regard to the impersonal nature of inmost creativity. In ordinary speech the term "creativity" is used much too loosely. In the context of spiritual life it has to do with compassionate meditation and metaphysical imagination. It is grounded in subjective realities that have nothing to do with anything external, though it may express itself in external ways. Spiritual creativity has to do with releasing the spiritual will, which is nothing less and nothing else than the light-energy of the *Atman*. It is universal, cosmic, unmodified and formless. Spiritual will is totally free. It is omnipotent. But it is also so universal that, like the light-energy of the *Atman*, it can be tapped only with complete mental purification.

It is necessary to create vital points of contact in the lower *manas* with higher *Manas,* centres for smooth transmission within one's manasic field of the subliminal energies of *Buddhi* and *Atman*. This naturally implies a great deal of theurgic work upon oneself, virtually all of which must take place in reverential silence and noetic secrecy. Though the cosmic will may be compared to the rushing wind, and faith to a rustic windmill, nevertheless, when one thinks of spiritual will moving the windmill of human faith, one should not think of that will as blowing from outside. In reality, one is thinking here of a benevolent spiritual breath which is only experienced within the sanctum of indrawn consciousness, when there is a complete quiescence of physical and mental activity, coupled with a slowing down of the rate of breathing and a calm withdrawal of attention from the lesser vestures. Through deep study and daily meditation upon these seminal ideas, through honest self-examination and cheerful self-correction, one may gradually come to clarify, at least in one's habitual conceptions, one's misty apprehension of spiritual creativity.

The true treasure-house of all cosmic creativity is the supernal realm of Akashic ideation. Just as there are many modes of refinement and specialization of intelligence in the different Rounds and Races on this globe, there must be many more on other globes, not only in the Earth Chain, but in all the chains of planets throughout the solar system. There is an incredible wealth to all the iridescent patterns of ideation and activity within the solar system, not to mention even vaster spheres of existence. All these patterns and potentialities for the variegated expression of Divine Intelligence have a definite impact, through the diffused *Akasha,* upon the creative potential of human beings. Through the sacred gift of the *Agnishvatta Pitris*, all human beings can draw freely from the Akashic realm. Those who are hierophants consciously invoke the highest hierarchies, and know how to tap those energies so as to advance human good on this terrestrial plane.

This is an exact and definite knowledge, inseparable in its awesome mastery and timely expression from the heroic courage associated with the divine hosts of Asuras. It is a courage to go beyond known limits, a daring refusal to settle down, a Promethean urge to redeem the human condition. It is sometimes only experienced as a confused disaffection with the earthly realm of personal existence, but in its origins it is a consistent refusal to settle on any sacrosanct finalities, to consolidate any final conception of human good, human progress and human perfectibility. This invaluable gift of the Asuras is revolutionary in the highest sense. But it is a revolutionary urge that is accompanied by such potent and profound compassion for every living being that it can hardly be compared with modern, mythified revolutions. Terrestrial revolutions sometimes arise from the altruistic urges of a few, but these rapidly become inverted. They are not, therefore, real revolutions. True revolutions in human consciousness are those initiated by Buddha and earlier by Krishna; they represent a fundamental alteration in the horizon of human consciousness. They affect classes of souls who become capable of reflecting their regenerative spirit throughout a series of civilizations. Those who voluntarily participate in these Copernican revolutions become courageous pioneers, true helpers consecrated to universal welfare (*Lokasangraha*).

This is the highest spiritual and revolutionary urge in humanity, and its inmost essence may be likened to the fiery presence of the Dragon of Wisdom. Unlike the Double Dragon – whose breath cannot make any difference to the external world because of its immense distance from this plane – the Dragon of Wisdom, reposing in man as *Buddhi-Manas,* can effortlessly master this field of differentiated elements and imperfect instruments. It can provisionally accept them and partake of them, while at the same time freely acting in the midst of them, to create a current of mental purification and spiritual regeneration. From time immemorial this has been associated with Shiva, the *Mahayogin*. The symbolic wearing of sackcloth and ashes expresses the spiritual truth that human beings are capable of experiencing exalted modes of renunciation and transcendence, of *tapas* and penance, even in their toughest conditions. All beings can release a revolutionary courage that is capable of moving into the Akashic realm and eliciting from the *Akasha* the concept of a golden age, the kingdom of heaven, a new humanity.

*Hermes*, October 1986
Raghavan Iyer

# INDEX

# *B*

# C

# D

# E

# F

# G

# L

# M

# N

# O

# P

# R

# S

# *T*

# U

# V

# W

# Y

# Z

Made in the USA
Las Vegas, NV
19 November 2022

59872329R00204